THE PRINCE OF THIS WORLD

THE PRINCE OF THIS WORLD

Adam Kotsko

Stanford University Press · Stanford, California

Stanford University Press
Stanford, California

Printed in the United States of America on acid-free, archival-quality paper

Library of Congress Cataloging-in-Publication Data

Names: Kotsko, Adam, author.
Title: The prince of this world / Adam Kotsko.
Description: Stanford, California : Stanford University Press, 2017. |
    Includes bibliographical references and index.
Identifiers: LCCN 2016024047 (print) | LCCN 2016025606 (ebook) |
    ISBN 9780804799683 (cloth : alk. paper) | ISBN 9781503600201 (pbk. : alk.
    paper) | ISBN 9781503600218 (e-book)
Subjects: LCSH: Devil--Christianity--History of doctrines. | Good and
    evil--Religious aspects--Christianity.
Classification: LCC BT982 .K68 2016 (print) | LCC BT982 (ebook) |
    DDC 235/.4--dc23
LC record available at https://lccn.loc.gov/2016024047

Cover photograph: Guilliame Geefs, *Lucifer*. Photo by Luc Viatour. Wikimedia
Commons.
Typeset by Bruce Lundquist in 10.25/15 Adobe Caslon Pro

League with you I seek
And mutual amity so strait, so close,
That I with you must dwell or you with me
Henceforth.

    Milton, *Paradise Lost*

The shift in level worked out by secularization often coincides not
with a weakening, but with an absolutization of the secularized
paradigm.

    Agamben, *The Use of Bodies*

TABLE OF CONTENTS

ACKNOWLEDGMENTS

Ted Jennings, Laurel Schneider, and Anthony Smith all read the full manuscript (and earlier drafts) in detail, providing sympathetic but rigorous critique. Bruce Rosenstock has been an invaluable dialogue partner from the earliest stages of this project, most notably for pointing me toward 2 Maccabees, and Brennan Breed steered me from the path of error in my reading of the Hebrew Bible. Both read early drafts and provided valuable comments. I owe all these readers a debt of thanks. I also had the privilege of teaching the materials treated in this book in multiple settings, and I thank Carol Anderson of Kalamazoo College, Barbara Stone of Shimer College, and Ken Stone of Chicago Theological Seminary for that opportunity—along with my students in all three classes. I am grateful as well to those who provided me the opportunity to work out my ideas through invited lectures: Frances Restuccia (Psychoanalytic Practices Seminar, Mahindra Humanities Center, Harvard University), Slavoj Žižek (The Actuality of the Theologico-Political Conference, Birkbeck Institute for the Humanities), Steve Shaviro and Ken Jackson (Wayne State University), and Marco Abel and Roland Vegso (Humanities on the Edge series, University of Nebraska–Lincoln). Finally, I express my profound thanks to Emily-Jane Cohen for her advocacy and help in bringing this project to fruition.

THE PRINCE OF THIS WORLD

WHY THE DEVIL?

In his testimony before the grand jury, Ferguson police officer Darren Wilson claimed to be terrified of Michael Brown, the unarmed black man he shot and killed. He returns to the topic frequently from a variety of angles, but one particular image stands out: "It looks like a demon."[1] Almost every word in this short statement is charged: the dehumanizing "it," the attempt at immediacy (and therefore audience identification) in the present-tense "looks," all culminating in the very literal demonization of his own victim.

Even leaving aside its apparent effectiveness, the fact that he could even utter such a thing and expect a jury of his peers to believe and sympathize with it speaks to the deep-seated racism of American society—for which there is already a tragic abundance of evidence. The alarming imagery of Wilson's remark, however, highlights another, less noted phenomenon: the prominence of theological language in the mainstream media discussion of the black victims of police shootings.

Again and again, we learn that the victims were "no angels." Now the same might be said of all of us, insofar as we are merely human. Yet the context in which this imagery is deployed shows that being "no angel" is effectively a euphemism for being a "demon"—a being hardwired for evil. The victims' records are invariably scoured for any hint of criminal activity, as though a single misdemeanor offense singles them out for summary execution. Their every word, action, and attitude during the police encounter are adduced as evidence of a dangerous rebelliousness that could be ended only with lethal force. What this line of inquiry aims to establish is not simply that the victims have committed a crime but that they are *criminals*. What they *do* is taken as a symptom of what they *are*—a point that becomes painfully clear when we recall how often victims' family connections are used as evidence of their supposedly inherent criminality.

The black victims are always presumptively criminals in this racist public discourse. Strangely, however, this ostensibly inherent inclination toward crime does not free them from moral culpability. As in the case of demons, who are still destined for eternal damnation despite being unable to do anything but evil, it instead exposes them to a particularly intense form of moral accountability in which they face arbitrary lethal punishments for their actions. Here the contrast with white mass shooters is striking. In mainstream media accounts, the sympathetic qualities of the shooter are highlighted, as though to reassure the public that this outburst of violence was truly random and unpredictable. The diagnosis is quick and absolutely uniform: the shooter was mentally ill, which—in sharp contrast to the supposedly intrinsic criminality of the black police-shooting victim—serves to absolve him of any straightforward culpability for his actions. The slightest infringement by a black victim serves, in the tortured logic of the mainstream media debate, to legitimate police brutality toward blacks, whereas every precaution is taken to make sure that nihilistic mass murders by white perpetrators are always regarded as isolated incidents. The actions of members of its most privileged demographic must never be allowed to raise the possibility that there is a problem with American society as a whole.

The question of agency becomes particularly fraught when we look to the police officers themselves. Here the rhetoric emphasizes the automatic, seemingly instinctive nature of the officer's action: "he just reacted." From the perspective of common sense, it is difficult to see how this helps the officer's case. Surely for a police officer—who is heavily armed, highly trained, and bound by oath to serve and protect the public—to follow blind impulse and murder someone is *more* morally culpable than it would be for a civilian to do so. The function of this seemingly counterintuitive defense is clear, however, when we note the contrast with the officer's victim, who always could have acted differently—who always "had a choice." In other words, the victim's actions are morally culpable because (within the media narrative) the victim has all the moral agency in the situation. In contrast, the officer's ostensible *lack* of any agency or choice places his action in the sphere of sheer necessity and thereby renders it morally irrelevant.

In short, in the mainstream media discourse on police shootings, the theological imagery of the demonic (or, euphemistically, the non-angelic) appears as part of a complex and seemingly contradictory discourse on moral agency. This discourse aims to legitimate, or at least explain away, unjustified and destructive actions taken by representatives of the powers that be—and to blame the victims for their own victimization.

This book aims to demonstrate that the place of theology in this heady mix is not accidental. This victim-blaming logic points back to a long theological heritage with which modernity has never fully grappled. This book provides an initial inventory, which will be necessary for taking any meaningful steps toward, if not escaping, then at least finding a new use for this explosive inheritance.

On one level, of course, theology has always been a victim-blaming discourse. The models here are the infamous friends of the long-suffering Job, who argue that since he is suffering, he *must* have sinned somehow. Yet Job's own defiance shows that theology has not always or only aimed to blame the victim. Indeed, theology has often served as a weapon against oppression and injustice. Perhaps surprisingly, that was initially the case for demonology, which emerged in Jewish communities facing persecution and violence at the hands of imperial conquerors. Their oppression was so severe that they simply could not make sense of it in any other way than by positing that their tormenters were the agents of some kind of spiritual force that was opposed in principle to God's justice and his plans for his people. This cosmic opponent, whom God would soon defeat, is the original form of the theological figure we know as the devil.

From the point of view of this theology, if anyone is the demon in this situation, it is surely Wilson, the embodiment of a racist structure of police violence that—as seen in the many similar cases that have come to light in the wake of the protests in Ferguson—is so arbitrary and implacable in its persecution of the black community in America that it is difficult to see it as motivated by anything other than sheer malice. This is a parallel that many contemporary black theologians have embraced, most notably James Cone, who openly refers to the racist American order as demonic while claiming that the black community enjoys a relationship to God similar to that of the Jews suffering under imperial oppression.[2]

Behind Wilson's testimony, then, there stands a profound theological reversal: the devil, having originated as a theological tool of the oppressed, has become a weapon of the oppressor. *The Prince of This World* is the story of that reversal and of its unexpected consequences for the modern world.

The book's two major divisions approach this story from different angles. The first, "Genealogy of the Devil," traces the devil's emergence out of the complex dynamics of the Hebrew biblical tradition and then the way the Christian tradition develops that demonic figure. It is a bitterly ironic story, full of tragic reversals. Fundamentally, it shows how the biblical God went from being the vindicator and liberator of the oppressed to being a cruel ruler who delights in inflicting suffering on his friends and enemies alike. In other words, it is the story of how God became the devil.

The second part, "Life of the Devil," explores the paradoxical figure of the devil who emerges out of this great reversal. The fully developed Christian devil is both the ultimate enemy and God's most capable servant, the representative and leader of all who rebel against God as well as the eternal executor of God's will. Having traced the devil's emergence in history, this part shifts perspective and explores the devil's own history in terms of the medieval theological consensus in which he plays such a decisive role— the devil's past (his initial fall from grace), his present (his identification with troublesome social bodies), and his future (his role as chief inmate and guard in the eternal prison of hell).

My guiding threads in both major parts are the ways in which questions of legitimacy and moral agency become intertwined in the theological figure of the devil. From this perspective, I draw many parallels to key concepts of modernity, including subjectivity, the social contract, the invisible hand, and racialization. In the conclusion I draw those threads together, arguing that the peculiar conceptual knot that ties together free will, blameworthiness, and legitimacy in medieval accounts of the devil becomes, in secularized form, one of the most powerful—and deeply questionable—legacies that Christianity leaves to secular modernity.

THE PROBLEM OF EVIL

At the root of both of my variations on the story of the devil stands what is known as the problem of evil, which has proven to be the most durable challenge to traditional monotheism. Stated schematically, it is the problem of how to reconcile something like the following three propositions. First, God is good, completely benevolent in all his goals and deeds.[3] Second, God is all powerful, superabundantly capable of doing all that he wills. Third, evil and suffering happen. If we view this problem from a purely conceptual perspective, it is clear that there is a conflict here and only two of the propositions can be true at the same time. If God wills only the good and is fully capable of carrying out his will, then only good should result. If God always intends the good and yet evil happens, then we must conclude that he is not actually almighty. Finally, if God is omnipotent and created a world filled with suffering, then it would appear that his intentions are less benevolent than we might have hoped.

Continuing in this vein, it seems that the only logical way to resolve this contradiction is to concede one of the first two points, since the testimony of universal human experience prevents us from discarding the third. Yet even at their most coldly logical, the theologians of the monotheistic traditions have almost always concentrated their efforts on demolishing precisely that most unassailable of propositions—indeed, the only one of the propositions for which we have any direct evidence at all. And the reason for this seemingly counterintuitive approach is that even at the rarefied level of the purest scholasticism, the problem of evil is not merely an intellectual problem. It is an existential problem, a problem that touches on the most profound questions of how we are to understand and respond to our experiences in the world. We will have occasion to examine the subtle and nuanced attempts of scholastic theologians to explain away our experience of evil and suffering in a later chapter. For now, though, it is best to begin by treating the problem of evil less as a puzzle and more as a kind of open wound.

This is in fact how the monotheistic tradition itself approaches it, as evidenced by the Book of Job. Job's impassioned speeches, which cycle through a variety of positions and even make shocking accusations against God, can ultimately be read as an anguished attempt to hold the three propositions together. His friends' speeches, in contrast, retrospectively seem to anticipate the theological tradition's attempt to explain away the experience of evil and suffering. As I have noted, their strategy is to claim that Job *must* have sinned, meaning that his suffering is a deserved punishment from God and hence not an act of sheer malice. Job agrees with his friends that God has caused his suffering, but he refuses to concede even an inch to the idea that it was somehow deserved.

In short, the Book of Job is grappling with an irresolvable deadlock— or better, a deadlock that it utterly *refuses* to resolve. This deadlock makes its mark on the text. The various speeches all circulate around the same unfixable problem, giving them a repetitive quality. The resolution, such as it is, comes in the form of a literal deus ex machina, as God appears to Job. While it is difficult to say with certainty what we are meant to think about God's intervention, from our perspective, we can say that God strongly affirms all three claims. First, God's lengthy monologue, which famously fails to directly address Job's complaint at all, asserts God's mighty power over even the most chaotic forces. He also tacitly admits that Job is right to regard his suffering as unjustified, insofar as he tells Job's friends, "You have not spoken of me what is right, as my servant Job has" (42:7). In fact, he even seems to view their pious explanations as blasphemy, which can be forgiven only if Job intercedes on their behalf (42:8–9). Finally, he does ultimately restore everything Job has lost and more, apparently to demonstrate his own goodness—or at least to show that the good outstrips the evil in God.

Even if modern readers tend to hold up the Book of Job as an exemplary effort to grapple with the problem of evil, it does not appear to serve as a model or starting point for discussions of the issue in the Hebrew Bible. Indeed, it is striking how much of an outlier Job is within the Hebrew biblical tradition. The text makes no mention of an explicit law revealed by God, nor does it specify that Job is an Israelite at all. There is no direct reference to any of the major events in Israel's history, and the exact time frame and country where the story takes place appear to have been left intentionally vague. Overall, even if it takes a narrative form and uses poetic language, the Book of Job is in a certain sense an abstract thought experiment.

The approach of the mainstream of the Hebrew biblical tradition to the problem of evil is very different. Above all, it is much more collective than individual in its focus. While we can still discern the general outline of the abstract problem of evil, it is always posed in terms of the concrete narrative of God's special relationship to the nation of Israel. That relationship is founded on God's loyalty to Abraham and his descendants, as portrayed in the Book of Genesis, but it reaches its definitive form only beginning with the Exodus from Egypt.

From the perspective of the problem of evil, the events surrounding the Exodus imply a full-throated endorsement of the first two propositions. In rescuing the people of Israel from their bondage, God shows himself to be powerful enough to defeat the mightiest of earthly powers, with astounding and devastating miracles. From the Israelite point of view, he shows himself to be good, vindicating their claim to justice out of sheer loyalty and generosity. On the issue of evil, however, things become more complicated, as God openly takes credit for hugely destructive acts. Between the ten plagues and the departure of the Israelites, in fact, Egypt arguably suffers from every major evil that afflicts humanity—military defeat, looting, disease, natural disaster, even the premature loss of children. Yet the clear implication is that these deeds were not properly evil insofar as the Egyptians were unjust oppressors who *deserved* to be punished.

The problem, then, is not really suffering as such but undeserved, unjust, or meaningless suffering. The God of Israel legitimates himself not simply by preventing or minimizing suffering—from the perspective of the Egyptians, he maximizes it—but by converting the brute fact of suffering into an experience that has meaning. And the ultimate horizon of this meaning is God's special relationship with his people, which means that in the Hebrew biblical tradition, the problem of evil is always necessarily a problem of political theology. Hence, unlike more abstract modern formulations of the problem, it always implies the existence of an enemy who must be overcome. When we ask about the origin of God's cosmic rival, Satan, we must therefore attend to his encounter with his first great earthly rival: Pharaoh. It is with this encounter that the first chapter begins.

METHODOLOGY

From a certain perspective, this starting point may seem to have very little to do with the devil at all. It would seem much more intuitive to start with figures that have often been identified with the devil, above all the serpent in the Garden of Eden or the shadowy figure known as the "accuser" or *ha-satan* from the Book of Job.

Both these literary figures are quite marginal within the Hebrew biblical tradition, however. Within the world of the text, Job's accuser fills a much more circumscribed role than we would associate with the fully developed figure of Satan or the devil. He appears to be a regular member of God's heavenly court (1:6), who fills a role analogous to that of the "devil's advocate" in the Roman Catholic canonization process, namely, casting doubt on a saint's moral rectitude. He does play a crucial role in setting events in motion, but after carrying out the attacks that God has authorized, the accuser completely vanishes from the scene. Neither Job nor his friends ever consider the possibility that an evil spirit is tormenting him, and God makes no reference to the accuser or even to the fact that Job was being tested.[4] Something similar happens with the tempting serpent in the Garden of Eden. While the Christian tradition will later make much of his role, the serpent, seemingly chastened by the divine curse, slithers into hiding and is never heard from again in the Book of Genesis, or indeed the Hebrew Bible as a whole.

Starting with such literary figures fits with the traditional expectations of intellectual history, where one starts from the earliest "precursors" of one's chosen topic and gives an account of the gradual accrual of ideas and themes around it until it arrives at its familiar form.[5] I do not deny that works in that vein can be very informative, but their method can never allow them to answer the deeper and more urgent question of *why* such ideas emerged and developed in the way they did. In the case of the serpent and the accuser, for example, it is undoubtedly significant that both figures come to be *identified* with the devil, but neither is substantial enough to *produce* a theological symbol as powerful and durable as the fully developed Satan that we are familiar with. To grasp the forces that made the development of a theological symbol like the devil seem both plausible and urgently necessary, we must proceed genealogically.

The genealogical approach finds its origin in *The Genealogy of Morals*, where Nietzsche propounds the following methodological credo:

> There is for historiography of any kind no more important proposition than the one it took such effort to establish but which really *ought to be* established now: the cause of the origin of a thing and its eventual utility, its actual employment and place in a system of purposes, lie worlds apart; whatever exists, having somehow come into being, is again and again reinterpreted to new ends, taken over, transformed, and redirected by some power superior to it; all events in the organic world are a subduing, a *becoming master*, and all subduing and becoming master involves a fresh interpretation, an adaptation through which any previous "meaning" and "purpose" are necessarily obscured or even obliterated. . . . The entire history of a "thing," an organ, a custom can in this way be a continuous sign-chain of ever new interpretations and adaptations whose causes do not even have to be related to one another but, on the contrary, in some cases succeed and alternate with one another in a purely chance fashion.[6]

In other words, the current form of any idea, practice, or institution does not stem from a logical or organic development but is instead the result of an ongoing power struggle. What does this mean?

It may help to think about the example Nietzsche is discussing in the context of this passage: ideas, practices, and institutions surrounding punishment. For many scholars, he points out, it suffices to learn the present purpose of punishment to comprehend its origin: if the purpose of punishment is to deter other criminals, for instance, then our ancestors must have invented punishment as a way to deter criminals. For Nietzsche, this approach is wrong on two counts. First, there is no *one* reason that we punish people. If anything, there is an overabundance of partly overlapping, partly contradictory reasons even within contemporary society, to say nothing of the differences between historical epochs. And that means that punishment cannot have a single origin. Instead, the perpetuation of punishment stems from its strategic location at a point where a number of contradictory forces converge—and depending on the situation or historical moment, the forces converging on punishment could be very different.

In contemporary society, for instance, motivations such as rehabilitation, the separation of an individual from the rest of society, and retaliation for the harm that individual has caused all converge on the same institution: prison. In different communities and in the context of different cases, the precise mix of those factors varies widely. That inconsistency does not undermine the institution of prison, as if it should "ideally" have one clear reason for existence, but is instead the very *source* of its social and political power in modern society. This means that the "same" idea, practice, or institution can and likely will have a very different meaning and function under different social, political, and historical circumstances. It would therefore be a mistake to claim that "all societies have prisons" simply because people in a wide range of times and places have found it expedient to occasionally lock people up in some way. To understand the role that imprisonment plays, one would have to understand the social tensions and pressures to which it constitutes a response in any given historical setting.

A further consequence of Nietzsche's argument is that an idea, practice, or institution can never be merely a result or end point of a power struggle. Rather, they are all *participants*. To stay with the example of prison, Foucault, one of the greatest twentieth-century practitioners of Nietzschean genealogy, has pointed out the ways that prisons have perpetuated themselves by actively producing the delinquents they supposedly exist to reform—which is only the most obvious way that the institution of the prison actively shapes the society it ostensibly serves.[7]

On one level, then, the genealogical method serves as a safeguard against the errors of anachronism and false universalism. Hence, for instance, we should not assume that the figure of the serpent in the Garden of Eden originated *in order to* symbolize the devil simply because it is typically used in that way now. Nor should we assume that the devil is a universal religious symbol simply because many mythological traditions include a "trickster" character who enjoys meddling in other gods' plans.

More important, however, the genealogical method requires us to keep digging below the surface. From a genealogical perspective it is not enough to follow the reasoning in a text, for instance. One must understand the tensions that made the particular approach of this text appear necessary, the forces that converge to render certain types of evidence and certain logical leaps acceptable and convincing. In short, one must learn to read texts as *strategies*, as interventions in a power struggle. It means accepting, with Foucault, that knowledge is not separate from power or even a mere tool of power but a form of power—and a particularly powerful one at that. It also means that contradictions and tensions within a text are not the sign of a lack of rigor but symptoms of a particularly fraught struggle.

Perhaps the best-known contemporary practitioner of genealogical inquiry is Giorgio Agamben. His work is of special relevance to my project because of the way he synthesizes the methodological tools of genealogy (particularly those developed by Foucault) with insights drawn from the field of political theology. This is above all the case in *The Kingdom and the Glory*,[8] where he seeks to demonstrate that the abstract theological debates surrounding the Trinity and the doctrine of providence actually reflect a deep struggle over how to make sense of the world in light of the claims of monotheism—and that the solutions theologians developed continue to shape our ostensibly secular modern world.

Agamben's relationship to the notion of "political theology"—itself a site of considerable struggle and contestation within contemporary academic debates—is complex. For our present purposes, however, it seems fair to say that his inquiry is indebted to the famous thesis of Carl Schmitt's *Political Theology*:

> All significant concepts of the modern theory of the state are secularized theological concepts, not only because of their historical development— in which they were transferred from theology to the theory of the state, whereby, for example, the omnipotent God became the omnipotent lawgiver—but also because of their systematic structure, the recognition of which is necessary for a sociological consideration of these concepts.[9]

Schmitt's claim has two main consequences. The first is that theological concepts can be somehow converted into political concepts *across time*, and the second is that theological and political concepts share a similar structure *at the same time*. This latter claim is foundational to the first, and it is the aspect of his thesis that Schmitt himself focuses on in the remainder of his chapter. His argument does not deal primarily with the impact of medieval theology on modern politics, for instance, but instead focuses on the parallels between deism and political absolutism, which were mutually contemporary phenomena in the early modern period.

For Schmitt, there are two primary reasons that theological (or metaphysical) and political thinking display such strong parallels. The first is that they are both "systematic" in the sense that both seek to render a consistent and total account of their respective fields. A theory of politics must ideally encompass the full range of human activities, relationships, and institutions, just as a theological or metaphysical doctrine aspires to a similarly complete reckoning of everything that exists. Hence they cover a similar range, meaning that comparing the two realms does not constitute the same kind of unhelpful reductionism that, for Schmitt, would be implied in deriving the contents of a legal doctrine from the personal idiosyncrasies of its author alone.[10]

The second and more fundamental is that both fields are responding to "the general state of consciousness" of a particular epoch,[11] that is, the deep convictions shared by a particular society about how the world does and should work. Foucault designates this same level of deep consensus by the paradoxical term "historical *a priori*," which he defines as

> what, in a given period, delimits in the totality of experience a field of knowledge, defines the mode of being of the objects that appear in that field, provides man's everyday perception with theoretical powers, and defines the conditions in which he can sustain a discourse about things that is recognized to be true.[12]

In genealogical terms, both Schmitt and Foucault are pointing to something like a field in which the power struggle takes place. But for both, this field is not a neutral background. Instead, it is something that is periodically decisively transformed, sometimes in a surprisingly short period of time.

The first major division of this book is organized around a series of such fields, which for convenience I call "paradigms." I interpret each of them as attempts to grapple with the specific articulation of the problem of evil in the Hebrew biblical tradition, meaning that they all struggle with a fundamentally unfixable problem. In approaching the theological tradition in this way, I am taking the lead of two contemporary theologians, Catherine Keller and Laurel Schneider. In *Face of the Deep*,[13] Keller argues that traditional theology can be read as an attempt to repress and subdue the forces of chaos symbolized by the "waters" mentioned in Genesis 1:2, as well as by Leviathan, the great sea monster from the Book of Job—whom Christian interpreters have traditionally understood to be symbolic of the devil. Schneider follows up on Keller's insights in *Beyond Monotheism*, where she traces the desire for a monotheistic God back to the experience of suffering and chaos among both Jews and Greeks.[14]

Where my approach differs from Keller and Schneider's is that I am not attempting to develop my own constructive theological position on the basis of my investigation. I have done such work previously,[15] but here my ultimate goal is to rethink some of the central concepts of modernity in light of their Christian theological roots. Hence my intention is more purely critical than constructive and more philosophical than theological.

At the same time that it is not a work of constructive theology, this book is not and cannot be a narrowly "scholarly" investigation. Any genealogical investigation is necessarily only one path among many that can be traced through our history to make sense of our present. Nietzsche's *Genealogy of Morals* is openly speculative in its approach for the bulk of the text, and even better-documented efforts like Foucault's *Discipline and Punish* and Agamben's *Kingdom and the Glory* cannot pretend to be exhaustive accounts of the phenomena they study. Though I of course acknowledge scholars to whom my argument is indebted, I make no explicit attempt to position my argument in terms of the existing literature on "devil studies" or on the specific texts and eras I address. Further, though I do occasionally alter translations or call attention to the original language of texts, my argument does not hinge on idiosyncratic translations, nor do I attempt to uncover neglected texts from the obscure nooks and crannies of the theological tradition. Even though my choice of texts may in some cases appear idiosyncratic due to my bias in favor of works that best illustrate the entanglement of the devil with questions of politics and freedom, my focus throughout is on the mainstream of the theological tradition, because I want to show that the narrative I am constructing has always been hiding in plain sight.[16]

That narrative is a distressing one, full of consequences that are no less destructive for being unintended. It casts a light on some of the ugliest corners of the Christian tradition and calls into question some of the most cherished concepts by which we continue to try to make sense of our world. This "negativity" leaves me open to the suspicion that I have some kind of alternative in mind, by which I am measuring our world and finding it lacking. In short, I might be called upon to answer the same question that Nietzsche anticipates at the end of the second essay of *Genealogy of Morals*: "What are you really doing, erecting an ideal or knocking one down?" My research for this project has convinced me of the truth of his response:

> But have you ever asked yourselves sufficiently how much the erection of *every* ideal on earth has cost? How much reality has had to be misunder-stood and slandered, how many lies have had to be sanctified, how many consciences disturbed, how much "God" sacrificed every time? If a temple is to be erected *a temple must be destroyed*: that is the law—let anyone who can show me a case in which it is not fulfilled![17]

Arguably, however, Nietzsche does not go far enough. As risky as it is to destroy a temple, more perilous still is the attempt to build one—above all because we never truly get to start from scratch. Even if no stone is left standing on another, the materials out of which our temple has been built are the materials we will inevitably use and misuse in building its replace-ment. And as we will see, they are dangerous and unstable materials indeed.

(PART I)
GENEALOGY OF THE DEVIL

CHAPTER 1

THE HEBREW BIBLICAL TRADITION

THE PARADOX OF MINORITY MONOTHEISM

In order to account for the origin of the devil, we need to answer two questions. First, why should the one and only God, creator of the heavens and the earth, have a rival? Second, why should that rival be regarded as morally *evil*? Both questions present significant difficulties. In the first case, it would seem that no meaningful rivalry against God is possible—he is in a category all his own, completely unsurpassable within the created world. Indeed, there are well-known forms of philosophical monotheism in which no possibility of rivalry can arise. Aristotle's Unmoved Mover, for instance, is so absorbed in his self-satisfaction that he neither knows nor cares that the universe exists. Although everything in the world is striving to emulate him to the extent possible, there is no sense in which they are trying to replace him. In these terms, even if we grant that the idea of rebelling against God could enter one's mind, it seems just as plausible—if not more so—to regard such an attempt as futile rather than evil and therefore to pity or scorn God's woefully unconvincing rival rather than revile him.

The God of the Hebrew Bible did not emerge from abstract philosophical reflection, however. He is the product of the concrete historical experience of a particular ancient Near Eastern people, an experience that produced a range of partly overlapping and partly contradictory traditions about their God and his place in the world. In some texts in the Hebrew Bible, for instance, it can appear that the Israelite God is merely one local god among others, albeit one with an unusual intolerance for theological promiscuity among his worshippers. The commandment "you shall have no other gods before me" (Exodus 20:3), for instance, could seem redundant if there simply are no other gods available.

Over time, however, the view emerged within the Hebrew biblical tradition that the God of Israel was also in some sense the God of all nations and that all the other purported gods were laughably inferior to him, if not entirely nonexistent. Even so, God remained very much the God of Israel, and his historical interventions on behalf of Israel—most notably the events of the Exodus, during which he liberated the Israelite slaves from oppression—were still central to his identity, arguably even more so than the greater, but less Israel-specific, achievement of creating the heavens and the earth. The Israelites did not somehow "transcend" their narrowly particular conception of God and embrace a more universal image of the divine. The God of all the universe *was* the God of their historical experience. To emphasize the contrast with the universalism of a philosophical monotheism like Aristotle's, then, the monotheism of the Hebrew biblical tradition can be characterized as a *minority monotheism*.

This short circuit of a local tradition with universal significance could appear to be an arbitrary self-assertion on the part of Israel, but the biblical authors attempt to vindicate their bold theological claim by highlighting the distinctive features of their God. On what we would regard as the more purely "religious" level, they frequently highlight the foolishness of worshipping idols (sculptural images of the gods), as in this classic statement from Isaiah:

> All who make idols are nothing, and the things they delight in do not profit; their witnesses neither see nor know. And so they will be put to shame. Who would fashion a god or cast an image that can do no good? Look, all its devotees shall be put to shame; the artisans too are merely human. Let them all assemble, let them stand up; they shall be terrified, they shall all be put to shame. (Isaiah 44:9–11)

The text then spells out in detail the physical process of creating the statue of the god, a process that makes use of the same materials with which the human artisan fulfills his own daily needs (44:12–16). A portion of this indifferent material "he makes into a god, his idol, bows down to it and worships it; he prays to it and says, 'Save me, for you are my god!'" (44:17). In these terms, idol worship is an absurd and delusional practice. In contrast to idols, which are merely human productions, the God of Israel transcends any form that we human beings can grasp (see Deuteronomy 4:15–16). For the biblical authors, it is therefore clear which God is truly worthy of worship.

More decisive in establishing the superiority of the God of Israel, however, is the fact that he is a God of *justice*. In contrast to the petty rivalries and arbitrary whims of the gods in other mythological systems, the God of Israel has consistent expectations that largely align with human intuitions about what is fair and proportionate (or at least the authors expect us to see him in that way). In principle, those standards apply to all nations, which are frequently presented as being subject to God's punishment for long-standing defiance of divine justice. This holds not only for Egypt but also for the nations of Canaan whom the Israelites are displacing in the Promised Land, nations that God claims to be "dispossessing" due to their "wickedness" (Deuteronomy 9:4).

Yet the divine claim to represent justice is intensified and elaborately articulated in God's relationship to Israel in particular, insofar as that relationship comes to be based upon an explicit covenant. In the Book of Deuteronomy, which concludes the Pentateuch and is presented as a long speech of Moses in which he recapitulates the historical narratives and legal codes of the previous books, the Israelites are faced with a stark choice:

> See, I am setting before you today a blessing and a curse: the blessing, if you obey the commandments of the Lord your God that I am commanding you today; and the curse, if you do not obey the commandments of the Lord your God, but turn from the way that I am commanding you today, to follow other gods that you have not known. (Deuteronomy 11:26–28)

This scheme became more elaborate in the encounter with historical experience, most notably in light of the apparently unpredictable time lag between acts of injustice and God's punishment. Nevertheless, it is fair to say that it provided the basic frame of reference for the retelling of Israel's history found in the Deuteronomistic history (the segment of the Hebrew Bible made up of Deuteronomy, Joshua, Judges, 1–2 Samuel, and 1–2 Kings).

In this paradigm, God's relationship to Israel bears all the marks of direct political leadership. He secures a territory for them, he promulgates the law, and in the view of the Deuteronomistic historian, he also enforces that law. Thus, the God of all nations is in practice the ruler of one particular nation—and a fairly marginal nation at that. The possibility of a rival to God emerges out of this contradiction between the God of Israel's claim to rule all the world and his often tenuous hold on power even within Israel itself. And from this perspective, it is no accident that the first great rival of the God of Israel is not a theological opponent but a political one: namely, Pharaoh.

The Pharaoh of Exodus is very clearly unjust. In ignorance of the Israelite patriarch Joseph's decisive contributions (Exodus 1:8)—not only to Egypt's power but to its very survival in the face of a seven-year famine—he comes to view the Israelites sojourning in Israel as a threat and begins oppressing them. First he enslaves them (1:11), and when their population continues to increase, he mandates that all male infants born to the Hebrews should be killed (1:22). Hence Pharaoh not only violates his predecessor's agreement that the Israelites can settle in Egypt (Genesis 47:4), but he subjects them to slavery and attempted genocide. The contrast with God's trustworthiness and justice could not be more stark.

Hence I propose that Pharaoh, who is presented as unambiguously evil and who is a clear rival to God for control of the Israelites, is the most relevant biblical antecedent for the devil. Neither of the other main candidates, the serpent in the Garden of Eden and Job's accuser, seem to fit the bill. The serpent is too lowly a creature to be God's rival, and even though his actions have destructive effects, his motives are too unclear to designate him as evil (without anachronistically identifying him as Satan). As for Job's accuser, he is apparently a permanent part of God's entourage, whose cynical outlook

God specifically seeks out. At no point does he emerge as a rival to God, for Job's loyalty or in any other way.

At the same time, Pharaoh is not *yet* the devil. In the terms set by the minority monotheism of the Hebrew biblical tradition, God's wicked rival can only be a rival king—but the devil is more than a worldly king. He is a *cosmic* rival, a spiritual power, not a mere human being. Nevertheless, the political charge of the concept of an evil rival to God will never be fully eradicated. The devil is not merely a theological symbol but a political-theological one. And as we will see, he emerges in the midst of a political crisis that is immediately and irreducibly a theological crisis.

THE PROBLEM OF EVIL
AND THE PROBLEM OF THEOCRACY

As noted in the Introduction, God's defeat of Pharaoh carries with it massive "collateral damage" to the people of Egypt. By the same token, his plan to settle the Israelites in the Promised Land necessarily entails a campaign of mass murder. In both cases, however, the biblical authors expect us to view these actions as just and necessary—not due to an arbitrary preference for Israel but due to the evil and injustice of the nations affected. Though God is merciful in allowing time for repentance, there comes a point when enough is enough and divine justice demands retribution. And even if their relationship with God is undoubtedly unique, the Israelites are ultimately every bit as subject to the divine justice as any other nation.

This political-theological scheme can be read as an initial attempt to account for the problem of evil within the terms of the historical experience of Israel. Suffering here is interpreted as deserved punishment. Up to a certain point, this punishment serves as a spur to repentance, but God's mercy has its limits—if the Israelites persist in rejecting God's blessing, they will be subject to his curse.

I call this solution to the problem of evil the Deuteronomistic paradigm, after the biblical book in which it is most clearly articulated. In principle, this paradigm is very robust. God inoculates himself against certain forms of protest by openly claiming responsibility for the very kinds of events—

war, disease, famine—that in other schemes might destroy his credibility. And since the majority of Israelites at any given moment apparently tended to keep their religious options open rather than give sole loyalty to God and his law, there were ample grounds for finding Israel to be in violation of the covenant and hence deserving of punishment.

There are, however, two primary points of tension in the Deuteronomistic paradigm. The first is the aforementioned paradox that the ruler of all the nations is apparently the ruler of only a single marginal kingdom. Though that contradiction will prove decisive for later developments, it did not emerge as central as long as the Israelites enjoyed self-rule. Under those circumstances, the more urgent source of tension was the necessary role of human intermediaries in making possible the rule of a human kingdom by a God who was beyond all human form.

Even during the Exodus itself, when God's presence among the people is most palpable (in the form of the pillar of fire by night and the pillar of cloud by day), God nonetheless relies on human intermediaries, most notably Moses and Aaron. The text repeatedly emphasizes the fact that Moses and Aaron are simply God's mouthpieces, delivering messages on his behalf. In case their subordination to God is unclear, the author implicitly reiterates it by setting up direct rivalries between Moses and Pharaoh's magicians—the proper rival to Moses is not Pharaoh himself but Pharaoh's underlings. Looking to the future, the Book of Deuteronomy envisions the possibility of a just king who serves as something like a faithful functionary for the divine ruler, submitting fully to the divine law:

> When he has taken the throne of his kingdom, he shall have a copy of this law written for him in the presence of the levitical priests. It shall remain with him and he shall read in it all the days of his life, so that he may learn to fear the Lord his God, diligently observing all the words of this law and these statutes, neither exalting himself above other members of the community nor turning aside from the commandment, either to the right or to the left, so that he and his descendants may reign long over his kingdom in Israel. (17:18–20)

Yet that same book also concludes with the death of Moses (chap. 34), who has been forbidden to enter the Promised Land due to an infraction whose precise nature the various strains of tradition gathered in the Pentateuch cannot seem to agree upon.

Even the most exemplary prophet of God cannot manage to live up to the necessary standard, it seems, so it is perhaps unsurprising that the remainder of the Deuteronomistic history is considerably less optimistic about the prospects for a faithful ruler. Moses's close associate Joshua, who leads the initial invasion of Canaan, appears to pass muster, but after his death, Israel goes through a long period without any stable human leadership at all. As related in the Book of Judges, this time was characterized by the appointment of ad hoc leaders of varying moral caliber, tasked with solving immediate crises.

Perhaps understandably, the Israelites grow impatient with this arrangement and clamor for the last of these temporary leaders, Samuel, to appoint a king for them. When Samuel consults God, God makes it clear that he regards the proposed Israelite king as a rival:

> Listen to the voice of the people in all that they say to you; for they have not rejected you, but they have rejected me from being king over them. Just as they have done to me, from the day I brought them up out of Egypt to this day, forsaking me and serving other gods, so also they are doing to you. Now then, listen to their voice; only—you shall solemnly warn them, and show them the ways of the king who shall reign over them. (1 Samuel 8:7–9)

The regime that Samuel then describes sounds less like the optimistic image of the submissive divine functionary and more like Pharaoh:

> These will be the ways of the king who will reign over you: he will take your sons and appoint them to his chariots and to be his horsemen, and to run before his chariots; and he will appoint for himself commanders of thousands and commanders of fifties, and some to plow his ground and to reap his harvest, and to make his implements of war and the equipment of his chariots. He will take your daughters to be perfumers and cooks and

bakers. He will take the best of your fields and vineyards and olive orchards and give them to his courtiers. He will take one-tenth of your grain and of your vineyards and give it to his officers and his courtiers. He will take your male and female slaves, and the best of your cattle and donkeys, and put them to his work. He will take one-tenth of your flocks, and you shall be his slaves. And in that day you will cry out because of your king, whom you have chosen for yourselves; but the Lord will not answer you in that day. (1 Samuel 8:11–18)

In the eyes of God and of Samuel, the Israelites' request, far from being a prudent political calculation, represents a repetition of the repeated pleas of their ancestors, who grew tired of the rigors of their long journey and begged God to allow them to return to Egypt. It is a rejection of their covenant with a God of liberation and justice in favor of a return to oppression and slavery. God has rescued the Israelites from Pharaoh once before, Samuel is claiming, but they should not expect him to do so again when they subject themselves to a new Pharaoh after having tasted freedom.

After this point, the relationship between Israel's king and its God becomes the crucial point at which the Deuteronomistic solution to the problem of evil is played out—in other words, the problem of evil becomes a problem of political theology. In practice, things are not as uniformly dire as Samuel predicts, and after a false start with the ill-fated King Saul, Israel is led by the legendary King David, "a man after God's own heart" (1 Samuel 13:14). While the tradition is surprisingly frank about David's many moral failings, he is nonetheless held up as the exemplary faithful king, perhaps the closest Israel would ever come to Deuteronomy's model of the king as divine functionary. The majority veered dangerously close to Samuel's prediction, however, particularly in the northern kingdom that emerged (and retained the name Israel) when Israel was split in two after the reign of David's son Solomon. There essentially all kings were unfaithful to God, while in the southern kingdom (known as Judah, from which the term "Jew" derives), at least a handful tried to return to the right course.

The most common accusation against the purportedly "evil" kings of Israel and Judah is that they lead the people astray to worship idols. We should not conclude from this that the idols themselves are God's primary rivals, however. While worshipping them constitutes a serious violation of the divine covenant, in the Deuteronomistic history it is the king who incites this behavior in the people and who bears primary responsibility. Even when we seem to be dealing with a purely "religious" conflict, then, the "political" rivalry between God and the king is the decisive element. As the Deuteronomistic history unfolds, however, it is often difficult to square the historical facts with the expectations of the Deuteronomistic paradigm. Kings who do what is wrong in the sight of the Lord often prosper, while few of the faithful kings stand out as especially accomplished or powerful. I will note only the most extreme examples.

On the positive side, King Josiah of the southern kingdom of Judah is said to have done "what was right in the sight of the Lord, and walked in all the way of his father David; he did not turn aside to the right or to the left" (2 Kings 22:2). Indeed, toward the end of his story, the text suggests he may have been even better than David: "Before him there was no king like him, who turned to the Lord with all his heart, with all his soul, and with all his might, according to all the law of Moses; nor did any like him arise after him" (23:25). During his reign, a court functionary had found a copy of God's forgotten law in some obscure corner of the Temple. This had a powerful effect on the king: "When the king heard the words of the book of the law, he tore his clothes" (22:11) and then proceeded to order that the kingdom be rededicated to the divine covenant. Yet even after all his efforts on behalf of the Lord, Josiah was cut down during a battle with the Pharaoh of his day. His reign amounted to thirty-one years, during much of which he was very young, having assumed the throne at the age of eight (22:1).

In contrast, Josiah's predecessor, Manasseh, stands out as the most profoundly evil king of Judah. He rebuilt idolatrous shrines that his forebears had destroyed (21:3, 7) and defiled the Temple in Jerusalem with sacrifices to other gods (21:4–5). He indulged in witchcraft, including a practice that required his son to "pass through fire" (21:6)—perhaps a reference to child sacrifice. Further, he "shed very much innocent blood, until he had filled Jerusalem from one end to another, beside the sin that he caused Judah to sin so that they did what was evil in the sight of the Lord" (21:16). Overall, Manasseh's crimes are so outrageous that the Lord declares through his prophets that he will abandon Judah altogether (21:10–15). The text subsequently references this declaration in accounting for why even Josiah's profound piety was deemed insufficient to stave off disaster (23:26–27). Nonetheless, Manasseh proved to be Judah's longest-serving king, ruling a total of fifty-five years (21:1) and apparently dying peacefully in his sleep (21:18).

Difficult as it may be to reconcile the details, however, the Deuteronomistic paradigm does work out as promised in the last analysis. The unfaithful Kingdom of Israel, which had long since abandoned the worship of God in favor of idols, was conquered by the Assyrians and its population liquidated. The Kingdom of Judah, episodically faithful though it was, did not adequately heed this warning and was finally conquered by the Babylonians, who exiled its political and intellectual elites to the imperial center. The covenant, it seemed, had been carried out to the letter—and now it was over.

"THE KING OF BABYLON, MY SERVANT"

In the face of this unthinkable loss, the Hebrew elites could have been forgiven for turning their backs on their defeated God and bowing down in worship to the gods of the new rulers who had so thoroughly demonstrated their superior power. Doubtless a good number of them did. Yet there was a critical mass who responded to the catastrophe with a bold theological risk. In the face of their God's apparent defeat, they claimed that their local God was actually the God of all the earth. Far from being defeated by the pagan empires, the God of Israel had orchestrated their rise. What appeared to be a geopolitical shift with Israel as collateral damage was actually God's plan to chastise Israel and preserve a faithful remnant who would one day be restored to the Promised Land. As for God's unwitting pawns, the rulers of this world, they would be suitably punished for their oppression and injustice once they had served their purpose.

It seems likely that ideas to this effect had been circulating even before the fall of Jerusalem, in certain circles centered around the prophets. While the term "prophecy" is normally associated with supernatural visions of the future, in the context of ancient Israel it amounted to something more like theologically charged political commentary, often incorporating some element of divination or omen reading. Predicting that Judah would eventually be overrun by one of the imperial powers who were periodically sweeping through the Fertile Crescent during that period did not require divine inspiration, however, particularly after their neighbor to the north had already suffered that fate. Ideological preparations had to be made. Hence, alongside the normal portents of doom, notions of a righteous remnant that would preserve Israel's heritage and special relationship with God began to emerge.

The conceptual roots of this stance are already present in the prior Hebrew tradition. God clearly played a major role on the international stage in the events surrounding the Exodus, thoroughly humiliating the greatest world power of the age. Deuteronomy also envisions the Israelite tribes playing a similar role with respect to the Canaanites that the prophets saw the imperial powers playing toward Israel:

> When the Lord your God thrusts [the Canaanites] out before you, do not say to yourself, "It is because of my righteousness that the Lord has brought me in to occupy this land"; it is rather because of the wickedness of these nations that the Lord is dispossessing them before you. (9:4)

More broadly, the prophetic gesture is homologous to that of the Deuteronomistic paradigm, which puts forward precisely the kinds of events that might endanger God's credibility as the greatest possible evidence of his control over the situation. In that sense, the prophetic move could even be seen as a direct logical consequence of the Deuteronomistic paradigm. Yet there is a crucial shift in emphasis. Where the Deuteronomistic paradigm tacitly relies on the existence of a substantial segment of Israelites being inobservant of the covenant—and as I have noted before, this segment likely represented a majority of ancient Israelites, most of the time—the prophetic paradigm focuses on the existence of a faithful minority. This remnant is the true bearer of God's promise, guaranteeing the continuity of God's special relationship to Israel even in the worst of circumstances.

The concept of the remnant would prove decisive in the development of Jewish and later Christian theology. More important from our perspective, however, is the shift in God's relationship with the earthly ruler. At least for the foreseeable future, there is no realistic prospect of a return to meaningful self-rule—and hence no room for the emergence of a Jewish ruler as a rival to God who leads the people astray. Perhaps paradoxically, the relationship between God and the ruler becomes much less fraught precisely *because* that ruler is not one of the Chosen People.

This dynamic is perhaps clearest in one of the oracles of the prophet Jeremiah, who lived through the end of the Kingdom of Judah and the beginning of the exile:

> Therefore thus says the Lord of hosts: Because you have not obeyed my words, I am going to send for all the tribes of the north, says the Lord, even for King Nebuchadrezzar of Babylon, *my servant*, and I will bring them against this land and its inhabitants, and against all these nations around; I will utterly destroy them, and make them an object of horror and of hissing, and an everlasting disgrace. And I will banish from them the sound of mirth and the sound of gladness, the voice of the bridegroom and the voice of the bride, the sound of the millstones and the light of the lamp. This whole land shall become a ruin and a waste, and these nations shall serve the king of Babylon seventy years. Then after seventy years are completed, I will punish the king of Babylon and that nation, the land of the Chaldeans, for their iniquity, says the Lord, making the land an everlasting waste. I will bring upon that land all the words that I have uttered against it, everything written in this book, which Jeremiah prophesied against all the nations. For many nations and great kings shall make slaves of them also; and I will repay them according to their deeds and the work of their hands. (25:8–14; emphasis added)

Although Nebuchadrezzar is objectively evil in the eyes of Israel's God—not only a worshipper of false gods but an oppressor and conqueror—the prophet can nonetheless call him God's "servant." The anxiety over whether the ruler will be God's functionary or his rival is here dissolved, or at least displaced. While formally he should be a rival to God in the mold of Pharaoh, his lack of any knowledge of God forecloses that possibility. The emperor serves God perfectly by doing what the emperor already wants to do for his own reasons. And because there is no relationship implying loyalty, the perfect functionary is also perfectly dispensable. Once he has served his purpose, he can be disposed of—as his just punishment for doing the very things that God's plan required him to do.

Not all of God's unwitting servants are so unceremoniously dispatched. The prophet Isaiah has high praise for Cyrus of Persia, for example, who financed the rebuilding of the Temple in Jerusalem as part of an imperial policy of supporting local religions in order to keep the peace. The discussion of Cyrus comes in the context of a song of praise to God, who will soon bring the exile to a close: "Comfort, O comfort my people, says your God. Speak tenderly to Jerusalem, and cry to her that she has served her term, that her penalty is paid" (Isaiah 40:1–2). In the pages that follow, God speaks of his mighty power over all creation and particularly over the world's rulers: "All the nations are as nothing before him; they are accounted by him as less than nothing and emptiness" (40:17).

This passage is among the best known of the Hebrew Bible and includes a segment that all four Gospels put in the mouth of John the Baptist, in his capacity as the forerunner to Jesus: "A voice cries out: 'In the wilderness prepare the way of the Lord, make straight in the desert a highway for our God'" (40:3; cf. Matthew 3:3; Mark 1:3; Luke 3:4–6; John 1:23). Hence it can be jarring to realize that it is all but a prelude to God's announcement that he has "roused a victor from the east, summoned him to service," a victor who "delivers up nations to him and tramples kings under foot" (41:2). This powerful servant turns out to be Cyrus, whom God calls "his anointed"—the root meaning of "Messiah" in Hebrew or "Christ" in Greek—and "whose right hand I have grasped to subdue nations before him and strip kings of their robes" (45:1). Yet even the great Cyrus, singled out for such an important role, remains an unwitting servant. As the Word of the Lord testifies in a paradoxical direct address to Cyrus, "You do not know me" (45:4).

Within this political-theological scheme, the Jews are encouraged to suspend judgment of the pagan rulers under whom they must live. God will continue to orchestrate geopolitical events to ensure that they get their just deserts. In the meantime, the Jewish community is called upon to be as faithful to the covenant as they can be under present circumstances and contribute positively to the society in which they are sojourning. Here again, Jeremiah's exhortation is exemplary:

> Thus says the Lord of hosts, the God of Israel, to all the exiles whom I have sent into exile from Jerusalem to Babylon: Build houses and live in them; plant gardens and eat what they produce. Take wives and have sons and daughters; take wives for your sons, and give your daughters in marriage, that they may bear sons and daughters; multiply there, and do not decrease. But seek the welfare of the city where I have sent you into exile, and pray to the Lord on its behalf, for in its welfare you will find your welfare. (29:4–7)

Within this framework, the model Jew is a figure like Joseph, Daniel, or Esther, who rises to a high government position while remaining faithful to God. The acknowledgment of Jewish acumen, even by pagan rulers, contributes to the prestige of the community, just as God's ability to make use of such august figures as pawns contributes to his glory.

Over the centuries that followed, this prophetic paradigm has proven remarkably durable, providing the primary framework through which Jewish communities have understood their relationship to earthly authorities. While Jewish self-understanding underwent significant changes in the period between the exile and the rise of the rabbis as the primary source of authority in the community in the wake of the destruction of the Second Temple in 70 CE, the prophetic political-theological strategy has remained a continual point of reference.

Like its Deuteronomistic predecessor, the prophetic paradigm is a very robust model for shoring up God's legitimacy in the face of human suffering. In both models, the community itself is encouraged to see events that might otherwise seem like inexplicable disasters as deserved punishment that cannot be regarded as evil. And in both models, there is a built-in, if tacit, assumption of some degree of unfaithfulness in the community. The main difference is that in the prophetic paradigm the religious pluralism of ancient Israel has been replaced by the temptation of assimilation. And it is the problem of assimilation that will provoke the first of many crises that would call the prophetic paradigm into radical question—a crisis so profound that the Jewish community could no longer make sense of the notion that they were to blame for their own suffering.

ASSIMILATION AND APOCALYPTIC

The Book of Daniel opens with a story about the tensions surrounding assimilation. Four Israelites who are among the exiled elites are singled out as "young men without physical defect and handsome, versed in every branch of wisdom, endowed with knowledge and insight, and competent to serve in the king's palace" (1:4) and enrolled in a training program for the Babylonian civil service. Their education includes learning "the literature and language of the Chaldeans" (1:5) and the assignment of new Babylonian names (1:7).

So far, it seems that the assimilation is total. These men have immediately recognizable virtues and should fit seamlessly into the apparatus of officialdom. Yet one of the trainees, Daniel, throws up resistance at the same point where the difference between outsiders and observant Jews most often presents itself up to the present day: the question of food. This potential conflict is resolved, however, when Daniel, not wanting to "defile himself with the royal rations" (1:8), receives permission for him and his three Jewish comrades to receive simple vegetables and water—a regime that turns out to have considerable health benefits (1:15). With the crisis thus averted, the four Jewish young men excel in their training (1:17) and enter into a promising career in public service (1:19–20). In the story that follows, Daniel distinguishes himself as a dream interpreter, leading the king to "worship Daniel" (2:46) and proclaim, "Truly, your God is God of gods and Lord of kings and a revealer of mysteries, for you have been able to reveal this mystery!" (2:47). As a result, Daniel is elevated to a very high governmental position and uses his influence to gain similar jobs for his three Jewish friends, Shadrach, Meshach, and Abednego (2:48–49).

So far, this story represents the best-case scenario under the terms of the prophetic paradigm. Not only have Daniel and his friends gained worldly success, but they have induced the king to offer homage to the God of Israel. Immediately afterward, however, a more serious crisis arises when King Nebuchadnezzar (an alternative spelling of the name Nebuchadrezzar from Jeremiah) erects a massive golden statue of himself and demands that everyone in the city worship him as a God, threatening that anyone who "does not fall down and worship shall immediately be thrown into a furnace of blazing fire" (3:6).

Loyal to their God, Shadrach, Meshach, and Abednego refuse to commit idolatry, leading some rival officials to inform on them to the king (3:9–11). When they are called in for questioning, they reiterate their refusal, so that the king is "so filled with rage against [them] that his face was distorted" (3:19). He orders the furnace to be "heated up seven times more than was customary" (3:19), resulting in temperatures so high that the guards ordered to throw the dissenters into the fire are killed (3:22). Nevertheless, Shadrach, Meshach, and Abednego, protected by a figure with "the appearance of a god" (3:25), survive unscathed. The king is so deeply impressed that he decrees that "any blasphemy against the God of Shadrach, Meshach, and Abednego shall be torn limb from limb, and their houses laid in ruins; for there is no other god who is able to deliver in this way" (3:29).

This story is a close call on the political-theological level as well as the obvious narrative level. It is not only the lives of three Jewish officials that are endangered by the king's fiery furnace—the entire prophetic paradigm is at stake. That paradigm had taught Jews to tolerate mistreatment as punishment indirectly meted out by God. Yet how can such a schema make sense of this case, where the Jews are being punished precisely for being uncompromisingly *faithful* to God and his covenant?

From the political direction, this story also seems to endanger the assumption that the foreign king is always God's unwitting servant. First, Nebuchadnezzar is no longer fully unwitting, as he has already acknowledged Israel's God in some sense in the preceding story and even pledges to defend God's honor at the end of this one. More troublingly, for most of the story, he seems less a servant than an outright rival of God. The narrative maintains a level of plausible deniability here insofar as it is never made explicit to Nebuchadnezzar that the God of Israel purports to be more than one god among others, and this ignorance leaves room for him to repent once he sees the error of his ways. In any case, however, the relatively anonymous and impersonal instrumentalization and punishment that Jeremiah had in mind no longer seem to apply here.

The Book of Daniel indicates that God's foreign policy has shifted in other ways as well. From the very first dream Daniel deciphers up to the enigmatic visions that make up the second half of the book (chaps. 7–12), we see repeated evidence that God has in mind a very specific sequence of imperial powers, variously symbolized by metals of declining quality (2:32) or bizarrely hybridized animals (7:4–8). Second, an additional layer of management has appeared between God and the worldly rulers, in the form of spiritual beings that we could (with only slight anachronism) characterize as angels. The being who saved Shadrach, Meshach, and Abednego, for example, is most likely meant to be an angel of some sort. In addition, Nebuchadnezzar has a vision that includes a "holy watcher" who hands down God's sentence that the king will be deprived of his reason and live the life of a wild animal (4:25), only to be restored afterward. Finally, the concluding visions make much of the figure of Michael (10:12–14; 12:1), who wars on Israel's behalf against rival spiritual powers.

The most decisive change, however, is that the stakes of God's interventions in world politics are vastly higher. Instead of simply orchestrating events to chastise Israel and ultimately restore the exiles to the Promised Land, God is leading all of world history toward a dramatic final confrontation that will culminate in the establishment of a completely new world. A brief passage from the end of Daniel's vision encapsulates this shift:

> There shall be a time of anguish, such as has never occurred since nations first came into existence. But at that time your people shall be delivered,

everyone who is found written in the book. Many of those who sleep in the dust of the earth shall awake, some to everlasting life, and some to shame and everlasting contempt. Those who are wise shall shine like the brightness of the sky, and those who lead many to righteousness, like the stars forever and ever. (12:1–3)

It is as though the restoration of Israel as a nation is no longer enough—now the dead must be raised and face a final, utterly irrevocable reckoning.

In sum, Daniel documents not only the breakdown of the prophetic paradigm but the emergence of its successor, the apocalyptic paradigm. This paradigm produces a kind of spiritual overlay to political events, using surrealistic symbolism to lend mystery and profundity to the dreary sequence of imperial conquerors who so frequently swept through the ancient Near East. The rhetorical strategy of the Book of Daniel is also common in the apocalyptic literature. It projects its vision onto a legendary figure from Jewish history, who then retrospectively "predicts" the events leading up to the author's present—and beyond that, into the final days that are surely at hand.

The decisive moment in Daniel's apocalyptic narrative comes when an earthly ruler sets himself up as a conscious rival to God. Outraged by political setbacks,

he shall be enraged and take action against the holy covenant. He shall turn back and pay heed to those who forsake the holy covenant. Forces sent by him shall occupy and profane the temple and fortress. They shall abolish the regular burnt offering and set up the abomination that makes desolate. . . . The king shall act as he pleases. He shall exalt himself and consider himself greater than any god, and shall speak horrendous things against the God of gods. (11:30–31, 36)

In a final campaign, however, "he shall come to his end, with no one to help him," defeated by "the great prince" Michael (11:44–12:1).

By all accounts, the evil king of this vision is Antiochus Epiphanes, ruler of one of the smaller empires that emerged after Alexander the Great's death. Antiochus gained control over the land of Judea at a time when Jews had been living there for generations, beneficiaries of King Cyrus's decision to return exiled elites to their native lands and financially support their local religions. The Book of Daniel was likely written or compiled during his reign, as his career can be neatly reconciled with the vision's "predictions" up until the decisive final campaign (11:40–45). A more literal presentation of the story of Antiochus's reign and the Jews' reaction to it is found in the Books of the Maccabees, named for the family of warrior-priests who defeated the foreign rulers and created the last independent Jewish state prior to the establishment of the modern state of Israel.

What distinguished Antiochus from previous rulers was that he was what we might call a Hellenistic fundamentalist—he insisted that the Jews be converted to the Greek way of life and religion. His plans met with some success, as he was able to recruit Jason, a corrupt high priest, to help implement his policies, starting with a Greek-style gymnasium (2 Maccabees 4:9–10). After making this initial inroad, Antiochus

> set aside the existing royal concessions to the Jews . . . and he destroyed the lawful ways of living and introduced new customs contrary to the law. He took delight in establishing a gymnasium right under the citadel, and he induced the noblest of the young men to wear the Greek hat [in tribute to the god Hermes]. There was such an extreme of Hellenization and increase in the adoption of foreign ways because of the surpassing wickedness of Jason, who was ungodly and no true high priest, that the priests were no longer intent upon their service at the altar. (4:11–14)

Later, Antiochus makes a point of entering the temple in person and profaning its holy vessels (5:15). Shortly thereafter, he takes advantage of the Jews' Sabbath observance to launch a brutal attack resulting in many deaths (5:25). In this and in many other ways, Antiochus establishes himself as a self-conscious enemy not simply of the Jews but of their religion—and hence their God.

These events utterly shatter the prophetic paradigm of the relationship between God and the earthly rulers. At this point, the faithful remnant of the Jewish community takes two paths. First, Judas Maccabeus, who will emerge as the leader of the revolt against Antiochus, escapes with some comrades into the wilderness (5:27), whence they will return to cleanse the Promised Land as their ancestors never did—effectively reestablishing the Deuteronomistic paradigm.

Second, those who remain in the city often submit to martyrdom. In some ways, this latter approach remains in line with the prophetic exhortation to submit to persecution by wicked rulers as a punishment from God, and the author of 2 Maccabees makes frequent editorial remarks to explicitly reaffirm this principle (e.g., 5:17–20, 6:12). Yet the same author records a famous account of martyrdom in which the victims themselves do not rest content with patiently bearing up under their sufferings (chap. 7). The martyrs in question are a mother and her seven sons, who refuse to violate the covenant by eating pork, even under pain of unbelievably horrific tortures. The mother is made to witness the torture and death of all seven of her sons before being murdered herself, and she is uncompromisingly defiant throughout the proceedings. Though she and her sons make occasional references to their sufferings as a punishment on the nation for unfaithfulness (7:18, 32, 38), it seems clear that the true source of the mother's courage is her unwavering conviction that God will ultimately raise their sons from the dead (7:9, 14, 23, 29).

Here the promise of the prophetic paradigm—that one's ancestors will eventually return to the Promised Land—is no longer operative. Not only are they already in the Promised Land, but their family line is being radically extinguished. Yet just as their Deuteronomistic and prophetic forebears had done before them, they respond to an event that could discredit God by doubling down. Their unjust, seemingly inexplicable deaths will be the occasion for God to show his power in the most profound possible way. As the mother says to her dying son,

> I beg you, my child, to look at the heaven and the earth and see everything that is in them, and recognize that God did not make them out of things that existed. And in the same way the human race came into being. Do not fear this butcher, but prove worthy of your brothers. Accept death, so that in God's mercy I may get you back again along with your brothers. (7:28–29)

If the Maccabees respond to the breakdown in the prophetic paradigm by forcing a reboot of the Deuteronomistic covenant, these martyrs are effectively demanding that God reboot creation itself, that he re-create them along with the world they live in. In other words, if the world no longer makes sense in light of the apocalyptic thinker's faith in a just and powerful God, then so much the worse for the world.

THE INSIDER-OUTSIDER

It was in the milieu of apocalyptic thought that Christianity arose, and centuries later, the early Islamic community would renew the spirit of apocalyptic protest in an age when Christianity had become all too comfortable in this world. Hence it would be no exaggeration to call the birth of apocalyptic one of the most decisive developments in world history. And it all came about because of the shortsighted cultural-religious policies of Antiochus Epiphanes, an all-but-forgotten king who ruled for just over a decade during the turbulent period between Alexander the Great's conquest and the rise of the Roman Empire.

The biblical texts seem to have an awareness of this strange disconnect. Daniel's vision is a vertiginous mixture of contempt and grandiosity. After a symbolic representation of the Persian Empire as a ram defeated by a goat (representing Alexander), Antiochus emerges as "another horn, a little one," which grew up after the goat's original horns were broken (i.e., when Alexander's empire broke apart after his death). Yet this incongruously anthropomorphized "little horn" is God's ultimate enemy, whose defeat ushers in the end of history.

Similarly, Antiochus's death as recounted in 2 Maccabees is not only painful but utterly humiliating—and at the same time, it is administered personally by God himself. The sequence begins when he meets with a military defeat (9:2) and decides to take out his frustration on the Jews. After boasting that he "will make Jerusalem a cemetery of Jews" (9:4), he receives an "incurable and invisible blow" from God himself, such that "he was seized with a pain in his bowels, for which there was no relief, and with sharp internal tortures—and that very justly, for he had tortured the bowels of others with

many and strange inflictions" (9:5–6). Yet he continues his railing against the
Jews so that "he fell out of his chariot as it was rushing along, and the fall was
so hard as to torture every limb of his body" (9:8). Even worse, "the ungodly
man's body swarmed with worms, and while he was still living in anguish and
pain, his flesh rotted away, and because of the stench the whole army felt re-
vulsion at his decay. Because of his intolerable stench no one was able to carry
the man who a little while before had thought that he could touch the stars
of heaven" (9:9–10). One can perhaps imagine the satisfactions derived from
imagining a mortal enemy in such a state, yet it seems somehow beneath
the dignity of God—and disturbingly reminiscent of the merciless cruelty of
Antiochus himself—to be administering such sadistic punishments.

Only when he can no longer "endure his own stench" does it occur to
him to repent, saying, "It is right to be subject to God; mortals should not
think that they are equal to God" (9:12). He decides to refrain from at-
tacking Jerusalem, to treat the Jews as full citizens, to restore all he had
plundered from the Temple, and even to "become a Jew and . . . visit every
inhabited place to proclaim the power of God" (9:18). When the pain does
not abate, he writes a fawning letter to "his worthy Jewish citizens" (9:19),
but even that is not enough to dissuade "the Lord, who would no longer
have mercy on him" (9:13). It is as though the purpose of the protracted
punishment is to force Antiochus to repent, in order to gain the further
satisfaction of verifying that he is beyond all hope.

From this perspective, Antiochus appears as the archetypal resident
of hell. The pain consuming his entire body anticipates the unquenchable
flames, he is tormented by worms in such a way as to make him repulsive
rather than pitiable, and the coup de grace of his punishment is his belated
and fruitless repentance. The apparatus of hell is not yet fully developed,
meaning that his suffering is finite. Yet Antiochus can perhaps anticipate
eternal torment insofar as his malicious actions inspired the hope for the
resurrection of the dead and the Last Judgment—both necessary precondi-
tions for the later idea of eternal physical suffering.

This connection makes sense if we realize that Antiochus is also the
model for hell's most famous inmate: the devil. He shares with the devil a

conscious rebellion against God, motivated by a mixture of wounded pride and sheer spite. This leads him to persecute God's faithful remnant with such ferocity that they can make sense of their world only by developing a complex spiritual overlay for political events. This apocalyptic vision transforms the vagaries of geopolitics into a cosmic drama culminating in a final confrontation between the head of God's heavenly host and God's greatest political-theological rival: Antiochus Epiphanes, the "little horn."

Despite the pragmatic benefits that may have come from speaking of ongoing political events in a kind of code, it is a mistake to assume that apocalyptic documents are "coded" in any reductive sense. It is not the case that the theological symbolism "really" refers to "real" political events, because in the Hebrew biblical tradition that reaches its fullest development and its limit in this historical moment, the political is always immediately theological. This is above all the case with Antiochus. We cannot say that the apocalyptic figure of the "little horn" merely "symbolizes" Antiochus, because it is Antiochus's horrific deeds that inspire the development of the entire system of apocalyptic symbolism, which initially exists in order to account for him.

In the centuries that followed, Jewish and Christian thinkers would reread (and in some cases rewrite) the Hebrew biblical tradition as though it had always been apocalyptic in intent. The prophetic writers would be transformed from political-theological commentators into visionaries giving us hints of God's mysterious plan, and even the early patriarchs would be pressed into service as apocalyptic preachers (most notably the enigmatic Enoch, who "walked with God" and then "was no more, because God took him"; Genesis 5:22–23). It would come to seem that there had always been an apparatus of angels and demons governing the world, that God had always had a plan culminating in the resurrection of the dead and the Last Judgment, and that God had always had an archrival plotting against humanity, even in the Garden of Eden itself.

Yet it was not always so. All of these theological developments had a concrete political origin that can be pinpointed with uncanny precision. Even if Antiochus seems little more than a forgettable imitation of

Pharaoh, the theological crisis his political agenda prompted sparked the development of the apocalyptic paradigm, in which he himself would play a starring role. Pharaoh may be the earliest relevant antecedent for the devil, but Antiochus ushers in the transition whereby the rival king becomes identified with a cosmic rival. In principle, the apocalyptic worldview came into being on the day that Antiochus Epiphanes committed his greatest crime against God and desecrated the Temple. And therefore we can say with only a slight exaggeration that on that day the devil was born.

Admittedly, not every scholar shares this view. Most notably, it is diametrically opposed to the theory recently put forth by Elaine Pagels in *The Origin of Satan*. Like me, she breaks with a history of ideas approach, instead offering what she characterizes as a social history of Satan, focused more on the sociopolitical background that gave demonic symbolism its plausibility than on the literary development of the symbolism itself. In her account, which covers the Hebrew Bible, the New Testament, and early Christian writings, the devil consistently appears as a ready tool to "demonize" *internal* enemies. Indeed, in her brief discussion of the Maccabean period, she barely mentions Antiochus, instead drawing attention to the many Jews who found his program of Hellenistic assimilation all too appealing.[1] Only when Christianity emerges as a predominantly non-Jewish movement, Pagels argues, do we find any identification between Satan and pagan rulers—because only at this point can the pagan rulers be meaningfully identified as internal to the same community as the gentile Christians.[2]

In my view, Pagels' theory, though it is elegant and in many ways convincing, misses a key point: from at least the time of the classical prophets if not before, the pagan ruler, although clearly "outside" God's people, was very much "inside" God's sphere of influence. This holds true even for Antiochus, who is the absolute enemy, beyond all hope of repentance or reconciliation—yet serves as the linchpin of God's plan to create a new heaven and a new earth.

We can make sense of this paradox if we return to the problem of evil as articulated in the framework of minority monotheism. The strategy for coping with that problem throughout the development of the Hebrew biblical tradition has been precisely to claim the unaccountable, uncontrollable events of life—disease, famine, natural disaster, and most of all the vagaries of imperial politics—as *part of the plan*. The Deuteronomistic, prophetic, and apocalyptic paradigms become apparatuses for integrating what is *outside* human control and using it to shore up the credibility of the *inside*. God's covenant with Israel is not called into question when a famine strikes but confirmed more powerfully than would be possible in the regular run of events. When foreigners ravage the land and deport Israel's leaders, that does not mean that the covenant has ended but that it has taken on an unexpectedly global scope. And even when the experience of the truly unthinkable—the persecution of the righteous for their very righteousness—threatens to tear the apparatus apart, it still manages to convert the ultimate outsider (God's eternal enemy) into the ultimate insider (the culmination of God's plan).

Here we can connect the political theology of the Hebrew Bible with the version most familiar to contemporary theoretical debates. When Carl Schmitt famously proclaims in *Political Theology* that sovereignty—for him, a mark at once of God and of the earthly ruler—consists in deciding on the state of exception,[3] he is repeating the same basic gesture of the Hebrew biblical tradition. Anything that qualifies as a state of exception, be it a natural disaster, an economic crisis, a state of internal unrest, or a foreign invader, is by definition something that one *cannot* predict or control. The sovereign does not "decide" whether an emergency will occur, because the very nature of an emergency is that it is unforeseen. Yet the Schmittian sovereign, just like the biblical God, uses precisely these events, which might seem to demonstrate his lack of control, as an occasion for asserting his control—indeed, for demonstrating the need for his continued existence and authority.

This parallel is possible because in the Hebrew biblical tradition, the problem of evil is not a question of bloodless metaphysical speculation. What is at stake in the problem of evil is the question of legitimacy, a legitimacy that is inseparably political and theological. Nevertheless, there is something surprising in Schmitt's formulation from the point of view of the Hebrew Bible: namely, that the earthly ruler should be comparable to God. As we have seen, it is precisely that possibility that the Hebrew biblical tradition is at pains to avoid. If there is any theological parallel to the earthly ruler within any of the paradigms we have examined, it is not God but his cosmic rival, the devil. And this demonic view of worldly powers continues to hold for the idiosyncratic apocalyptic movement that would come to be called Christianity.

THE THREE PARADIGMS

The next two chapters are devoted to the changes that Christianity introduces into the apocalyptic political-theological scheme that it inherits from the Hebrew biblical tradition. Before complicating the last of them, however, it may be beneficial to briefly review the paradigms that grew out of the Hebrew biblical tradition's series of distinctive attempts to deal with the problem of evil in changing historical circumstances (see Table 1).

TABLE 1. Political Theological Paradigms from the Hebrew Biblical Tradition

	Deuteronomistic	Prophetic	Apocalyptic
Political context	Israelite self-rule	Jewish diaspora under indifferent or good rulers	Jewish diaspora under self-consciously hostile rulers
Meaning of suffering	Punishment as retribution	Punishment as purification	Necessary part of divine plan
Meaning of delayed judgment/punishment	Time for repentance	Using earthly rulers' evil deeds for good	Necessary part of divine plan
Place of earthly ruler	Potential rival to God	Unwitting tool of God	Cosmic enemy of God

Compared to the apocalyptic paradigm, the Deuteronomistic and prophetic paradigms have an admirable simplicity. In both, suffering that might threaten to undermine God's authority is converted into deserved punishment, which can be acknowledged as suffering without being evil. In both schemes, God's moral standards hold in principle for all nations: Canaan and Babylon both receive their just punishment in the end. Over time, however, the difference between Israel and the other nations becomes more pronounced. The Deuteronomistic paradigm already singles out Israel as the only nation with an *explicit* covenant with God, and in the prophetic paradigm, God punishes Israel in the hope of restoring them but seems to have no such corrective purpose when he punishes other nations. The divergence comes to a head in the apocalyptic paradigm, as Antiochus Epiphanes' terrible fate includes the pain of fruitless repentance.

There is a similar articulation of the meaning of suffering. In the Deuteronomistic paradigm, it can seem that the punishment is simply an end in itself and that even Israel will be justly destroyed if it defies God's law. In the prophetic paradigm, the punishment of the other nations retains this character, and while Israel's suffering remains punitive, it takes on the additional purpose of purification or purgation. A time lag was undoubtedly involved between sin and retribution, but that very deferral could appear as evidence of God's mercy, allowing time to repent—or of his power and glory, insofar as he could make use of the depredations of the conquerors before giving them their due punishment. Despite these important differences, within both the Deuteronomistic and the prophetic paradigm, the overall strategy remains the same: denying the very existence of unjust suffering.

In the apocalyptic paradigm, however, that strategy is decisively abandoned. The suffering of the martyrs is explicitly acknowledged as unjust—indeed, that is the entire point. Nevertheless, that suffering is still asserted to be *necessary* insofar as it is a part of God's plan. The nature of this necessity is never directly specified, and so this move can be characterized as a promise, and therefore deferral, of meaning. Suffering becomes *meaningful* even as it is denied any concrete *present meaning*. Perhaps for this very reason, the time lag becomes less and less tolerable as patience under unjust suffering comes at the price of a radical demand for final and definitive justice in the form of the Last Judgment and the new heaven and earth.

Even more problematic is the role of the apocalyptic enemy, who between the Maccabean and early Christian periods comes to be clearly identified as our familiar figure of Satan or the devil. To the extent that he relieves God of responsibility for unjust suffering, he also diminishes God's power and control. Yet insofar as the devil's wickedness is inscribed into

God's mysterious plan as a necessary element, it becomes more and more difficult to avoid attributing his deeds directly to God, undermining God's goodness. In short, by introducing the devil, the apocalyptic paradigm opens up the possibility that God will become identified with him—utterly failing at the goal of the entire political-theological tradition that gave rise to apocalyptic, which is to relieve God of responsibility for evil.

CHAPTER 2

THE NEW TESTAMENT
AND EARLY CHRISTIANITY

APOCALYPTIC AND ITS CHRISTIAN VICISSITUDES

There is a passage from Isaiah that in many ways anticipates the apocalyptic stance toward suffering exemplified in the martyrdom of the Jewish mother and her seven sons in 2 Maccabees. It recounts the unanticipated prosperity and exaltation of God's servant (52:13), despite his "marred . . . appearance, beyond human semblance" (52:14). This servant is "a man of suffering and acquainted with infirmity; and as one from whom others hide their faces, he was despised, and we held him of no account" (53:4). All of his suffering is not in vain, however, for "he was wounded for our transgressions, crushed for our iniquities; upon him was the punishment that made us whole, and by his bruises we were healed" (53:5). Perhaps out of awareness of this redemptive mission, the suffering servant does not share Job's defiance: "He was oppressed, and he was afflicted, yet he did not open his mouth; like a lamb that is led to the slaughter, and like a sheep that before its shearers is silent, so he did not open his mouth" (53:7). And for this silent and patient obedience in the face of unjust punishment, we are told, God will greatly reward him (53:10–12).

This passage is most famous in Christian circles as a purported prophecy of Jesus's redemptive suffering and death for human sins. In its original context, however, it makes little sense to associate this figure with the messiah or anointed one. Not only is that role already occupied by the good

Persian emperor Cyrus, who is to restore Israel to the Promised Land after its long exile, but the Suffering Servant is very explicitly the opposite of a mighty liberator, utterly lacking in majesty and strength. He may be promised a "portion with the great" and the opportunity to "divide the spoil with the strong" (53:12), but the poetic and rhetorical force of the passage depends on the fact that this is a surprising reversal.

The most likely referent for this figure, many interpreters agree, is the downtrodden and oppressed Jewish community itself, as represented by its righteous remnant. And here another difference from traditional ideas about Christ surfaces: the suffering is not vicarious but collective. Even if we limit the Suffering Servant to the remnant, they are not suffering in order to somehow take on punishment deserved by others. Instead, they are suffering precisely *as* part of the people of Israel—and the whole people of Israel benefits from their righteousness just as the whole people must be punished for the sins committed by certain other members.

Their patient suffering in exile is part of God's plan to purify and restore Israel, which in the context of Isaiah is to be brought to completion by God's anointed servant, Cyrus. The role of the community's suffering becomes much more difficult to understand in the apocalyptic context, however. It can no longer be viewed as a purification, since they are suffering for their very faithfulness to God. On the narrative level, therefore, its role is fundamentally negative: the magnitude of the suffering serves to make God's rival all the more villainous while rendering God's victory and the restoration of Israel all the more striking and glorious. God's chosen people must suffer because that makes for a better story.

Once the apocalyptic paradigm forecloses the possibility of identifying the pagan ruler as God's anointed, it becomes necessary to read Isaiah differently. The messiah's role must be reconceived, and this opens up the potential for identifying the messiah and Suffering Servant. As Daniel Boyarin has shown, this view was considered a live option within Jewish theology even before Jesus's time.[1] Obviously it was an especially attractive view for those faithful to Jesus of Nazareth, who also remained faithful to the strategy we have seen time and time again in the preceding chapter: doubling down. Far from representing Jesus's defeat, they claimed, his shameful execution was actually the greatest possible proof that he really *was* the messiah.

As represented in the New Testament literature, early Christian defenses of this bold and counterintuitive claim took two basic paths. The first strategy was to join in the broader trend of rereading (and rewriting) the Hebrew biblical tradition from an apocalyptic standpoint—but with a Jesus-focused twist. Examples of this approach can already be found in Paul's epistles, which essentially all scholars regard as the earliest extant Christian literature. In many passages, Paul deploys a strategy of typology, seeking out symbolic parallels and counterpoints to Christ in the Hebrew Bible. Among the most important of these is Adam, the first human being, "who is a type of the one who was to come" (Romans 5:14), meaning Jesus. The Gospels take a much less nuanced approach, retrospectively reading selected passages from the Hebrew Bible as "predicting" events of Jesus's life. Their chosen snippets often seem to have been cherry-picked with little regard to their original context and meaning, and in some cases, one begins to suspect that certain events in Jesus's career may have been invented precisely *because* there seemed to be a suitable "prediction" in the scriptures.

The second and most important evidence that Jesus was the messiah was the testimony that he had risen from the dead and had given evidence of this, first to his most intimate associates, then to a wider group—and finally, "as to one untimely born," to the apostle Paul (1 Corinthians 15:8), who had never met Jesus during his earthly life but would become one of the most energetic missionaries and intellectuals of the early Christian movement. For Paul as for many others, this event was decisive evidence that Jesus, as God's chosen messiah, had set the apocalyptic sequence in motion. Jesus is "the first fruits of those who have died" (1 Corinthians 15:20), a sure sign that God will soon bring about the resurrection of all, the Last Judgment, and the new messianic kingdom. Indeed, apparently Paul's preaching was so emphatic on the imminent approach of the eschatological fulfillment that he needed to reassure a group of his followers that those who had died since declaring their loyalty to Jesus would not miss out on the resurrection (1 Thessalonians 4:13–18).

In short, not only was Jesus predicted in the Hebrew scriptures, but his resurrection shows that he is an integral part of the apocalyptic sequence. Overall, then, early Christians embraced the same strategy as the apocalyptic literature, explaining unjust suffering—first of all Christ's, but also that of his followers—as having been part of the plan all along. In so doing, they posit that suffering as *meaningful* in a way that will be revealed in due course. In other words, they repeat the gesture of deferral that I described in the previous chapter—suffering is given no present meaning, though a future meaning is promised.

The one major exception to the strategy of deferral is found in Paul's epistles, where Christ's crucifixion has an immediate present function. In Paul's view, the messiah's execution at the hands of the Roman Empire, with the complicity of the Jewish authorities, showed that all systems of law—the laws of the Jews and of all the other nations, as represented by Rome—were incapable of achieving justice and were therefore fundamentally illegitimate. By taking upon himself the curse of the law, Jesus had made it possible for all people, Jewish or Gentile, to take part in God's promises (Galatians 4:10–14). And while the majority of the Jews had rejected Jesus for the time being, Paul—in keeping with the political-theological tradition in which he stands—believes that this apparent setback is actually *the greatest possible proof* of God's intention that "all Israel will be saved" (Romans 11:26). As he explains it, "Through [the Jews'] stumbling salvation has come to the Gentiles, so as to make Israel jealous" (11:11)—and when they see the Gentiles enjoying the promises of God, they will surely be brought back into the fold, bringing about the final consummation of history, the resurrection of the dead.[2]

The devil is not a major presence in Paul's teachings, because for Paul the devil—in his role as symbol for worldly systems of legitimacy—has already in principle been defeated on the cross. The major eschatological event that remains in the future for Paul is not the defeat of the devil but the resurrection, and all his apocalyptic narratives focus exclusively on the resurrection (1 Thessalonians 4:13–18; 1 Corinthians 15).[3] While the devil still holds de facto power and must be reckoned with, Paul urges his followers to live "as if not" bound by the legal and social status defined by earthly power structures as they wait for the final vindication of God's justice (1 Corinthians 7:25–31),[4] which by all evidence Paul expected to arrive very soon. In the meantime, his communities would serve as a vanguard of God's messianic kingdom, anticipating in this life the form of life of the world to come.

As this chapter shows, few other early Christian authors were as successful as Paul in mastering the apocalyptic tensions associated with a suffering messiah. In part, this stems from historical events that rendered Paul's optimistic stance toward the Jewish community less and less plausible to the communities represented by the New Testament literature. This was above all the case after the Romans destroyed the Temple in Jerusalem in 70 CE— an event that Paul almost certainly did not live to see but that seemed to many Gentile Christians to be a definitive sign of God's curse upon the Jews for rejecting the messiah. In a perverse step, the very apocalyptic logic that had grown out of the Jews' attempts to make sense of their special relationship to God was deployed to show that God had rejected them.

In short, the unique balance of an apocalyptic hope that can make sense of unexpected and counterintuitive events, in such a way as to found a genuine alternative to the demonic rulers of this world, proved increasingly elusive. This deadlock led some early Christian thinkers to significantly revise the apocalyptic paradigm, generating a new paradigm that broke with the previous tradition by severing the nexus between the political and the theological—or at least attempting to.

THE HALL OF MIRRORS

Even if the identification of Jesus as the messiah necessitates a retroactive reconsideration of the details of the apocalyptic sequence, the nature of the messiah's apocalyptic mission remains the same: the defeat of God's cosmic adversary, the devil, whom Jesus directly confronts in all four of the canonical Gospels. This move involves a decided raising of the stakes—in other words, a further doubling down. No longer are we dealing with a petty king like Antiochus who, if not for his fateful decision to antagonize the Jewish community, may well have been relegated to the footnotes of a mostly forgotten transitional era. Now the political representative of the cosmic enemy is Rome, the greatest empire that part of the world had ever known.

Nowhere in the New Testament is the polemic against Rome more unmistakable than in the Book of Revelation. Alongside the majority of biblical scholars, thinkers as different as Nietzsche and Engels have recognized the deeply political message of Revelation. Nietzsche concludes the first essay of *The Genealogy of Morals* by asserting that the ultimate "symbol of the struggle" between master and slave morality, "inscribed in letters legible across all human history, is 'Rome against Judea, Judea against Rome,'" and he puts forward the Book of Revelation as the ultimate expression of Jewish hatred against the Roman masters.[5] Engels claims that "Christianity was originally a movement of oppressed people: it first appeared as the religion of slaves and emancipated slaves, of poor people deprived of all rights, of peoples subjugated or dispersed by Rome."[6] As in Nietzsche's case, his primary example is the Book of Revelation, and he goes on to interpret it in detail using the most recent scholarship available to him.

Beyond this historical question, for both authors, Revelation proves to be a site for thinking through the conflict that is most central to their understanding of their contemporary moment. For Nietzsche, it symbolizes the triumph of slave morality in the French Revolution, while for Engels, it portends the inevitable victory of socialism over the forces of the bourgeoisie. In this regard, they stand in a long and durable tradition of readers who have found this baffling collection of heterogeneous visions to be of urgent contemporary relevance. As Elizabeth Schüssler Fiorenza points out, both conservative American Christians and liberation theologians have drawn on Revelation as a potent weapon in their respective political-theological struggles.[7] And while Schüssler Fiorenza is clearly more sympathetic with liberation theologians than with their more reactionary counterparts, she reads Revelation as a complex rhetorical performance meant to call forth precisely such reflections on the readers' own political situation.

In this regard, the rhetorical strategy of Revelation is fundamentally similar to that of the Book of Daniel. Its purported "predictions" of recent events serve to inscribe the present into the apocalyptic sequence, providing hope in a seemingly hopeless situation. The primary difference—aside from its much more elaborate symbolism—is in the timescale. Where Daniel's vision of successive empires spanned generations and its "predictions" were put in the mouth of a long-dead legendary figure, Revelation compresses its vision into the lifetime of most of its audience and is attributed to an otherwise unknown John, who is a contemporary and fellow sufferer with his readers.[8] This is clearest in a direct reference to Daniel: "I saw a beast rising out of the sea, having ten horns and seven heads; and on its horns were ten diadems, and on its heads were blasphemous names. And the beast that I saw was like a leopard, its feet were like a bear's, and its mouth was like a lion's mouth" (Revelation 13:1–2). As Schüssler Fiorenza points out, "The depiction of this bizarre creature combines in surrealistic fashion all the features of the four beasts of Daniel 7, which represents different kingdoms and political powers" so that "the beast embodies all political powers of the time."[9]

The rise of this beast, compressing a whole history of political oppression into itself, is presided over by the "dragon," which is explicitly identified as a symbol of the devil (12:9). The chapter prior to the rise of the beast had documented the dragon's harassment of "a woman clothed with the sun, with the moon under her feet, and on her head a crown of twelve stars," who "was pregnant and was crying out in birth pangs, in the agony of giving birth" (12:1–2). Later Christian tradition has identified this woman with the Virgin Mary, but most scholars agree it refers to Israel, perhaps as embodied in the messianic community (here playing the role of the remnant). Though the dragon sought to "devour her child [Christ] as soon as it was born" (12:4), he was thwarted, then further humiliated in a heavenly war against "Michael and his angels" (12:7). Again, the timescale is compressed, as Jesus's birth is the earliest historical event clearly depicted in the vision. At the same time, however, this abbreviated time scale seems to compress all of human history into itself, as the war in heaven is often associated with an era before the creation of the material world.

In the face of this defeat, the dragon decides to attempt to produce the beast as his own quite literal Antichrist, including a resurrection: "One of its heads seemed to have received a death-blow, but its mortal wound had been healed" (13:3). Here we receive a clue to the specific identity of the beast (or rather of the relevant head) as the emperor Nero, who seems to inherit the mantle of Antiochus Epiphanes. Nero was the first emperor to incite significant persecution against Christians, blaming them for a major fire in Rome. Like most Roman emperors of the first century, Nero was assassinated, but as Schüssler Fiorenza points out, "Rumor had it that Nero did not really die but would return with the Parthian army to take revenge."[10] This Antichrist also gets his own anti–John the Baptist in the person of the false prophet who "makes the earth and its inhabitants worship the beast" (13:12; cf. 19:20).

This play of mirrors repeats itself throughout Revelation, leading Schüssler Fiorenza to claim that it is structured around a series of antitypes. The righteous Jerusalem is counterposed to the wicked Babylon, a symbolic code name for Rome that is appropriate given that both cities "shared the dubious distinction of having destroyed Jerusalem and the temple."[11] Similarly, the heavenly woman who gives birth to the messiah has as her counterpart the "Whore of Babylon," a personification of Rome's promiscuous idolatry and general injustice. She is depicted as "seated on many waters" (17:1), the precise opposite of the heavens in biblical imagery,[12] and as "drunk with the blood of the saints and the blood of the witnesses of Jesus" (17:6). The angel clarifies to John that the waters "are peoples and multitudes and nations and languages" (17:15), that is, Rome's international power, and later visions of Rome's downfall make much of its demonic religious practices (18:2) as well as its unjust economic policies—including the trading of "human lives" (18:13; cf. 18:2, 11–12). Here as in the Hebrew Bible, the problems that we would regard as political and economic are *immediately* theological in their significance.

The intention behind this play of mirrors, it seems clear, is that the devil and his demonic forces have attempted to usurp God's place, though their efforts are so obviously doomed as to constitute an unintentional parody. The Whore of Babylon cannot truly match the glorious beauty of the Woman of Heaven, just as the beast appears hideously grotesque compared to the actual messiah. It is here, however, that a certain ambivalence enters in, because it can at times seem as though the mirror effect is reversed—as though Rome is the model for the heavenly Jerusalem. I am not thinking merely of the fact that God does his fair share of destruction throughout the visions, since such manifestations of divine justice are familiar from as far back as the Deuteronomistic paradigm. In some cases, however, the violence reaches such a disturbing pitch that it can be difficult to remember that we are dealing with the God of justice rather than the wicked empire:

> Then I saw an angel standing in the sun, and with a loud voice he called to all the birds that fly in midheaven, "Come, gather for the great supper of God, to eat the flesh of kings, the flesh of captains, the flesh of the mighty, the flesh of horses and their riders—flesh of all, both free and slave, both small and great." Then I saw the beast and the kings of the earth with their armies gathered to make war against the rider on the horse and against his army. And the beast was captured, and with it the false prophet who had performed in its presence the signs by which he deceived those who had received the mark of the beast and those who worshipped its image. These two were thrown alive into the lake of fire that burns with sulfur. And the rest were killed by the sword of the rider on the horse, the sword that came from his mouth; and all the birds were gorged with their flesh. (Revelation 19:17–21)

One is almost tempted to call this depiction of cruelty, brutality, and cannibalism a parody of the Christian rite of the Last Supper—except that it is carried out by the angelic rather than demonic forces. Rome's parody of God is answered with self-parody.

We have noted that apocalyptic writings tend to use the present sufferings of the righteous community as a negative counterpoint, rendering God's subsequent victory all the more glorious. Here we can detect a further reversal, where the sufferings of the wicked serve to enhance the joy of the saints. In some cases, this duality can be jarring, as when God declares, "Death will be no more; mourning and crying and pain will be no more; for the first things have passed away" (21:4), and almost immediately goes on to say, "But as for the cowardly, the faithless, the polluted, the murderers, the fornicators, the sorcerers, the idolaters, and all liars, their place will be in the lake that burns with fire and sulfur, which is the second death" (21:8). Suffering is no more—unless you deserve it, in which case it is infinitely extended. This seems an uncanny parallel to Antiochus's elaborate torture of the martyrs, or indeed the Roman practice of crucifixion, both of which sought to keep their victims alive and in utter agony for as long as possible. Is the stark opposition of good and evil beginning to break down?

The same question arises from another angle in another seemingly incongruous image, which occurs after a detailed description of the dimensions and unimaginable wealth of the heavenly city:

> I saw no temple in the city, for its temple is the Lord God the Almighty and the Lamb. And the city has no need of sun or moon to shine on it, for the glory of God is its light, and its lamp is the Lamb. The nations will walk by its light, and the kings of the earth will bring their glory into it. Its gates will never be shut by day—and there will be no night there. People will bring into it the glory and the honor of the nations. (21:22–26)

Who are these "kings of the earth" and these "nations"? Why does God need to derive glory from them—apparently eternally? Here, as with the wealth of the city, the model for glory seems to be Rome, a model that the vision of Revelation can exceed but not escape. And given the immediate identity of the political and the theological, we can say the same on a theological level: the devil may be presented as a parody of the divine, but the divine ends up looking like an exaggeration of the devil.

In other words, apocalyptic, which began as the most radical demand for the entire world to be entirely remade, seems to be at risk of simply remaking the world as it is. As Engels and Nietzsche recognized, the Book of Revelation is a book about revolution—and at this point we are confronted with a fundamental question: Is a revolution doomed to install a new form of oppression? On the surface, Revelation can be read as saying that the problem is not persecution as such but persecution with the wrong victims; not a worldwide rule of all the nations as such but a worldwide rule with the wrong rulers; not amassing wealth as such but an economic system that makes the wrong people rich. The New Jerusalem is to be preferred to Babylon/Rome, it seems, simply because it is ruled by God and God is definitionally in the right.

Even if Revelation presents it in an unmistakably stark way, this basic tension has been present from the very beginning of our investigation. As early as the Exodus, God is openly taking credit for natural disasters and acts of cruelty, and the biblical authors intend for us to view such objectively destructive acts as good because God is carrying them out against the *right* targets. The tension is ratcheted up in the prophetic paradigm, where God takes credit for the actions of the pagan rulers who were formally his enemies—so it is perhaps not a surprise that God would ultimately collapse into a mirror image of the earthly systems of rule that embody his cosmic enemy, the devil.

"ALL THESE KINGDOMS WILL I GIVE YOU"

Even the harshest critics of Christianity normally contrast its less attractive manifestations to the authentic teachings of Christ. However, those seeking sharp distinctions between the outlook of Revelation and that of the canonical Gospels are likely to be disappointed. All four evangelists are unanimous in presenting Jesus as living in a demon-haunted world. Particularly in Matthew, Mark, and Luke—which are grouped together as the "Synoptic" Gospels because of the similarity of their narratives, in contrast to the very different approach of John—we learn that Judea and Galilee are absolutely infested with demons, and exorcism is one of Jesus's most frequently performed miracles.

As in Daniel and Revelation, the demonic forces are a spiritual counterpart to the political situation—in this case, the situation of Roman rule. This is clearest in the case of a notorious demoniac from the region of Garasenes (Mark 5:1–20). When Jesus confronts the evil spirit who is possessing him in the Gospel of Mark, he responds, "My name is Legion; for we are many" (5:9). A "legion" is of course a well-known Roman military unit—indeed, one often refers to the Roman army simply as "the Roman legions." To any reader of the time, the Roman reference would have been immediately evident. Mark reinforces this connection by later having Jesus assemble and feed a crowd of five thousand men, the average size of a Roman legion (Mark 6:30–44). In case the reader has not gotten the message, Mark then goes further and has Jesus repeat the feat by later feeding four thousand men (Mark 8:1–10)—a smaller legion but a legion nonetheless.[13]

More important, all three of the Synoptic Gospels have Jesus confront the devil himself in person at the beginning of his career, at the end of an intensive forty-day fast in the desert (Matthew 4:1–11; Mark 1:12–13; Luke 4:1–13). While Mark's account of this incident is characteristically brief and elliptical, Matthew and Luke go into considerable detail. In both cases, the format is similar: the devil presents Jesus with temptations, which he rejects by quoting a relevant passage of scripture.

Both begin with the most immediately relevant temptation for a man who has been fasting for over a month: to turn stones into bread (Matthew 4:3; Luke 4:3). Jesus easily repulses this initial attack, and the devil quickly escalates with two further temptations: to jump off the pinnacle of the Temple in Jerusalem, virtually daring God to rescue him and thereby show his messianic role indisputably (Matthew 4:5–6; Luke 4:9–11), and to bow down to the devil, at which point the devil will grant him power over all the kingdoms of the world (Matthew 4:8–9; Luke 4:5–7). These two temptations, which could be characterized as "religious" and "political," respectively, are presented in reverse order in Matthew and Luke, perhaps providing a clue to the different emphases of these two evangelists. Yet there is a deeper interchangeability at work here, insofar as the religious and political temptations both break down the boundaries between the two realms. After all, the devil is offering Jesus political power in exchange for worshipping him, while Jesus's religious authority would hypothetically be confirmed by an indisputably *public* display of God's favor.

Particularly interesting from our perspective is that Jesus does not respond to the devil's offer of political power by denying that the devil has the authority to grant it. Instead, in both Matthew and Luke he quotes a key teaching from Deuteronomy: "Worship the Lord your God and serve him only" (6:13). One might say that Jesus is opting for the more important principle here, so that loyalty to God counts for more than quibbling about political power. Yet the narrative logic demands that the devil's claim to have dominion over the political world must be true, just as it demands that Jesus would actually be able to turn bread into stones and that God would prevent Jesus's suicide. If any of these conditions were false, then the temptation would not be a temptation but a charade.

The confrontation does not end here, of course. No ruler can tolerate disrespect and insubordination, particularly a ruler as proud as the devil, and so it is not surprising that at the end of Jesus's ministry, he is portrayed as being on a collision course with the rulers of this world. In this case, he deals primarily with the devil's earthly representatives, and as in the first temptation, so in the last, the political and religious are tangled together. While the events surrounding the night before Jesus's death are portrayed in convoluted and contradictory ways across the Gospels, the general sequence is as follows: one of his disciples, Judas Iscariot, betrays him and hands him over to the Temple authorities, who then hand him over to the Roman procurator, Pontius Pilate, to be crucified. This collusion between religious and political authorities reflects the inseparably religious and political nature of Jesus's crime, which comes to be summarized in the accusation that he claimed to be "King of the Jews" and thereby made himself equal to God.

It has been frequently noted that the later Gospels tend to become ever more sympathetic to Pilate and try to place as much blame as possible on the Jewish authorities. In this respect, scholars agree that they depart ever further from the historical Jesus's own self-understanding as a faithful Jew.[14] Already in Mark, the most overtly anti-Roman of the Gospels, however, there is very much a sense of shared responsibility. This emphasis on Jewish complicity with Jesus's death, along the correlative downplaying of the fact that a Roman official ultimately had him executed using the distinctively Roman practice of crucifixion, has played into the tragic history of Christian anti-Judaism and anti-Semitism, as well as the tendency to use Christianity to legitimate oppressive political powers. In the original context, however, it makes sense that the evangelists focus their sights on the Jewish authorities, because they are the ones who will understand what is at stake on a political-theological level. In contrast, Pilate elaborately performs his ignorance of the subtleties of Jewish religious squabbles.

The debate that plays out narratively in the Gospels is essentially that between the prophetic and the apocalyptic paradigms. From the evangelists' point of view, the Jewish authorities do not recognize that the apocalyptic sequence—including the arrival of the messiah—has begun. Instead, they live with the illusion that they are living under "normal" prophetic conditions and proceed, quite sensibly from their perspective, to use the same strategy of compromising with foreign rulers that by that time had preserved Jewish cultural and religious identity against all odds for centuries. Sometimes the compromises involved may turn out to be unsavory—as when they feel constrained to hand over an apocalyptic rabble-rouser to the Roman authorities in order to make it as clear as possible that he does not represent their views—but from the Jewish authorities' point of view, they are undoubtedly necessary.

This kind of complicity with God's apocalyptic foe is not entirely without precedent. Certain Jewish leaders cooperated with Antiochus's efforts to Hellenize Judaism, though 2 Maccabees presents them as isolated bad actors. Handing over Jesus to be executed, however, is clearly much more extreme and definitive than the opportunism of a handful of leaders—from the evangelists' standpoint, it represents a rejection of God's chosen messiah by essentially the entire religious leadership and, at least as presented in the New Testament literature, by the mainstream Jewish community as a whole.[15] As I have already noted, this rejection seemed in a sense more paradoxical and alarming than Jesus's death as such, all the more so when Gentiles quite unexpectedly began to respond much more eagerly than their Jewish peers to the messianic message. How could the chosen people reject God's plan for them? From this perspective, it was hard not to conclude that they had turned against God.

Within the New Testament literature, this identification of Jews as God's enemies culminates in the Gospel of John. Here the evangelist presents Jesus as continually associating the Jews with the devil and introduces the detail that the devil "personally" possesses the betrayer Judas (13:27)—whose name in Greek could also mean simply "Jew." In place of the confrontation with the devil in the desert, John's Jesus repeatedly confronts the devil in Jerusalem, and in true apocalyptic style, John has Jesus "predict" the destruction of the Temple, which most likely took place decades prior to the finalization of the Fourth Gospel. In this way, Jesus's conflict with the devil is cast in almost completely "religious" terms, as the devil's earthly representatives, the Jews, are characterized primarily by a refusal to adopt the appropriate beliefs about Jesus.

John's account of Jesus's encounter with Pilate is by far the most detailed and sympathetic of any of the Canonical Gospels and even presents Pilate as handing Jesus over to the Jews to be crucified (19:16). Along the way, Jesus explicitly minimizes Pilate's responsibility and blames the Jews: "You would have no power over me unless it was given you from above; therefore the one who handed me over to you is guilty of greater sin" (19:11).

What is the nature of this power granted to Pilate? As Giorgio Agamben has recently demonstrated, that authority does not include exercising judgment over Jesus. None of the evangelists portray Pilate as following accepted Roman legal norms, even the more flexible norms governing colonial administrators.[16] From this perspective, Jesus's death seems less like a legal execution and more like the outcome of a complex power play between Pilate and the Jewish authorities. Jesus submits to this exercise of power, which does indeed fulfill divine ends—but as in the prophetic paradigm, the divine purpose does not fully exculpate God's chosen tool. We might say that Jesus submits to Pilate and the Jewish authorities de facto but not de jure. And even if Jesus's statement is often read as relieving Pilate of responsibility, he only says that the Jews—who from the evangelists' perspective should have recognized Jesus—are guilty of a *greater* sin, implying that Pilate is guilty of a lesser one.

A similar dynamic can be found in the letters of Paul, though customary translations tend to obscure it somewhat. One of the most infamous lines of the Pauline corpus is Romans 13:1, which reads in the New Revised Standard Version: "Let every person be subject to the governing authorities; for there is no authority except from God, and those authorities that exist have been instituted by God." The Greek text is more ambiguous and could also be translated as "let every person be subject to those exercising powers over you; for there is no power except from God, and those that exist have been arranged by God." If we read it in this way, the verse seems compatible with the words the John puts in the mouth of Jesus, claiming that God has arranged for the outcome of certain power struggles—above all, the one that culminates in Jesus's public execution—without necessarily legitimating them in any absolute sense.

The difference is important because for Paul, the earthly powers emphatically *do not* have legitimate authority over the Christian community. As noted previously, they forfeited any legitimacy they may have previously possessed when they "crucified the Lord of Glory" (1 Corinthians 2:8). Indeed, he chastises some of his followers for taking their disputes to court:

> When any of you has a grievance against another, do you dare to take it to court before the unrighteous, instead of taking it before the saints? Do you not know that the saints will judge the world? And if the world is to be judged by you, are you incompetent to try trivial cases? Do you not know that we are to judge angels—to say nothing of ordinary matters? If you have ordinary cases, then, do you appoint as judges those who have no standing in the church? (1 Corinthians 6:1–4)

Just before this passage, Paul had recommended expelling an immoral member from the community, an action that he refers to as "hand[ing] this man over to Satan" (1 Corinthians 5:5). Clearly the world is still the devil's domain for Paul—a fact that Karl Barth has underlined by grouping his discussion of Romans 13:1 with that of the preceding verse: "Do not be overcome by evil, but overcome evil with good" (12:21).[17]

Drawing in part on Barth's commentary, Jacob Taubes has more recently claimed that "the Epistle to the Romans is a political theology, a *political* declaration of war on the Caesar."[18] The same could be said of the Book of Revelation, and so here as well we could ask the question of whether we have any indication that the new boss will be any different from the old boss. I emphasized the negative in my initial discussion of Revelation, but as Schüssler Fiorenza points out, a counter-reading is possible. If we turn our attention away from hell for the time being, there is a case to be made that the New Jerusalem is in some respects a radically different social order from that in Babylon/Rome: its fabulous wealth is shared with the entire city and available to be freely enjoyed by all, and its perpetually open gates are a striking counterpoint to political systems premised on exclusion. The movements of the oppressed that have drawn upon it—including the workers' movement, Latin American liberation theologians, and the US civil rights movement, to focus only on the last century—have been responding to a genuine promise: "See, I am making all things new" (Revelation 21:5). The fact that the text often seems to betray that promise does not negate the fact that it is there to betray.

The same can be said for much of the rest of the New Testament. Principles of nonviolence (modeled on Jesus's submission to his crucifixion), of radical egalitarianism (including what we might call "affirmative action" measures to invert the social hierarchy of the outside world), of nonacquisitiveness (most dramatically illustrated by the communism practiced by the early Christian community as portrayed in Acts 4:32–5:11)—all these contrast sharply with the violent, hierarchical, and greed-driven Roman Empire. Hence, if we could say that in the New Testament worldview the devil has de facto power over the world while God has legitimate authority, the same may be said for their respective earthly representatives: Rome undeniably has power and wields it freely, but the Christian community has authority—above all, *moral* authority.

DEMONIC DOCTRINES

Over the centuries that followed, many Christians attempted to exercise that moral authority in the public square. A substantial proportion of the early Christian literature that has come down to us consists of "apologies," in which the author attempts to defend the Christian community from persecution by pleading with the authorities. More dramatically, the steadfastness and patient endurance of martyrs seemed to make a significant impression on the Roman public.

Meanwhile, within their own communities, Christians began disputing about authority in the more conventional sense. The faction that would ultimately prove most successful set about creating a self-perpetuating authority structure centered on bishops, who ultimately drew their authority from that of the twelve apostles, who in turn drew their authority from Christ. One of the earliest theorists of this position was Irenaeus of Lyons, a second-century bishop writing in modern-day France. He is most famous for his massive work *Against All Heresies*,[19] in which he attempts to refute a wide range of views on the significance of the Christian message and then offer his own, presumably more authentic, position. As in the Gospel of John, the question of appropriate beliefs takes center stage.

Interestingly, however, his own exposition of the correct Christian view—which begins only in the third of the five books of this sprawling tome—does not start off with a creedal statement or doctrine. Instead, Irenaeus points to the unbroken chain of succession from contemporary bishops back to Jesus and his apostles, with all of them publicly preaching the same consistent message. In contrast, the heretics or sectarians are constantly proliferating new and outlandish doctrines and claiming secret sources of knowledge (the word "heresy" stems ultimately from a Greek term meaning "choice" and in pre-Christian usage referred to philosophical schools).

There is more at work here than a simple contrast between unity and multiplicity, however. Irenaeus had already claimed in the first book of the work that the heretics, too, have a single founder, namely, Simon Magus, a magician who appears briefly in the New Testament and attempts to purchase the power of the Holy Spirit from the apostles (Acts 8:9–24). While the biblical author has him repent, Irenaeus claims that Simon later "set himself eagerly to contend against the apostles, in order that he himself might seem to be a wonderful being, and applied himself with still greater zeal to the study of the whole magic art, that he might the better bewilder and overpower multitudes of men." The result was that Caesar Claudius set up an idol to him, prompting Simon to put himself forward as an incarnation of the Holy Spirit, alongside Christ's incarnation of the Son of God (1.23.1).

In short, Simon became an Antichrist, who then set up his own succession of followers, beginning with a man named Menander (1.23.5). Despite their apparent variety,

> all those who in any way corrupt the truth, and injuriously affect the preaching of the Church, are the disciples and successors of Simon Magus of Samaria. Although they do not confess the name of their master, in order all the more to seduce others, yet they do teach his doctrines. They set forth, indeed, the name of Christ Jesus as a sort of lure, but in various ways they introduce the impieties of Simon; and thus they destroy multitudes, wickedly disseminating their own doctrines by the use of a good name, and, through means of its sweetness and beauty, extending to their hearers the bitter and malignant poison of the serpent, the great author of apostasy. (1.27.4, alluding to Revelation 12:9)

And as befits an Antichrist—here all but equated with the Beast of Revelation—his successors do not publicly confess his name but keep it a secret. Furthermore, they do not teach a unified message but constantly modify it: "Many offshoots of numerous heresies have already been formed from those heretics we have described. This arises from the fact that numbers of them—indeed, we may say all—desire themselves to be teachers, and to break off from the particular heresy in which they have been involved" (1.28.1). The very fact that they deviate from their teachers proves them to be his best possible followers, insofar as he deviated from the one true teacher.

This antichurch of the heretics, then, is unified in its very dissension, faithful to its founder precisely in its betrayal. And behind it all is the devil, who in these last days plans "to render men disbelievers in their own salvation, and blasphemous against God the Creator" (4.pref.4). From this point of view, the existence of a variety of doctrines in Christian circles is not a simple difference of opinion or even a question of people being incorrect or misinformed: it is a Satanic conspiracy.

As a result of this projection of the model of the church onto the various sects of heretics, their doctrines come to seem more and more unified, with petty differences obscuring their overall purpose: denigrating the creator of this world as an inferior God and claiming to have access to another, higher God. In most sects discussed, this creator God or demiurge is identified with the God of Israel as described in the Hebrew Scriptures, necessitating a complete break between Christianity and Judaism. This view of creation as the product of an evil or inferior being leads logically to a denigration of the flesh in favor of the spiritual realities purportedly made accessible by esoteric teaching.

Modern scholars would rely heavily on Irenaeus's description in constructing the religious worldview known as "gnosticism," a construction that more recent scholarly work has demonstrated to be artificial at best.[20] For our immediate purposes, however, the accuracy of Irenaeus's construction is less important than the role it plays in his thought. We have already observed that Irenaeus's heretical antichurch reflects the structure of what he takes to be the true church—though to a naïve reader, that connection becomes clear only retroactively, as Irenaeus presents us with the antichurch before the true church. I believe that something similar is at work with the lesser "gnostic" creator God: he is an exaggeration of the role of the devil in Christian thought.

This connection is more immediately clear in a short text by one of Irenaeus's near contemporaries, Tertullian. Entitled "On the Shows" (*De Spectaculis*),[21] it sets out to answer the seemingly narrow question of whether Christians are allowed to enjoy certain forms of entertainment, but it begins with an ambitious theological prolegomenon. Responding to the claim that the entertainments in question must be good, given that they are part of God's good creation, he concedes: "Now nobody denies what nobody is ignorant of—for Nature herself is teacher of it—that God is the Maker of the universe, and that it is good, and that it is humanity's by free gift of its Maker." Yet he believes that we have more to learn from God's explicit self-revelation. First, he has specific demands of human beings: "But having no intimate acquaintance with the Highest, knowing Him only by natural revelation, and not as His friends—afar off, and not as those who have been brought near to Him—men cannot but be in ignorance alike of what He enjoins and what He forbids in regard to the administration of His world."

Second—and seemingly more important—he has an enemy: "They must be ignorant, too, of the hostile power which works against Him, and perverts to wrong uses the things His hand has formed; for you cannot know either the will or the adversary of a God you do not know" (chap. 2).

It is clear from what ensues that Tertullian's emphasis falls decidedly on the second point: the revelation of the devil. In his view, this is a specifically *Christian* knowledge, even if he does not use the explicit term:

> We, therefore, who in our knowledge of the Lord have obtained some knowledge also of His foe—who, in our discovery of the Creator, have at the same time laid hands upon the great corrupter, ought neither to wonder nor to doubt that, as the prowess of the corrupting and God-opposing angel overthrew in the beginning the virtue of man, the work and image of God, the possessor of the world, so he has entirely changed man's nature—created, like his own, for perfect sinlessness—into his own state of wicked enmity against his Maker, that in the very thing whose gift to man, but not to him, had grieved him, he might make man guilty in God's eyes, and set up his own supremacy. (chap. 2)

Thus, anyone can see that there is a creator, but Christians realize that this world has been effectively *re*-created by the devil. This achievement falls short of that of Irenaeus's gnostic creator God, who created the world all on his own, but the practical result is the same: the devil is responsible for the created world as we actually know it.

Having established this point, Tertullian goes on to describe virtually all of human culture as saturated with the demonic, primarily through the mediation of pagan gods. Today, most secularists and Christians would likely agree that the pagan gods simply did not exist, a view that the Hebrew tradition of idol critique would also embrace. For most of the early Christian writers, however, they were all too real—more specifically, they were *demons* who actively misled people into worshipping them. To be fair, Tertullian's critique of Roman culture is not entirely based on a guilty-by-association argument. He has a great deal to say about the violence of much Roman entertainment, where competitors routinely fought to the death and where, he reminds his audience, Christian victims are often fodder for the fun. Nevertheless, the bulk of the argument is given over to demonstrating that any aspect of culture related to religion is infected with the demonic, and Tertullian provides detailed genealogies connecting contemporary Roman practices with specific demonic religious rites.

This identification of demons with the gods of the nations is a natural outgrowth of the apocalyptic paradigm, with its spiritual overlay for worldly politics. And by the end of the text, Tertullian enters into an apocalyptic reverie—made famous by Gibbon and Nietzsche, who both quote it at length—that seems to completely undermine his moral critique of Roman entertainments. After briefly mentioning the attractions of the New Jerusalem, he mentions "other sights":

> That last day of judgment, with its everlasting issues; that day unlooked for by the nations, the theme of their derision, when the world hoary with age, and all its many products, shall be consumed in one great flame! How vast a spectacle then bursts upon the eye! What there excites my admiration? What my derision? Which sight gives me joy? Which rouses me to exultation?—as I see so many illustrious monarchs, whose reception into the heavens was publicly announced, groaning now in the lowest darkness with great Jove himself, and those, too, who bore witness of their exultation; governors of provinces, too, who persecuted the Christian name, in fires more fierce than those with which in the days of their pride they raged against the followers of Christ. (chap. 30)

Here Tertullian is in line with the political focus of most apocalyptic literature, but he goes on to expand his vision to include the educated and artistic elites as well:

> What world's wise men besides, the very philosophers, in fact, who taught their followers that God had no concern in ought that is sublunary, and were wont to assure them that either they had no souls, or that they would never return to the bodies which at death they had left, now covered with shame before the poor deluded ones, as one fire consumes them! Poets also,

trembling not before the judgment-seat of Rhadamanthus or Minos, but of the unexpected Christ! I shall have a better opportunity then of hearing the tragedians, louder-voiced in their own calamity; of viewing the play-actors, much more dissolute in the dissolving flame; of looking upon the charioteer, all glowing in his chariot of fire; of beholding the wrestlers, not in their gymnasia, but tossing in the fiery billows; unless even then I shall not care to attend to such ministers of sin, in my eager wish rather to fix a gaze insatiable on those whose fury vented itself against the Lord. (chap. 30)

Finally, he turns more directly on Christ's tormenters, seeming to conflate the Jews and Romans:

This, I shall say, this is that carpenter's or hireling's son, that Sabbath-breaker, that Samaritan and devil-possessed! This is He whom you purchased from Judas! This is He whom you struck with reed and fist, whom you contemptuously spat upon, to whom you gave gall and vinegar to drink! This is He whom His disciples secretly stole away, that it might be said He had risen again, or the gardener abstracted, that his lettuces might come to no harm from the crowds of visitants! (chap. 30)

These gruesome and unending entertainments are what Christians have to look forward to, and in the meantime, "we in a measure have them by faith in the picturings of imagination" (chap. 30). Yet again, it seems, we are in an apocalyptic hall of mirrors.

The situation is very different in Irenaeus, who turns to apocalyptic reflections toward the end of *Against All Heresies*. He draws on Revelation at great length, believing that its prophecies must come to pass soon, as John's vision "was seen no very long time since, but almost in our day" (5.30.3). Reflecting on the infamous number 666, he cautions against insisting on any particular interpretation but offers three possibilities. The meaning of the first, Evanthas, is obscure—perhaps a random name chosen because it fit the numerical code. His second is the Greek equivalent of "Latins," that is, the Romans, but he sets this meaning aside as a possible coincidence. Finally, he settles on the Greek term for "Titan." In the end, he comes close to acknowledging the anti-Roman thrust of Revelation but stops short.

A few chapters earlier, Irenaeus had also downplayed the political significance of another text we have examined. Quoting Paul against the clear implication of the gospel story of Jesus's temptation, he claims, "As, then, 'the powers that be are ordained of God,' it is clear that the devil lied when he said, 'These are delivered unto me; and to whomsoever I will, I give them'" (5.24.3). Having established this, Irenaeus presents views that the prophets Isaiah and Jeremiah could well approve of:

> For by the law of the same Being as calls men into existence are kings also appointed, adapted for those men who are at the time placed under their government. Some of these rulers are given for the correction and the benefit of their subjects, and for the preservation of justice; but others, for the purposes of fear and punishment and rebuke: others, as the subjects deserve it, are for deception, disgrace, and pride; while the just judgment of God, as I have observed already, passes equally upon all. (5.24.3)

The devil does not have political power, in other words, but only persuasive power: all he can do is "deceive and lead astray the mind of man into disobeying the commandments of God, and gradually to darken the hearts of those who would endeavor to serve him, to the forgetting of the true God, but to the adoration of himself as God" (5.24.3).

The devil's human agents, therefore, are not the kings of this world but the antibishops of the antichurch of heresy. Jesus's apocalyptic role is still to defeat the devil, but the stakes are radically different than in Paul, Revelation, or Tertullian: in Irenaeus's mind, defeating the devil means defeating the heretics. Hence Jesus becomes incarnate to disprove the gnostic rejection of this world, and he dies on the cross to fulfill biblical prophecies and demonstrate that the redeemer God and the creator revealed in Jewish scripture are one and the same. As in the Gospel of John, the apocalyptic polemic has been fully shifted onto the plane of belief—the political theology of the tradition culminating in the apocalyptic paradigm has lost its political thrust and become purely theological.

THE DEVIL CONVERTS TO CHRISTIANITY

What Irenaeus is trying to do here, I would argue, is to make peace with earthly rulers in order to shift Christianity away from the unstable apocalyptic paradigm and toward something like the relatively sustainable prophetic paradigm. As I noted in the previous chapter, this is the path that the Jewish community took after the great disaster of the destruction of Jerusalem. Yet a simple reversion to the prophetic paradigm is not available within the Christian perspective, because Jesus has already set the apocalyptic sequence irrevocably in motion through his death and resurrection. Going back on apocalyptic can only mean going back on Christianity as such.

Peace with the ruling authorities therefore comes at the price of *displacing* the demonic apocalyptic role of earthly rulers onto some other group—usually a religiously defined group such as Jews or heretics, representing a displacement from the political-theological to the theological as such.[22] While this displacement may have had practical strategic benefits in that it headed off a potentially fatal confrontation with the Roman Empire, it had a significant cost as well. In breaking the connection with the political, it also began to uproot the tradition from its foundation in the problem of evil. In particular, it threatened to render the central event of Christian apocalyptic, Jesus's death on the cross, increasingly arbitrary and unintelligible—does God really need to become incarnate, suffer, die, and rise from the dead in order to prove that some particular group holds incorrect religious views?

In the first section of this chapter, I argued that while the identification of Jesus introduced important changes relative to previous apocalyptic thought, the suffering messiah was still fundamentally within the range of plausible options. In other words, early Christianity was a variation on the apocalyptic theme rather than a totally new paradigm—and in this sense, I would count Paul, Mark, and Revelation as still in fundamental continuity with previous apocalyptic thought. The displacement of the demonic from the political, however, marks a decisive mutation as well as a break from the Jewish tradition that led up to it.

I call this new political theological construction the patristic paradigm, after the patristic writers or "Church Fathers" who developed it. It is in many ways exemplified in Athanasius's *On the Incarnation*,[23] written amid the tumultuous events surrounding Constantine's embrace of Christianity. The second half of a two-part work, it follows up on his *Against the Heathens*, which consists largely of what had by that time become standard critiques of pagan religious practices centered on idol worship. What has changed, however, is the tone. Where previous apologetic tracts had been fighting an uphill battle against ingrained imperial practices, Athanasius seems to be kicking idolatry when it's down, presumably after it had been dealt the crushing blow of the Edict of Milan in 318. In this context, Athanasius backs away from previous arguments based on the moral authority of Christian practice, claiming instead that the defeat of the idols is the proof of Christ's divinity—and nowhere is this proof more definitive than the triumph of the cross.

There is a striking note of resentment in Athanasius's description of the cross, "which Jews traduce and Greeks laugh to scorn, but we worship," and it grows as he dwells on the theme of mockery:

> For the more he is mocked among the unbelieving, the more witness does he give of his own Godhead. . . . And what men, in their conceit of wisdom, laugh at as merely human, he by his own power demonstrates to be divine, subduing the pretensions of idols by his supposed humiliation—the cross— and those who mock and disbelieve invisibly winning over to recognize his divinity and power. (§ 1)

All this resentment is arguably misplaced. As recently as 311, Athanasius's home city of Alexandria had suffered deeply from the final persecution of Diocletian, losing their bishop, and it is difficult for me to believe that, for example, pagan priests and educated philosophers were playing a significant role in the killing. A similar displacement is at work in his discussion of the cross, where he initially insists that Christ's death must be public—but instead of drawing the seemingly more natural political conclusion from this act, he attributes the necessity of publicity to the perfidy of the Jews, who would otherwise be able to deny that Jesus had really died (§ 23). This displacement onto the Jews continues as Athanasius moves on to another reason for the crucifixion—it was more appropriate for Jesus to let his enemies pick the method of death, lest he appear weak, because his enemies are sure to pick the most fearsome method. Though he is not as explicit in naming the Jews as Christ's enemies here, the invocation of John the Baptist and Isaiah's deaths point in that direction, and the quotation "Cursed is he that hangs on a tree" (Deuteronomy 21:23; qtd. in Galatians 3:13) almost makes crucifixion out to be a distinctively Jewish punishment.

In keeping with the Hebrew biblical tradition, Athanasius does present God as a political liberator. For instance, in discussing the incarnation, he claims that

> like as when a great king has entered into some large city and taken up his abode in one of the houses there, such city is at all events held worthy of high honor, nor does any enemy or bandit any longer descend upon it and subject it; but, on the contrary, it is thought entitled to all care, because of the king's having taken up his residence in a single house there; so, too, has it been with the monarch of all. (§ 9)

Here he has in mind God's liberation of humanity from the curse of death, which had gained "a legal hold over us" (§ 6). He continues to develop the image by envisioning a king who finds his house or city "beset by bandits from the carelessness of its inmates" and "avenges and reclaims it as his own work, having regard, not to the carelessness of the inhabitants, but to what beseems himself" (§ 10). Athanasius reaffirms his view that Christ's overcoming of death represents such a righteous vengeance, then highlights Christ's teaching as another prong in this attack, emphasizing the characteristic patristic theme of belief. The political imagery is becoming just that: imagery, with less and less grounding in concrete political concerns.

Athanasius's account of the necessity of the cross also focuses on purely symbolic interpretations, such as the idea that Christ's outstretched hands show that he was sent to unite Jews and Gentiles and finding scriptural reasons for his elevation into the air. I have noted that the apocalyptic paradigm tends to assert the *meaningfulness* of suffering, particularly the cross, while refraining from attributing a concrete present meaning. As the apocalyptic paradigm begins to collapse among the patristic writers, that promise of meaning is fulfilled, but the meaning is purely symbolic and remarkably unsatisfying. Does Jesus really need to undergo an agonizing death simply to spread his hands toward the east and the west and symbolically embrace all people?

As we have seen, in the Hebrew biblical tradition, the devil arose as part of the political-theological rhetoric of the oppressed. The conceptual apparatus of demonology was a mode of political-theological critique, denouncing current political arrangements as contrary to God's justice and demanding divine—and human—action to utterly overthrow them. The devil remained a tool of the oppressed in the properly apocalyptic strain of early Christianity (represented by Paul, Mark, and Revelation). However, preserving what is in essence an apocalyptic movement over the course of multiple generations was a truly unprecedented challenge. As Athanasius illustrated, the memory of the political thrust of apocalyptic thought remained, but it was increasingly drained of any literal political content. Displacing demonic rhetoric from political enemies to religious rivals inevitably presented itself as a possible survival tactic, giving rise to the patristic paradigm.

From this practical perspective, it is possible to view all of the moves that resulted in the patristic paradigm as understandable and even well intentioned. The displacement of the devil from the political to the purely theological realm was motivated by a desire for a peaceful coexistence with the powers that be. Purely symbolic or theological explanations of the cross followed naturally as a way of filling the explanatory gap opened up by dissociating crucifixion from its political context—a gap that, if left open, may collapse and generate the very political confrontation they aimed to prevent. All in all, we are dealing with survival strategies developed under very trying circumstances.

In Athanasius, these strategies begin to display their inherent dangers. The outrage of the cross, made all the more real in Athanasius's own experience of persecution a few years earlier, is obviously at work in the angry tone that pervades the work. Yet within the patristic strategy of displacing the political-theological into the purely theological, that anger can vent itself only on proxy targets. Even more perversely, now the favor of the empire that killed Jesus becomes the ultimate revenge against all of Christianity's imagined enemies, and the triumph of Christianity is interpreted through the lens of military conquest, with the enemy's gods replaced by *our* triumphant god. We are once again trapped in the apocalyptic hall of mirrors.

In the final chapter of *The Gift of Death*,[24] Jacques Derrida analyzes a series of paradoxical sayings of Jesus from the Sermon on the Mount, sayings that are often put forward as a demonstration of the promise of Christianity. These sayings urge Jesus's hearer to renounce treasure on earth, to shun recognition for their piety, to abstain from seeking vengeance, opening up a space for a genuine alternative to practices of domination and oppression. Yet as Derrida points out, all of these sayings operate by displacing what is negated into a transcendent realm: if you renounce earthly treasures, you will have treasures in heaven; if you do not seek recognition, God will give you the best form of recognition; if you abstain from revenge, God will provide the surest revenge.

The danger of such a displacement is obvious: if practices of domination and oppression always remain the point of reference, there is no guarantee that such practices will not ultimately be adopted. Such an eventuality was unlikely when Christianity was a small, persecuted sect, so one might forgive Tertullian's rhetorical indulgences, for instance, and focus on his thoroughly justified critique of the pervasive and callous violence of Roman society in his time. The situation changes radically, however, when the Roman Empire adopts Christianity.

Within the apocalyptic framework, this quite unexpected event was tantamount to the devil's conversion to Christianity. And it is at this point that we witness one of the great reversals that the genealogical method teaches us to expect—namely, the great world-historical reversal whereby the devil becomes a tool of the oppressor rather than the oppressed. Strategies meant to maintain an uneasy peace with the political enemy become the basis for embracing that enemy as a friend and protector. Hermeneutical approaches meant to generate meaning for a theological symbol torn from its native political soil come to actively obfuscate its political stakes.

The patristic paradigm sought to deactivate the political, but it merely deferred it. And as we will see in the next chapter, its practical effect was that just as the community claiming to represent him on earth begins to adapt itself to the Roman Empire, so too does God increasingly adopt the methods of the devil—to the point where the two can at times appear indistinguishable.

CHAPTER 3

MONASTICISM AND MEDIEVAL CHRISTIANITY

THE RANSOM PAID THE DEVIL

The fateful moment of transition between Roman persecution and Roman favor opened up the space for a remarkable theological reflection that can be read as a kind of threshold between the apocalyptic and patristic paradigms: Gregory of Nyssa's "Address on Religious Instruction," also called the "Great Catechism."[1] The text is presented as a guide for catechists seeking to instruct the presumably large number of new converts flooding into the church as a result of official Roman sponsorship, and hence it addresses the central patristic problem of belief. Yet those with differing beliefs are not demonized but welcomed as open and persuadable. Far from denouncing false doctrines, Gregory recommends that catechists keep in mind their students' starting point, as converting a Jew or heretic will require different arguments from converting a Greek (preface). His focus is primarily on the latter, whose emphasis on philosophical reason renders them naturally open, in his view, to the reasonable claims of Christianity. And he is remarkably optimistic about what philosophy will enable them to accept, including very nuanced theological claims about the Trinity (§§ 1–3).

At this point in the argument, Gregory pauses to briefly address techniques for converting Jews, which he views as a relatively easy task due to the existence of a shared scriptural point of reference (§ 4). His optimistic presentation comes up against an obstacle, however: "Neither Greek nor Jew, perhaps, will contest the existence of God's Word and Spirit—the one depending on his innate ideas, the other on the Scriptures. Both, however, will equally reject the plan by which God's Word became human, as something incredible and unbefitting to say of God" (§ 5). Addressing this issue requires him to start again from the very beginning: creation. He argues that God has a natural desire to share his goodness, leading him to create humanity. Yet he agrees with Tertullian that we do not see the original state but "an unnatural condition" (§ 5).

What went wrong? To answer this, Gregory deploys two arguments that will continue to occupy us throughout the rest of the book. The first is that God could not possibly deprive humanity of "the most excellent and precious of blessings—I mean the gift of liberty and free will. For were human life governed by necessity, the 'image' would be falsified in that respect and so differ from the archetype. For how can a nature subject to necessity and in servitude be called an image of the sovereign nature?" (§ 5). Our fellowship with God, the very reason that we were created, depends on sharing in God's freedom. Yet precisely this divine gift opens up the possibility of breaking the divine fellowship, insofar as it opens up the possibility of evil, which occurs when "the soul withdraws from the good" (§ 5). A version of this claim will prove decisive for Christian attempts to solve the problem of evil: evil does not truly exist in itself but is only the absence of good.

We see this in the story of Genesis, which Gregory claims "is not a fanciful story; but our very nature makes it convincing" (§ 6). Anticipating that philosophically educated Greeks will be inclined to favor the spiritual over the material, he claims that in God's creation of humanity out of the dust, "the earthly was raised to union with the divine, and a single grace equally extends through all creation, inasmuch as the lower nature is blended with that which transcends the world" (§ 6). Part of this divine order, the angels, was fully spiritual, and one of these angels, Satan, was appointed to govern over the earth. Upon learning of God's special relationship with a material being, whom Satan (sharing Greek philosophical prejudices) regarded as inferior to himself, he "begot envy" and quickly fell to the very lowest possible level of evil (i.e., as far as possible from God). There he began to hatch his plan to deceive humanity and pull them away from God as well: "Cunningly he cheats and deceives man by persuading him to become his own murderer and assassin" (§ 6)—not by force but by obtaining their free consent to disobey God and thereby obey the devil.

Gregory's account is a variation on what is known as the "ransom theory" of redemption, which is prevalent throughout the early Christian era.[2] In this view, the problem that Christ comes to solve is not primarily or only human sinfulness but our bondage to the devil—in other words, it is not merely a religious or theological problem but a political one. Jesus does not come to pay the price for our sins but to secure our freedom from a political-theological oppressor. In this way, Gregory rejoins the apocalyptic strand of the Christian tradition by identifying the devil as a political power.

Having set up the problem in this way, Gregory comes up against another obstacle. Even if someone will concede that entering into a human body is not per se unworthy of God, given the original impetus behind our creation, the concrete facts of the incarnation may nevertheless seem wrong: "owing to the unworthiness connected with the death, they do not admit that the resurrection of the dead was worthy of God" (§ 9). After considerable discussion of what exactly is worthy or unworthy of God (§§ 10–14), Gregory claims that the crucifixion was necessary because "the prisoner was looking for someone to ransom him, the captive for someone to take his part" (§ 15).

While one might object that God could simply rescue the devil's human captives by force, such an action would not represent the full range of God's divine attributes. It may be good, but it would not be just, and "separated and taken by itself, justice is not goodness" (§ 21). In this case, God's justice is found "in his not exercising an arbitrary authority over him who held us in bondage." If the whole purpose of providing humans with free will is to have fellowship with them, then simply ignoring their free choice to go over to the devil's side is not an option.

This means that our bondage to the devil has a kind of de facto legitimacy that must be reckoned with, and God's strategy initially seems to take the form of buying humanity back from the devil to set them free again. Judging from the devil's character, God can infer that he might be willing to accept a particularly remarkable human being as payment, and Jesus fits the bill: "When the enemy saw such power, he recognized in Christ a bargain which offered him more than he held. For this reason he chose him as the ransom for those he had shut up in death's prison" (§ 23).

Yet as in the Synoptic Gospels and Paul, the devil's de facto power does not have the last word. God enters into the devil's system only in order to subvert it. In fact, his plan is not to pay off the devil's claim but to render it completely null and void. From this perspective, the incarnation becomes a kind of trick, luring the devil into overreaching by asserting the ruler's ultimate power—the power of life and death—over God himself: "In that way, as it is with greedy fish, he might swallow the Godhead like a fishhook along with the flesh, which was the bait" (§ 24). Gregory further claims that this deception, far from being morally problematic, is actually profoundly just: "Justice is evident in the rendering of due recompense, by which the deceiver was in turn deceived" (§ 26). Moreover, it is merciful, insofar as Christ's act of undermining the devil's claim "benefited, not only the one who had perished, but also the very one who had brought us to ruin. . . . He freed humanity from evil, and healed the very author of evil himself" (§ 26). In other words, Christ's saving work does not save only humanity but the devil as well.

This optimistic vision will represent a decidedly minority position in the Christian tradition, as most theologians will instinctively regard the salvation of the devil as missing the entire point of having a devil in the first place. Yet compared to other solutions for resolving the apocalyptic tensions while making peace with the earthly authorities—above all, the scapegoating of heretics and Jews—it has an obvious attraction, preventing the descent into the apocalyptic hall of mirrors.

Just like Paul's optimistic apocalyptic outlook, however, Gregory's solution to the distinctively Christian form of the problem of evil will have a narrow window of historical plausibility. It is the product of a member of the first generation of Christians to grow up in the wake of Constantine's

||| |||| |||| ||| |||| |||||| ||| ||||||

000475661 50

**Sell your books at
sellbackyourBook.com!**
Go to sellbackyourBook.com
and get an instant price
quote. We even pay the
shipping - see what your old
books are worth today!

embrace of Christianity—a wholly unexpected event that from an apocalyptic perspective was tantamount to the devil converting to Christianity. In the generations to come, however, Gregory's attempt to shift the devil back into the political arena, even if only figuratively, will not have much staying power. Instead, the patristic displacement will lead a newly empowered Christianity to take the opportunity to kick the devil when he's down, again and again.

THE SATANIC SOCIAL CONTRACT

For all its seemingly mythological trappings, Gregory of Nyssa's account of how Christ saves us from bondage to the devil is in one sense strikingly modern: it anticipates social contract theory. Adam and Eve represent the primeval human community, in a literal "state of nature"—a condition that, in both Gregory and in social contract theory, is now inaccessible to us. Through their own free consent, they choose a ruler, effectively binding themselves and their future descendants to obey the devil as their sovereign in perpetuity. And initially, even God recognizes the legitimacy of this situation, because the possibility of submitting to the devil is inherent to human freedom, just as for social contract theorists the establishment of a concrete political order is at once a contingent historical achievement and a natural outgrowth of human needs and capacities.

From a certain perspective, the patristic version seems most akin to that of Hobbes. One of the key steps in his argument for sovereign absolutism is the insistence that promises made under duress are still binding—a provision that would presumably cover Adam and Eve's promises made under false pretenses. The fact that humanity cannot simply vote to remove their Satanic sovereign from office also anticipates Hobbes's insistence on the irreversibility of the social contract. Yet there is at least one key element in the Hobbesian scheme that cannot be mapped neatly onto Gregory's account: the place of death.

For Hobbes, the ultimate motivation to adopt the social contract and submit to a single sovereign is the fear of death. In the Hobbesian state of nature, every individual is under constant threat of violence from every

other individual, a situation that can be remedied only if everyone surren-
ders his or her right to arbitrary violence simultaneously and entrusts it to
a single sovereign. For Gregory, however, it is only *after* our first parents
submit to the devil as their new sovereign that they become susceptible to
death. Perhaps even more surprisingly from a Hobbesian perspective, death
here figures as an act of mercy on God's part, restraining the chaos and
destructiveness that would result if humans, now corrupted by evil, would
have remained immortal as they were in the Garden of Eden. More than
that, the intervention of death is ultimately therapeutic in intent. And it is
here that Gregory—having already decisively transformed the apocalyptic
theme of God's cosmic enemy by introducing the possibility of the devil's
salvation—achieves a parallel transformation of the other great apocalyptic
theme: the resurrection of the dead.

Before introducing the devil's role in the drama of salvation, Gregory
had put forth humanity as a kind of microcosm of creation, in which "the
earthly was raised to union with the divine" so that "a single grace equally
extends through all creation, inasmuch as the lower nature is blended with
that which transcends the world" (§ 6). Satan's deception threw off this
perfect balance, causing humanity to fall into sensuality (§ 7). In order
to restore humanity—and hence all of creation—to its intended state,
God must restore the appropriate balance between body and soul in the
human being. The first step is to destroy the body that had been corrupted
(§ 8). The next is to purify the soul, which Gregory believes can be accomplished either through baptism (which means spiritually sharing in
Christ's death) in the present life or by the fires of purgation after it (§ 35).
Finally, body and soul must be reunited in a durably perfect form in the
resurrection of the dead.

At its inception, the demand for the resurrection was a demand for
restitution in the face of unjust suffering and death at the hands of political oppressors. That connection still exists insofar as the devil's rule over us
prompted the development of death, yet it is fair to say that Gregory makes
every effort to "depoliticize" death. He does this through a twofold motion
of universalization and individualization. That is to say, death is depoliti-

cized first by claiming that the problem is not historically specific unjust deaths but death in general, death as experienced by everyone regardless of historical situation. Second, this universalization makes death into a more or less purely internal affair, centered on the appropriate relationship between body and soul within each individual human being.

From the perspective of the tradition we have been tracing out of the Hebrew Bible, Gregory's move here represents perhaps the most ambitious doubling down yet. After all, death could be seen as the ultimate challenge to the divine order—it is utterly inescapable and most often apparently meaningless. Yet Gregory converts it into the greatest possible proof of God's wisdom and mercy, even going so far as to claim that redeeming humanity from death is a greater and more glorious achievement than creating humanity in the first place (§ 8). Further, like the most robust previous theories, it effectively blames humanity for its own suffering, insofar as death is God's response to our free choice to follow the devil and our own sensual desires.

Gregory's theory arguably avoids the most unattractive elements of previous apocalyptic and patristic views, insofar as he does not envision the existence of eternal punishment—nor, indeed, any punishment at all in the strict sense, since suffering and death are ultimately therapeutic in his view. From a contemporary perspective, his capacious universalism, big enough to embrace even the devil himself, certainly presents a compelling alternative to the vengefulness of apocalyptic and the scapegoating of the patristic paradigm. At the same time, however, the radical demand for justice—and political change—that resonates throughout the entire previous tradition, even in its arguably more misguided forms, seems here to be virtually inaudible.

In place of a polemic against an unjust human ruler, here we see a critique of the sensual, the bodily, the material. Doubtless some of this suspicion of the body comes from the Greek philosophical culture in which Gregory was educated and to which he explicitly addresses himself in the text. Compared to the desire to escape the body outright in certain Platonic traditions, Gregory's position may even count as moderate. Yet even if the body has a legitimate role to play in the drama of salvation, even if we are not being saved *from* the body, the presumption throughout is that the body is questionable and somehow inherently in need of redemption. When God unites soul to body in the human being, for instance, that step is seen as necessary to elevate the earthly and material into some form of union with God, with which it would otherwise be incompatible. This disjunction seems obvious to Gregory, but it is far from self-evident that an element of God's own creation would be inherently incompatible with God.

Furthermore, even if evil is defined as a lack or negation of the good, and hence as nonexistent in the strict sense, it is still closely associated with the body. When our first parents choose to obey the devil, they are motivated by sensual desire, which leads to a degradation of the body so thorough that the body must be completely destroyed and remade: "since our judgment of the good went astray by the prompting of the senses and this departure from the good produced a contrary state of things, that part of us which was rendered useless by partaking of its opposite is dissolved" (§ 8). And this can occur because the devil himself, having fallen to the lowest level of evil, levels his attack on humanity's sensual desires—apparently paradoxically, given that his disdain for the body motivated his fall in the first place and that he is constrained to use persuasion (seemingly the realm of the intellectual) rather than force (the realm of the bodily).

Hence the body becomes closely associated with evil and with the author of evil. And although Gregory himself does not take this step, the broader tradition will conclude from this that the devil is also more closely associated with woman, who is regarded as more bound to the body and whom the devil targets first. (We will return to this point in the discussion of witchcraft in Chapter 5.)

On an intellectual level, this link between evil and the body is a natural outgrowth of a hierarchical ontology in which the bodily is regarded as "lower" than the spiritual. The notion of an ontological hierarchy is most closely associated with Neoplatonism, but it represents something like the cultural common sense of the late classical period. This broad intellectual consensus includes the more philosophically minded patristic thinkers, who were often quite eager to point out the compatibility between Christian doctrine and various forms of Platonism. Even if the patristic tradition asserts that everything—including Satan himself—is good insofar as it has been created by God, it seems difficult to distinguish between the lower *relative level* of good that is still good and the *deprivation* of good that is evil.

Yet it is not enough to point out the influence of Neoplatonic thought on the patristic writers. The more interesting question from the perspective of our present genealogical investigation is why they would be so receptive to that influence.

One key reason is surely Christianity and philosophy's shared affinity for asceticism. The two traditions converged on such practices for different reasons. Where the philosophical tradition was suspicious of the body in general, in Christianity asceticism was often figured as an imitation of Christ—above all in martyrdom. This imitation could be quite literal during the era of persecution, and ascetic exercises often functioned as a form of training to endure the deprivation and torture that persecutors deployed in the attempt to get Christians to renounce their faith. As a result, Christianity could claim to have met the philosophical goal of overcoming the fear of death—and indeed, to have done so even for women, slaves, and children, for whom the elite philosophical approach was unattainable.

Beginning with the age of Constantine, when persecution against mainstream Christians largely came to a halt, asceticism would become less a preparation for martyrdom than a substitute for it. This handoff appears dramatically in Athanasius's *Life of Antony*, the first extended biography of an ascetic saint to come down to us.[3] Like Athanasius himself, Antony lived through the transition between the age of persecution and the Constantinian settlement, and Athanasius presents him as leaving his wilderness retreat in order to participate in the final round of persecution. As one would expect from any exemplary Christian, Antony "yearned for martyrdom, but because he did not wish to hand himself over, he rendered service to the confessors both in the mines and in the prisons." This service extended to the "law courts" as well, where "he showed great enthusiasm, stirring to readiness those who were called forth as contestants, and receiving them as they underwent martyrdom and remaining in their company until they were perfected" (§ 46).

For all his provocative behavior, however, Antony's prayers for martyrdom were never answered because, as Athanasius makes clear, he was being saved for an even greater role:

> He seemed, therefore, like one who grieved because he had not been martyred, but the Lord was protecting him to benefit us and others, so that he might be a teacher to many in the discipline that he had learned from the Scriptures. For simply by seeing his conduct, many aspired to become imitators of his way of life. (§ 46)

Even before the persecution began, the results of Antony's powerful example were striking. Like most ascetic saints, Antony was inspired to leave behind the civilized world and seek God in the wilderness. Yet when people learned of his heroic self-denial, they flocked to join him, forming a community of imitation centered on the great man. This is the origin of the term "monasticism," which etymologically refers to a solitary life but came to refer to entire ascetic communities.[4] And as Athanasius presents it, Antony's spontaneous community was an idyllic place:

> So their [monastic] cells in the hills were like tents filled with divine choirs—people chanting, studying, fasting, praying, rejoicing in the hope of future boons, working for the distribution of alms, and maintaining both love and harmony among themselves. It was as if one truly looked on a land all its own—a land of devotion and righteousness. For neither perpetrator nor victim of injustice was there, nor complaint of a tax collector. (§ 44)

Here as in social contract theory in its most optimistic forms, we see the hope of a purely voluntary social bond that can eliminate oppression and injustice. If Gregory's familiarity with monastic asceticism renders his distrust of the body understandable, then perhaps it also explains his affinity toward understanding apocalyptic political theology in terms of something like a social contract.

This connection is not limited to the case of Antony. In *The Highest Poverty*, Agamben has claimed that the founding document of one monastic group, known as the "Pact of Fructuosus," "constitutes, perhaps, the first and only example of a social contract in which human beings in a group subject themselves unconditionally to the authority of a *dominus* [lord], attributing to him the power to direct the life of the community . . . in all its aspects."[5] Agamben notes briefly that this agreement, which places strict limits on the powers of the abbot, compares favorably to Hobbes and Rousseau's visions of unfettered sovereignty. Yet his larger point is that this pact is not actually a *contract* at all, in the sense of a binding and irreversible agreement. He makes a similar point when he is at great pains to claim that monastic vows do not originally represent anything like a binding oath and that the introduction of the oath represents a compromise with the worldly powers that monks had sought to escape.[6] For Agamben, monks are not constrained by monastic rules as by some external law. Rather, their rule is, at least initially and ideally, an organic expression of the shared way of life into which each has freely entered and in which each freely remains. Agamben is arguing that monasticism, more than an alternative social contract, represents an alternative *to* the social contract—an important distinction if we recognize, with Carole Pateman, that every contract, whether freely entered into or not, is effectively an instrument of subordination and constraint.[7]

A crucial feature in Agamben's argument is the fact that monastic communities, at least in their most promising forms, are not defined oppositionally. Throughout *The Highest Poverty*, Agamben presents monasticism as a form of life that simply goes about its business, in more or less total indifference to the worldly powers from which it has fled. Only when those powers come to see monastic communities as a threat and hence seek to co-opt them do we begin to see the emergence of features like binding oaths that assimilate monasticism to more traditional forms of power. If Athanasius is to be believed, however, the earliest monastic communities are not so studiously neutral. When they ventured into the wilderness, they found the devil there waiting for them—and they were all too happy to engage him in combat.

A NEW TEMPTATION IN THE WILDERNESS

Athanasius's biography of Antony begins by exhorting the "profit and assistance" that derives from recalling the life of this great man, whose "way of life provides monks with a sufficient picture for ascetic practice" (introduction). He then briefly recounts Antony's early life as the naturally abstemious child of a prosperous Christian couple (§ 1) who both died when he was a young adult (§ 2), leaving him in charge of the household. Shortly after their death, Antony spends his walk to church pondering "how the apostles, forsaking everything, followed the Savior, and how in Acts some sold what they possessed and took the proceeds and placed them at the feet of the apostles for distribution among those in need, and what great hope is stored up for such people in heaven." When he arrives, he finds that the Gospel reading is the story of Jesus exhorting rich man, "'If you would be perfect, go, sell what you possess and give to the poor, and you will have treasure in heaven.' It was as if by God's design he held the saints in his recollection, and as if the passage were read on his account" (§ 2, quoting Matthew 19:21). Immediately, he sells all his possessions and "devote[s] himself from then on to the discipline rather than the household, giving heed to himself and patiently training himself" (§ 3).

Scarcely has Antony's life of heroic asceticism begun, however, when he begins drawing the wrong kind of attention: "The devil, who despises and envies good, could not bear seeing such purpose in a youth, but the sort of things he had busied himself in doing in the past, he set to work to do against this person as well" (§ 5). His initial onslaught is remarkably thorough:

> First he attempted to lead him away from the discipline, suggesting memories of his possessions, the guardianship of his sister, the bonds of kinship, love of money and of glory, the manifold pleasure of food, the relaxations of life, and, finally, the rigor of virtue, and how great the labor is that earns it, suggesting also the bodily weakness and the length of time involved. So he raised in his mind a great dust cloud of considerations. (§ 5)

All these practical obstacles have no effect, and so the devil, observing that Antony is still a young man, turns to sexual temptations. Initially they are of a purely mental variety, but after failing to achieve his goal, "the beleaguered devil undertook one night to assume the form of a woman and to imitate her every gesture, solely in order that he might beguile Antony"—all to no effect (§ 5). At this point, Athanasius is quick to point out that Antony's spiritual endurance is of more than purely personal significance:

> All these were things that took place to the enemy's shame. For he who considered himself to be like God was now made a buffoon by a mere youth, and he who vaunted himself against flesh and blood was turned back by a flesh-bearing man. Working with Antony was the Lord, who bore flesh for us, and gave to the body the victory over the devil, so that each of those who truly struggle can say, It is "not I, but the grace of God which is in me." (§ 5, quoting 1 Corinthians 15:10)

The goal of Antony's ascetic achievements, then, is not merely his own personal edification—what is ultimately at stake, as in the apocalyptic and patristic schemes, is the defeat of the devil.

We noted previously that the patristic paradigm had displaced the role of the devil from the political realm to the more purely theological question of belief, so Christ's defeat of the devil takes place by means of a defeat of Christianity's theological opponents. We also saw how Athanasius, in *On the Incarnation*, had presented the spread of Christianity in terms of the defeat of Jews and pagans. In what I will call the monastic paradigm another, parallel displacement is at work. Here the field of battle is not the realm of belief but the body itself, with all its needs, desires, and vulnerabilities. And in *The Life of Antony* as in *On the Incarnation*, the outcome of this battle is a decisive and even humiliating victory over the devil.

After the failure of his explicit sexual temptation, "the dragon"—in an echo from Revelation that confirms the apocalyptic stakes of monasticism—"altered himself, taking on the likeness of his mind, . . . the visage of a black boy" (§ 6). The editor suggests that this image could be a reference to the practice of pederasty, but the context makes it clear that this is not another sexual temptation on the model of the illusion of a woman. Instead, the devil directly and explicitly challenges Antony, boasting of his past victories in driving people to fornication. In response, Antony says, "You, then, are much to be despised, for you are black of mind, and like a powerless child. From now on you cause me no anxiety, for 'the Lord is my helper, and I shall look upon my enemies'" (§ 6, quoting Psalm 117:7). As in Jesus's temptation in the desert, the quotation from scripture proves to be the decisive stroke, and "hearing these words, the black one immediately fled, cowering at the words and afraid even to approach the man" (§ 6). Far from representing a new temptation, the enigmatic image of a black boy is an instance of the devil showing his true colors despite himself—both his evil intentions and his pitiable weakness.

This shameful defeat only leads the devil to redouble his efforts. One day, when Antony had taken up residence among the tombs outside the village—perhaps a reference to the demoniac named "Legion," who lived in a graveyard—the devil makes another desperate attack:

> When the enemy could stand it no longer—for he was apprehensive that Antony might before long fill the desert with the discipline—approaching one night with a multitude of demons he whipped him with such force that he lay on the earth, speechless from the tortures. He contended that the pains were so severe as to lead one to say that the blows could not have been delivered by humans, since they caused such agony. (§ 8)

The next morning, a friend visits and finds Antony all but dead. After being nursed back to some minimal level of health, Antony returns to the scene and openly defies the devil to try again. Outraged, the devil "summoned his dogs"—presumably a reference to his fellow demons—and plots with them to develop an even more terrifying attack:

> Now schemes for working evil come easily to the devil, so when it was nighttime they made such a crashing noise that that whole place seemed to be shaken by a quake. The demons, as if breaking through the building's four walls, and seeming to enter through them, were changed into the forms of beasts and reptiles. The place immediately was filled with the appearances of lions, bears, leopards, bulls, and serpents, asps, scorpions, and wolves, and each of these moved in accordance with its form. The lion

roared, wanting to spring at him; the bull seemed intent on goring; the creeping snake did not quite reach him; the onrushing wolf made straight for him—and altogether the sounds of all the creatures that appeared were terrible, and their ragings were fierce. Struck and wounded by them, Antony's body was subject to yet more pain. (§ 9)

Antony's response is to defy and mock the devil, saying that "it is a mark of your weakness that you mimic the shapes of irrational beasts" (§ 9). As with the reference to "the dragon" of Revelation, I believe that Antony's vision is meant to echo Daniel, with its apocalyptic visions of the rulers of this world as fearsome animals and its strange account of the Babylonian king's descent into an animal-like state. And in keeping with the fundamental gesture of the monastic paradigm, these apocalyptic visions are displaced from the political to the bodily. Far from representing the rapacity and ferocity of oppressive rulers, these demonic animals represent the weakness and vulnerability of the flesh, which Antony easily overcomes.

In the passage that follows, Athanasius presents us with an even more decisive scriptural echo, this time of the Book of Job. When Antony dismisses the animalistic demons, he is treated to a vision of God descending from above and dispelling his demonic tortures. Antony is relieved but asks God, "Where were you? Why didn't you appear in the beginning, so that you could stop my distresses?" This calmer reiteration of Job's defiant questioning receives a more satisfying and direct answer: "I was here, Antony, but I waited to watch your struggle. And now, since you persevered and were not defeated, I will be your helper forever, and I will make you famous everywhere" (§ 10).

One could thus read the *Life of Antony* as a kind of rewriting of the Book of Job, with all the parts that challenge a complacent piety written out. Antony is the Job who voluntarily parts with all of his belongings and family obligations and voluntarily submits to bodily deprivations. The sufferings are not meaningless catastrophes that must be reversed but the very substance of righteousness itself. Perhaps most crucially, in this version of the Job story the devil never drops out of sight—he remains clearly in view throughout, always available to take the blame when Antony's suffering becomes excessive and at the same time to serve as an occasion for Antony's endless triumphs.

It is at this point that Antony begins recruiting large numbers of followers, to whom he delivers a lengthy sermon that makes up the bulk of the text. Recapitulating in miniature Athanasius's own presentation, it begins with a brief consideration of the value of monastic discipline before turning to the monks' "terrible and villainous enemies—the evil demons" (§ 21). He starts his treatment of the demons with a brief theology lesson that is broadly similar to the accounts found in Tertullian and Gregory of Nyssa:

> The demons were not created as the figures we now identify by "demon," for God made nothing bad. They were made good, but falling from the heavenly wisdom and thereafter wandering around the earth, they deceived the Greeks through apparitions. And envious of us Christians, they meddle in all things in their desire to frustrate our journey into heaven, so that we might not ascend to the place from which they fell. (§ 22)

He proceeds to detail the wide range of demonic tactics, including "imitating women, beasts, reptiles, and huge bodies and thousands of soldiers" (§ 23)—reiterating the association between the devil and the body, represented both by women and animals, and once again repurposing the political imagery of traditional apocalyptic.

The Book of Job becomes an increasingly important source in this discourse, which straightforwardly identifies the Leviathan and Behemoth, the fearsome beasts with which God wrestles in his final monologue, as the devil. This allows Antony to weave imagery from Job together with tropes traditionally associated with the ransom theory of redemption:

> Although he speaks such and so many things, and is overbold, never mind—like a serpent [Leviathan] he was drawn with a hook by the Savior, and like a beast of burden [Behemoth] he received a halter around the snout, and like a runaway he was bound by a ring for his nostrils, and his

lips were pierced by an iron clasp. He was also bound by the Lord like a sparrow, to receive our mockery. And, like scorpions and snakes, he and his fellow demons have been put in a position to be trampled underfoot by us Christians. The evidence of this is that we now conduct our lives in opposition to him. (§ 24)

Here God's enigmatic and disturbing monologue to Job is rewritten as a boast of his defeat of the devil, represented by Leviathan and Behemoth, and Antony calls his throng of new Jobs to join God in his work of continually subduing and humiliating his demonic foe.

The remainder of the speech provides increasingly detailed information on repulsing demons, culminating in the devil's ultimate defeat at the hands of Antony:

Once someone knocked at the door of my cell. And when I went out, I saw someone who seemed massive and tall. When I asked, "Who are you?" he said, "I am Satan." I said, "What are you doing here?" And he asked, "Why do the monks and all the other Christians censure me without cause? Why do they curse me every hour?" When I replied, "Why do you torment them?" he said, "I am not the one tormenting them, but they disturb themselves, for I have become weak. . . . I no longer have a place—no weapon, no city. There are Christians everywhere, and even the desert has filled with monks. Let them watch after themselves and stop censuring me for no reason!" Marveling then at the grace of the Lord, I said to him: "Even though you are always a liar, and never tell the truth, nevertheless this time, even if you did not intend to, you have spoken truly. For Christ in his coming reduced you to weakness, and after throwing you down he left you defenseless." Upon hearing the Savior's name, and being unable to endure the scorching from it, he became invisible. (§ 41)

And the lesson of this incident, in Antony's view, is that Christians should continue to kick the devil when he's down: "Now if even the devil himself confesses that he is able to do nothing, then we ought to treat him and his demons with utter contempt" (§ 42).

It is only after this stirring reminder of victory over the devil that Athanasius presents us with the idyllic picture of the monastic community cited
earlier in this chapter. Far from the simple withdrawal from society envisioned by Agamben, Athanasius presents the monastic movement as a
second front in the ongoing war against the devil. We learned in *On the Incarnation* that he had been all but driven out of the city, and now the monks
are pushing back his territory in the wilderness as well. These two fronts
are not solely geographical in nature, however. They can also be conceived
as a war for control over both the mind—represented by the city, which
has been purged of the competing belief systems targeted by the patristic
paradigm—and the body—represented by the wilderness, where the monastic paradigm sets its sights.

Toward the end of the text, Athanasius repeatedly emphasizes that the
two paradigms are completely compatible. Most notably, Antony "honored
the rule of the Church with extreme care, and he wanted every cleric to be
held in higher regard than himself. He felt no shame at bowing the head to
the bishops and priests" (§ 67). Furthermore, "he was truly wonderful and
orthodox" in his beliefs and warned against heretics, "saying that their doctrines were worse than serpents' poison" (§ 68) and claiming that the heretics
"are no more numerous than those demons with whom we wrestle on the
mountain" (§ 70). Just like the church fathers, he debates philosophers, who
concede victory because "they saw that even demons feared Anthony" (§ 72),
and he critiques the follies of the demonic Greek gods (§ 76). And just like
the church itself, he was sought out by the emperors (§ 81) and judges (§ 87)
of this world.

In reality, of course, the relationship between church authorities and
monastic movements was seldom as seamless as Athanasius portrays it here.
We have to take into account the fact that *The Life of Antony* is written by
a thinker who, despite his obvious attraction to monastic spirituality, remains in the end a churchman—and a remarkably combative one at that.
Agamben is right to point out that the picture is more complicated in the
monastic sources themselves, which are often remarkably indifferent to ecclesiastical rites, offices, and doctrines, and he is also right to emphasize the

fact that monasticism represented a significant and durable site of resistance to the dominant political-theological order throughout the medieval period.

From the perspective of our genealogy of the devil, however, more decisive than the conflict between church and monastery—or in my terms, between the patristic and monastic paradigms—will be their alliance. Before investigating the distinctively medieval approach to the devil that grows out of this alliance, however, it will be helpful to review them in the schematic form laid out in Table 2.

TABLE 2. Political Theological Paradigms from Early Christianity

	Apocalyptic	Patristic	Monastic
Meaning of the Cross	Necessary part of divine plan	Demonstration of theological truths	Mortification of the flesh
Earthly representative of the devil	Earthly rulers, especially Roman Empire	Religious rivals: Jews, heretics, pagans	Bodily desires and earthly attachments
Attitude toward earthly rulers	Hostility and resentment	Placation	Indifference

The table is partly misleading, in that we are not really dealing with three separate paradigms. Compared with the Hebrew biblical paradigms, the three Christian options are much more formally similar—the patristic and monastic paradigms could even be viewed as subsets of the apocalyptic paradigm. This is so first of all because both paradigms continue to hold to the Christian conviction that Christ's death and resurrection have opened up the apocalyptic sequence and that this sequence will one day come to a dramatic conclusion with the resurrection and Last Judgment.

More than that, however, the patristic and monastic paradigms are structurally identical to the apocalyptic paradigm and simply redeploy its logic into a new field. And that includes the tautological aspect of apocalyptic, which gestures toward the *meaningfulness* of human suffering without granting it any immediately comprehensible *meaning*. Why are correct beliefs important, for instance? The early patristic writers gesture toward the notion that correct beliefs produced better moral practice, but that argument falls by the wayside as the struggle over heresy increasingly plays out between groups whose day-to-day practices are indistinguishable. In the end, the only answer is that correct beliefs are important because God says so.

Similarly, why should suffering in itself be considered righteous? There are many perspectives according to which Antony, far from being morally exemplary, was being self-indulgent and negligent of his family duties (including his duty to society to form his own family). Again, the answer here is that suffering is righteous because God says so, most emphatically when he presents himself for crucifixion. And in both paradigms, in case the appeal of obeying God is not enough, we receive the supplemental encouragement that our correct beliefs and heroic asceticism are helping defeat and humiliate the devil. The resentment that Nietzsche saw at the heart of the apocalyptic paradigm is still at work, but it has been redirected at targets that are much less deserving, and arguably even nonsensical.

THE RANSOM PAID TO GOD

While Eastern and Western Christianity diverged in many ways in the medieval period—theologically, politically, and spiritually—there was one point on which there developed a firm consensus: the ransom theory of redemption could not possibly be right. One can see this in the work of John of Damascus, whose *Orthodox Faith* represents the classic synthesis of Eastern Orthodox theology. He presents the meaning of Christ's death as follows:

> And so for our sake he submits to death and dies and offers himself to the Father as a sacrifice for us. For we had offended him and it was necessary for him to take upon himself our redemption that we might thus be loosed from the condemnation—for God forbid that the Lord's blood should have been offered to the tyrant! Wherefore, then, death approaches, gulps down the bait of the body, and is pierced by the hook of divinity.[8]

The use of Gregory of Nyssa's striking "bait-and-switch" metaphor only highlights the profound shift in the Damascene's approach. The replacement of the devil by death is perhaps not entirely unprecedented, given the close parallel between humanity's bondage to death and its bondage to the devil in Gregory's scheme. More momentous is the notion that Christ, rather than being a ransom offered to the devil is now a sacrifice offered to God. The motivation for this epochal shift is a changed attitude toward the devil. Instead of a quasi-legitimate ruler who had obtained humanity's consent, he is a tyrant—with no rights of any kind. Yet in an echo of the apocalyptic play of mirrors we observed in the last chapter, it seems that this exaggerated rejection of the devil leads directly to God playing the same role.

This dynamic can also be found in the work of Anselm of Canterbury, one of the most ambitious and creative theologians of the Latin West. One of the founders of the distinctive synthesis of tradition and reason that would be known as Scholasticism, Anselm broke with his predecessors by attempting to demonstrate the truth of Christianity using logical arguments rather than authoritative citations. In *Why God Became Human*,[9] he turns his attention to the very problem that had stymied Gregory of Nyssa in his attempt to prove Christian doctrine using logic alone: the necessity for the incarnation and crucifixion. And while his argument is indeed logically elegant, from our perspective his attempt at bracketing all presuppositions is less important as a philosophical exercise than as an inadvertent revelation of the deepest and most unquestioned presuppositions of the Western medieval worldview.

Anselm begins this treatise, which takes the form of a dialogue between a teacher and a student, by laying out his goals (I.1–2) and then stating the common objections to the incarnation and crucifixion. The latter are broadly similar to the ones Gregory anticipates, namely, that the incarnation and crucifixion seem unworthy of God (I.3) and that the biblical account seems mythological rather than reasonable (I.4). Before proceeding to his argument proper, however, he feels constrained to respond, not to unbelievers but to something "which we [believers] are in the habit of saying: that God, in order to set humankind free, was obliged to act against the devil by justice rather than mighty power" (I.7). He summarizes the argument in favor of this view in a fairly even-handed way, then declares, "I do not see what validity there is in that argument" (I.7).

In Anselm's view, there are two primary counterarguments against the ransom theory. The first, which could be considered the more secular argument, denies outright that the devil could ever gain legitimate authority over humanity or that humanity could legitimately assent to such authority: "For they were both thieves, since one [humanity] was stealing his own person from his master at the instigation of the other [the devil]" (I.7). The second argument against the ransom theory is much more overtly theological, in that it echoes God's approach to the earthly rulers in the prophetic paradigm:

> Alternatively, suppose that God, the judge of all, finding humanity thus in the devil's possession, were to seize him from the power of the one who was so unjustly possessing him, either with a view to punishing him by some means other than the agency of the devil, or with a view to sparing him— what would be unjust about that? For although humanity was being justly tormented when he was tormented by the devil, the devil himself was not acting justly in tormenting him. . . . Rather than being reluctantly drawn to act thus out of love of justice, [the devil] was impelled by the force of malice. . . . For the devil was not acting in this way at the command of God, but with the permission of God's incomprehensible wisdom, by which he orders even bad things in a way that is good. (I.7)

Hence there is a kind of legitimacy to the devil's hold over humanity, "because God permits this justly, and humanity suffers it justly," but there is no implication that the devil has any rights that need to be respected (I.7). Instead, like the unwitting pagan king of the prophetic paradigm, he can be unceremoniously dispatched at any moment—for precisely the evil actions that made him so useful to God.

Even if God is not bound to avoid the coercion of the devil, however, Anselm insists repeatedly that God was in no way coercing Christ. Rather, "Christ himself of his own volition underwent death in order to save mankind" (I.8), and the obedience he displayed toward God was "an obedience consisting in his upholding of righteousness so bravely and pertinaciously that as a result he incurred death" (I.9). Hence one might say in a Derridean vein that Christ's obedience is an obedience-without-obedience—a freely voluntary action that conforms to God's will and is called obedience only by analogy, as it were.

This distinction is important, because as Anselm later clarifies, God can and *does* demand absolute obedience from his creatures. Anselm characterizes this obedience, which every rational creature (angelic or human) owes to God unconditionally and perpetually, as a way of giving God his proper honor. By disobeying God, the creature is depriving God of the honor due to him, and not only does this create a debt to God, but it digs the sinner ever deeper into the hole:

> As long as he does not repay what he has taken away, he remains in a state of guilt. And it is not sufficient merely to repay what has been taken away: rather, he ought to pay back more than he took, in proportion to the insult which he has inflicted. . . . It is not sufficient for someone who violates someone else's honor, to restore that person's honor, if he does not, in consequence of the harmful act of dishonor, give, as restitution to the person whom he has dishonored, something pleasing to that person. (I.11)

For Anselm, God cannot simply forgive the debt without punishing it, because that would represent a challenge to God's uniqueness: "It makes sinfulness resemble God. For, just as God is subject to no law, the same is the case with sinfulness" (I.12). Yet even if God is not subject to a superior law, it is not fitting that he should "do anything in an unjust and unregulated manner" (I.12), above all by tolerating "something which it is the greatest injustice in the universe to tolerate, namely: that a creature should not give back to God what he takes away" (I.13). Later, Anselm will even claim that disobedience to God is of such infinite consequence that it would be worth destroying "an infinite multiplicity of universes" in order to avoid disobeying God in even the most trivial point (I.21).

It is at this point that Anselm, in an apparent non sequitur, addresses "God's plan to make up for the number of angels who had fallen, by drawing upon the human race, which he created sinless" (I.16). This opens up a wide-ranging discussion of God's plans to create a perfect heavenly city— here again, the political reemerges—which is thwarted by the demons' rebellion and by the devil's subsequent seduction of the human beings who were to replace the fallen angels in God's city. And it is only in this context that Anselm will concede that Christ's death has something to do with the devil, because humanity cannot "be reconciled with him so long as he is subject to the charge of having inflicted this insult upon God—unless he has previously honored God by conquering the devil just as he has dishonored him by having been conquered by the devil" (I.22). The devil's rights might not necessitate his involvement in the drama of salvation, but God's besmirched honor does.

It is worth pausing to consider the image of God that we are being offered here. The mercy, generosity, and love traditionally associated with the biblical God are radically absent. God is jealous of his honor—which is to say, proud—and he is absolutely unforgiving of any debt or obligation. This sounds much like the devil as we know him from the ransom theory. Furthermore, Anselm specifies that were God to allow his city to remain incomplete, he would seem to be less than God—and so, just like the devil in Gregory's telling of the ransom theory, God is initially motivated by a perceived loss of status and by wounded pride.

At this point, God is in a double bind. On the one hand, only a human being can repay humanity's debt, or else God's justice would not be fulfilled. On the other hand, humanity is in no position to pay the infinite debt of insulting God's infinite honor, even in the best of circumstances. And as we discuss in more detail in a subsequent chapter, circumstances are remarkably unfavorable, because human rebellion from God has resulted in a situation where every single human being is *born* already in debt to God. Even if human beings were able to begin obeying God properly from this moment forward, they would be fulfilling only their baseline obligation, leaving them with no way to deal with their trailing debt.

In this scenario, Christ's role with respect to God is remarkably similar to his role with respect to the devil in Gregory's theory. In both cases, humanity is held in bondage to sin by the one who is ruling over them, and in both cases, Christ must intervene according to the rules of this system in order to subvert it. And as for Gregory, so also for Anselm it is the dual nature of Christ as fully God and fully human that allows him to pull off his complicated heist. First, God contrives to have Christ born without the stain of original sin, allowing him to meet the baseline human obligation. Then Christ gives himself over to death—which is something over and above his existing obligations, since only those who have sinned are subject to death in Anselm's view. This bonus merit is infinitely multiplied due to Christ's divine nature, meaning that it can cover all of humanity's debt. This being achieved, human beings can be saved, because "God rejects no one who approaches him on this authority" (II.19).

It has often been observed that Anselm presents God as acting like an earthly ruler, and I would argue that this straightforward identification between the two is only possible in the wake of the patristic displacement of the devil from the political realm. From a certain perspective, Anselm's parallel between God and the earthly ruler represents a step beyond the patristic paradigm, which sought a kind of uneasy truce with the rulers—a Constantinian paradigm perhaps. (As we see in Chapter 5, this is the narrow space within which Schmittian political theology remains confined.) From the perspective of our investigation, however, the Constantinian move only intensifies the basic patristic move of identifying the devil with religious rather than political opponents. Anselm is able to do this quite casually, almost as an aside, when he compares the fallen angels to the Jews who were replaced by Gentiles in God's favor (I.18). Correlatively, he absolves the Romans of any guilt for Christ's crucifixion by noting that Christ's humanity covered over his divinity, so the sin of killing God "is capable of being pardoned because it was committed through ignorance" (I.15).

Yet the patristic paradigm cannot account for the most crucial part of Anselm's argument, which is the notion of accruing additional merit before God. In discussing this possibility, Anselm's chief example is what happens "when someone of his own free will makes a vow about holy living" (II.5)—in other words, when someone joins the monastic spiritual elite. Here Anselm falls far short of his goal of arguing from premises that will be shared by all reasonable human beings, but he provides an invaluable window into the deepest presuppositions of his time. It is this monastic perspective that makes it intelligible that Christ's death should be taken, ipso facto, as a meritorious act, because within the monastic paradigm, as we have seen, God rewards physical deprivation as such, simply for its own sake. Hence it is natural that in the unique case of Christ, who is not obligated to die, death could appear as the pinnacle of monastic asceticism. With a perfect circularity, then, the monastic discipline that had emerged out of an imitation of Christ's death comes to retrospectively explain the logic of that very death.

In the penultimate chapter of the work, having established the complex strategy by which God managed to redeem us from our bondage to God, Anselm addresses the devil once more. Shortly before, he had reiterated that Christ is obligated to defeat the devil *solely* as a matter of humanity's honor before God: "Certainly God did not owe the devil anything but punishment, nor did man owe him anything but retribution—to defeat in return him by whom he had been defeated" (II.19). Now he returns to the controversial question of "the reconciling of the devil," and he makes triply sure that such a thing is impossible. On the one hand, he notes that just as humans needed a human savior, so also "the condemned angels cannot be saved except by an angel-God who would be capable of dying and who would restore by his righteousness what the sins of the others have stolen." Yet even *this* would itself be impossible, because "angels are not of one race as human beings are. For angels are not all descended from one angel in the same way that human beings are descended from one man." Beyond that, Anselm claims that "just as they fell without having as the cause of their fall injury from someone else, similarly they ought to rise once more without the assistance of anyone else—and this is impossible for them" (II.21).

In short, to be saved, the demons would need an angel-Christ, which is impossible, and in any case they are obligated to save themselves without any outside help. Anselm claims that "unalterable logic opposes the granting of relief to the fallen angels" (II.21), but his argument is clearly an ad hoc attempt to exclude the odious possibility of the salvation of the devil by any means necessary. Yet there is a deeper logic dictating this conclusion than the tortured arguments in this paragraph: it makes perfect sense that God would not be merciful to the devil, because *he is not even merciful to humans.* Christ has not brought it about that humanity's debt is forgiven but that it is paid. The regime that led to humanity's indebtedness remains in place for all of eternity, with no escape and no appeal. Unlike in the ransom theory, the important thing is not that we have been saved but that God has saved face.

GOD BECOMES THE DEVIL

By the medieval period, the apocalyptic apparatus that grew out of the attempt to explain and compensate for suffering had become an apparatus for *demanding* suffering. Far from being an unintended side effect of God's plan or a purification in service of some higher goal, suffering is increasingly an end in itself and can sometimes seem to be the whole content of righteousness. In Anselm's scheme, it is no longer even a necessary evil due to the fall, because the entire logic of his argument depends on suffering (to the point of death) being intrinsically pleasing to God even in the absence of original sin—otherwise Christ's death would not have been meritorious. The God of medieval Christianity inflicts suffering on his enemies, and he uses his enemies to inflict it on his friends. He uses it to restore his own honor and humiliate all who oppose him. And when all is said and done, the saints will enjoy the beatific vision of God—the spectacle of his punishment of all wrongdoers in hell, endlessly and to no rational end.

In short, the God of medieval Christianity is a God who delights in suffering, a God who has become demonic. And there is no one whose suffering pleases him more than the devil's, that cosmic enemy who serves as God's eternal punching bag. He is always thwarted, always humiliated. Perhaps most humiliating of all is the fact that his very attempt to rebel against God is undercut at every turn, because everything he does fulfills God's plan—but just as with the actions of his closest allies, the Jews, the devil's very fulfillment of God's plan only confirms that he is unredeemable. As the Scholastic philosopher Peter of Poitiers writes,

> And the devil serves God and God approves the works that he has done,
> but not the way in which he has done them: the works done, as one is

accustomed to saying, not the doing of the works, which are all evil, since they do not proceed from charity. So God approved of the passion of Christ carried out by the Jews, insofar as it was the Jews' work done, but did not approve the Jews' doing of the work and the actions by which they worked that passion. God is offended by the devil's action, but not by the act itself; God does not want the devil to do that which God commands him to do in the way he does it. If one reads in the Scriptures that God commands the devil to do something . . . this must not be understood to mean that he commands it as he wants it. Rather, if he wants him to do it, he does not, however, want him to do it as he does it. Even if the devil does what God wants, he does not do it as God wants and for that reason, he is always sinning.[10]

If Christ's obedience on the cross was an obedience-without-obedience, an obedience without threat or coercion, then the devil's unwitting obedience is obedience-without-obedience from another direction: obedience without free consent and therefore without reward.

We have come a long way from the mysterious "accuser" of the Book of Job, who seemingly preys on God's insecurities in persuading him to subject his servant Job to a test of dubious significance, only to disappear when it comes time to explain what has happened. Here God is openly taking credit for the devil's actions, which contribute to God's glory (in no small part because they humiliate the despised enemy who carries them out). Yet from another perspective, there is a return to Job's model, insofar as the devil is somehow "on staff" with God, doing his dirty work for him. We can see this in the work of Peter Abelard, who like Anselm disproves the ransom theory of redemption but from the opposite direction: the devil *does* have legitimate—and eternal—jurisdiction over at least some human beings, as their "jailer or torturer" in hell.[11]

Apocalyptic had grown out of the Jews' horror at the torture of the innocent faithful, and now God is in the business of hiring the devil to torture on his behalf, as a kind of divine military subcontractor. Yet just like the original demonic torturer, Antiochus, the devil will receive his own torture—not in turn but simultaneously, as the devil is at once inmate and guard in hell. This image could be viewed as the most extreme outcome of the apocalyptic hall of mirrors, where the torturer becomes the tortured in a vicious circle, world without end.

Now one could argue that the seed of this scenario was already present from the very beginning, because even Antiochus was in a sense "on staff," a necessary part of God's plan. What has changed in the meantime is the character of God. The God of the Hebrew Bible and the New Testament was jealous and often violent, but he was also the vindicator of the oppressed who represented a demand for justice in an unjust world. By the medieval period, that face of God has largely fallen by the wayside in the mainstream Christian tradition. God has become indistinguishable from the arbitrary and cruel rulers against whom the apocalyptic tradition protested—or in political-theological terms, he has become the devil.

Meanwhile, the devil has become the representative of all that is oppressed and marginalized in medieval culture: primarily social groups like Jews, heretics, pagans, Muslims, and women but also the increasingly repressed and reviled demands of the physical body itself. Indeed, in the merger between the patristic and monastic paradigms, the devil has become a point of communication allowing all those heterogeneous social bodies to be associated with one another: so that, to give just a few examples, Jews can be conceived as definitionally more bodily, Muslims as heretics, and women as the site of reemergence of the pagan customs tarred as witchcraft. Yet the memory of the original apocalyptic paradigm persisted, with perverse effects. In the eyes of medieval culture, their very association with the devil rendered these oppressed and marginalized social bodies the real oppressors, despite appearances—and God would get his just revenge in the end, without end. Indeed, the entire life of the devil, as we will see in the chapters that follow, is overshadowed by divine vengeance, which the devil both suffers and carries out.

⟨ PART II ⟩
LIFE OF THE DEVIL

CHAPTER 4

THE FALL OF THE DEVIL

The three chapters of the first major part of the book traced the emergence of the paradoxical figure of the medieval devil, who is essentially the same devil handed down to secular modernity and therefore the devil best known to contemporary Western culture. The three chapters that make up the next major division take a different approach, charting the devil's own history as perceived by the medieval theological system—from his fall from grace, through his ongoing meddling in the present world, all the way to his ultimate fate as the jailer and chief inmate in hell. While I still proceed via the close reading of representative texts, my organization is primarily thematic rather than chronological.

Nevertheless, my investigation in this and the following chapters still continues the genealogical account begun in the first half. Already we have seen several of the surprising twists that are so characteristic of the genealogical approach. Who could have predicted, for instance, that reflections on the relationship between Israel and its God could have produced the conceptual space for something like the devil or that the figure of the devil would ultimately be taken up most enthusiastically by a group claiming to supersede the Jewish covenant with God? And who would have guessed that the Christian God would increasingly take on the characteristics of his cosmic opponent or that a series of attempts to explain the problem of suffering would evolve into an apparatus for demanding and sacralizing suffering?

My hope is that my approach has already proven its worth by casting a new and unexpected light on the development of Christian theology. My ultimate goal in this genealogical investigation is not simply to expose the flaws in a long-dead theological system, however. I want to show that it is still *living*—in the last places anyone would ever suspect. In support of this goal, I continue to build on the modern political concepts discussed in previous chapters (sovereignty, revolution, social contract) and introduce new connections. And it is arguably in this chapter, on the theological debates surrounding the devil's fall from grace, that the connections to modernity are most prominent—and most surprising.

Before connecting my argument to our present, however, I must connect it to what has come before by grounding this discussion in the most important figure in the transition between the patristic and medieval periods in the Latin West: Augustine. Arguably the first true theological genius to write in Latin, Augustine exercised an incalculable influence over medieval theologians, who for several generations largely contented themselves with transcribing, commenting upon, and imitating his sprawling body of work. Even when more creative theologians arose and began speaking in their own voice, Augustine remained an indispensable point of reference. Behind Anselm's arguments from reason rather than authority, the echo of Augustine's approach is often unmistakable, and though Thomas Aquinas is best known for his bold synthesis of Christian theology and Aristotelian thought, Augustine remains a powerful influence in his theological system. Even when the medieval synthesis began to break down during the Reformation, it is only a slight exaggeration to say that the debate was less over the proper interpretation of Scripture than over the proper interpretation of Augustine.

Few thinkers have had such a profound and long-lasting influence, and fewer have placed such a personal stamp on Western thought. Augustine is best known today for his spiritual autobiography, *The Confessions*, in which he documents his relentless quest for truth. His guiding question is also the guiding question of this book: the problem of evil. His attempts to grapple with it take him initially to a sect known as the Manicheans, who taught that there were two principles at work in the world, one good and one evil. When their teachers prove unable to answer Augustine's increasingly probing questions, he is then drawn to Platonism. Finally, he returns to the Catholic Christianity of his upbringing, because he finds the orthodox Christian answer to the problem of evil, namely, that evil does not exist in itself but is a deprivation of the good, to be the most intellectually satisfying.

For Augustine, however, the problem of evil is not merely an intellectual puzzle but an existential challenge. He is seeking more than the solution of a logical conundrum—he wants to know how to live. He does not simply ponder Manichean ideas but associates himself with their sect, and when he is drawn to philosophy, he sets up a retreat with his friends. Once he embraces Christian doctrine, then, he feels that he must join the church and live in earnest as a Christian. Yet even as he abstractly believes in Christian doctrine, Augustine somehow cannot bring himself to make the final act of will necessary to convert. When his conversion does come, Augustine experiences it as a miraculous result of divine intervention. His final act of surrender was not anything he could have achieved or even contributed to—his salvation occurred at God's sole initiative, as a pure gift.

As a phenomenological account of his own spiritual experience, Augustine's narrative is deeply moving. As the basis for a systematic theology, however, it immediately raises disturbing questions. What about the people God chooses not to save? Has God created them for the sole purpose of sending them to hell? How can they be considered culpable for actions that God preordained? And how can any of us, damned or saved, be considered free in any meaningful sense?

From a certain perspective, this problem of predestination had been hiding in plain sight throughout the patristic era. At least since Irenaeus, the overwhelming consensus among theologians was that *everything* that exists is God's creation. God's power and independence are so radical and unquestionable that he does not even need preexisting raw materials. Rather, God creates ex nihilo, out of nothing. At the same time, however, every patristic writer fully affirmed the freedom of human and angelic wills as the basis for authentic relationship with God and as the only possible grounds for legitimate moral judgment.

These two premises are at least incipiently in conflict: How can God have such overwhelming power over all things and still leave room for the kind of creaturely autonomy implied in the notion of free will? The demands of logical consistency were not enough to force the issue, but at least for the Latin West, Augustine's profound religious experience was. The result was that the problem of evil increasingly hinged on the vexed relationship between divine and creaturely wills. This is true above all of the will of the devil at the moment of his inscrutable rebellion from God, and so the problem of the fall of the devil comes to serve as a kind of laboratory for thinking through the meaning of freedom—with lasting consequences for the modern West.

UNTAMED WILLS

In contemporary theology, the doctrine of predestination is most closely associated with Calvinism, and Protestant polemics against the supposed Roman Catholic doctrine of "salvation by works" may give the impression that predestination would be incompatible with Catholicism. Yet predestination was in fact the consensus view throughout the Latin West during the medieval period. Many theologians were uncomfortable embracing what is known as "double predestination," the view that both the saved and the damned were preordained to their respective conditions. This hesitation did not indicate a rejection of the overall concept of predestination, however—instead, they claimed that only the saved were predestined, while the damned were simply passed over. This solution is typical: a convenient conceptual division, in this case between God's action and nonaction, serves to absolve God of responsibility for the evil fate of the damned.

Nor indeed did the embrace of predestination do anything to challenge the overwhelming conviction among Christian theologians that moral responsibility is possible only on the basis of free will. Unlike the patristic thinkers, however, who either failed to notice the problem or brushed it aside, medieval theologians increasingly tackled it head-on, often deploying a dizzying array of fine logical distinctions. Anselm's late work *De Concordia* is exemplary in this regard. He begins by conceding that "it certainly seems as though divine foreknowledge is incompatible with there being human free choice. For what God foreknows shall necessarily come to be in the future, while the things brought about by free choice do not issue from any necessity." His solution to this dilemma is to claim that "if something is going to occur freely, God, who foreknows all that shall be, foreknows this very fact. And whatever God foreknows shall necessarily happen in the way in which it is foreknown. So it is necessary that it shall happen freely" (I.1).

Anticipating that his reader will find this distinction to be hollow, Anselm proceeds to introduce a further division into the concept of necessity itself, between logical necessity (such as the necessity that anything God fore*knows* must necessarily be going to happen, or else God's foreknowledge would not be authentic knowledge) and the necessity of force (I.2). Hence, "when we say that what God foreknows is going to happen is necessarily going to happen, we are not asserting always that it is going to happen by necessity but simply that it is necessary that what is going to happen is going to happen" (I.3). This distinction, too, rings hollow—can God passively "know" something about a universe that he alone has caused to arise from nothing?

Later in his argument, Anselm turns from the problem of God's foreknowledge and addresses the more difficult conundrum of his predestination, which "is the equivalent of pre-ordination or pre-establishment; and therefore to say that God predestines means that he pre-ordains, that is, to bring it about that something happen in the future" (II.1). To resolve the conflict between predestination and free will, he introduces a division into God's will between what he actively predestines and what he permits. The former is the realm of grace, which "coexists with" free choice "and cooperates with it" (III.1), whereas the latter is the realm of God's benign neglect, where he chooses not to intervene to stop a freely willed evil act. Nevertheless, God's decision not to act is also in a sense an act of God's will, so that "there is no problem in saying that in this sense God predestines evil people and their evil acts when he does not straighten them out along with their evil acts" (II.2). Once again, the carefully constructed division collapses in on itself.

At no point in this complex argument does Anselm let go of the principle of the freedom of the will. Indeed, one of his core postulates is that every will, if it is truly a will, is radically undetermined. This holds equally for divine and human wills: "just as it is not necessary that God wills as he does, it is not necessary that you or I will as we do" (I.3). Yet in Anselm's earlier treatise *On the Fall of the Devil*, this postulate of a completely self-causing will comes under considerable pressure. Ultimately Anselm will be able to save it only by introducing a fresh division into the concept of will itself.

This text, which like *Why God Became Human* is presented in a dialogue format, begins with the seemingly abstract question of whether any creature "has anything of itself," that is, apart from God. The answer is unequivocal: in line with the doctrine of creation ex nihilo, God "alone has of himself all that he has, while other things have nothing of themselves. And other things, having nothing of themselves, have their only reality from him." The student then asks whether the realm of non-being also falls under God's sway. Here Anselm anticipates *De Concordia*'s division between God's active and permissive will, claiming that no action involving non-being can be properly attributed to God, even if we do sometimes use such figures of speech:

> In this way God is said to do many things that he does not, as when he is said to lead us into temptation when he does not prevent temptation that he could, and to cause what is not since he could make it be and does not. But if you consider the things which pass into non-being, you will see that it is not God who causes them not to be. For not only is there no essence he does not make, but nothing he does make could last if he did not preserve it, for when he stops preserving what he made, it is not the case that he turns what was a being into non-being, as if he caused non-being, but only that he stops causing it to be. (§ 1)

In other words, the devil had blessedness initially but failed to persevere in it.

Since perseverance is something good, it could have come from God only according to the terms Anselm sets up. Hence, the student points out, "he does not have it because he did not receive it, and he did not receive it because God did not give it to him. So tell me what his fault is, seeing that he did not persevere because he was not given perseverance, without which gift he could do nothing" (§ 2). To save God from this apparent negligence, the teacher—in conformity with the pattern established at every step so far—posits a division within the very idea of not receiving. On the one hand, one can fail to receive something because it was never given. On the other hand, one can fail to receive something because one refuses it when offered. The case of the devil's nonreception of perseverance falls into the latter category. Indeed, he refused perseverance so radically that he actually abandoned justice without having retained it for even an instant.

What is this justice that the devil abandoned? As the teacher says, "No one serves justice except by willing what he ought, nor abandons it save by willing what he ought not. . . . Therefore by willing something that at the time he ought not to will, he abandoned justice and thus sinned" (§ 4). When the student presses him as to *what* the devil concretely willed so as to merit damnation from all but the instant of his creation, the teacher clarifies that "he inordinately willed to be God," insofar as he refused his place in the ontological hierarchy. Yet the teacher does not go so far as to say that the devil literally willed the thought, "I should be God, not you." Indeed, as the student points out, no one who truly understood what God is could wish to be God, because God is by nature unique. Thus, the devil's will to be God was more a matter of form than of content:

> Even if he did not will to be wholly equal to God, but something less than God against the will of God, by that very fact he inordinately willed to be like God, because he willed something by his own will, as subject to no one. It is for God alone thus to will something by his own will such that he follows no higher will. (§ 4)

In short, as we already saw in *Why God Became Human*, justice consists in subordination and obedience, which God unconditionally demands of all his creatures.

At this point, the discussion turns to the other angels, who either imitated the devil or persevered in justice. Anselm is certain that the good angels could equally have sinned initially (§ 5) but claims that once the initial decision whether to reject or accept perseverance is made, both the good angels and the evil demons are "locked in"—the good angels can never sin, while the evil demons can never regain the justice they abandoned. And in a bitter irony, God rewards the good angels by fine-tuning their will so that "they could have whatever they willed and not see what more they could have willed"— in other words, they get to enjoy precisely the absolute freedom of the will (at least from their own perspective) that the devil and his followers wished to attain (§ 6). To the good angels, then, there belongs a life of perfect fulfillment, while the demons' initial impatience dooms them to an eternity of frustration.

It is at this point that the student notes an inconvenient fact: the will, which allows the devil to take the blame for his own fall, must have come from God as well. As he puts it:

> Indeed, although I see clearly that the perverse angel could not have fallen into an immoderate demand of the good except through some immoderate desire, I am not a little worried as to whence comes this immoderate will. For if he was good, then he fell from so much good into so much evil on account of a good will. . . . If he willed what God gave him to will, how did he sin? Or if he had this will of himself, he had some good that he did not receive. (§ 7)

After a lengthy discussion of the theory of evil as deprivation (which gives the impression of stalling for time in the face of this difficult question), the teacher finally arrives at an answer—and yet again, it consists in making a division, this time within the devil's own will.

This division is premised on a prior division within the concept of the good between "the moral good, which is called justice to which the evil that is injustice is opposed, and the good that it seems to me can be called the useful, to which the harmful is opposed" (§ 12). All living creatures have a will toward the latter, which Anselm calls the animal will, but only rational creatures are capable of a will toward the former, which is designated as the will to rectitude. The animal will is logically prior to the will to rectitude, and it is in a sense amoral, a will-without-will that is more like a necessity, insofar as it stems directly from the living creature's nature to pursue what it perceives as good. Only in a second moment does God bring in the will to rectitude, "harmoniz[ing] the two wills in [the creature] such that he wills to be happy but wills it justly"—which is to say, in appropriate submission to the limits imposed by God (§ 14).

Justice, then, is not merely conformity with the nature God has created. In keeping with Anselm's monastic outlook, it requires some form of deprivation or restraint of one's natural happiness. The will must efface itself before God in order to be just. And with this division, Anselm believes he has squared the circle whereby the devil's will can only have come from God yet can still be regarded as unjust. Precisely by willing what it was in his created nature to will, the devil wills in an unrestrained way, and therefore, according to the formalism established previously, "he wills to be like God" (§ 13). If God had not imposed the requirement of the will to justice or rectitude upon him, the devil would be neither good nor evil. Indeed, the devil still is in this amoral state—and *for that very reason* he is evil: "what is blameworthy in that will is not that it did not remain in justice, but that it does not have justice" (§ 16).

The devil is therefore marked by his relation to the order of justice even as he is radically excluded from it. He does not enjoy a simple animal life—although it is not accidental that here, as in Gregory and Athanasius, a supposedly purely spiritual entity is being paradoxically associated with animality—but instead represents a derelict third form of life, excluded from both the innocence of instinct and the rectitude of the just order.

What is strange about this setup is that Anselm seems to be proposing that *every* creaturely will is necessarily in rebellion against God from the very beginning. Insofar as it is self-causing, every will by definition wills from out of itself and is therefore in a state of formal rivalry to God by Anselm's standards. If will is to be will, then it cannot be created "presubdued." It must be subdued in a second moment—and it may conceivably take longer than an instant to tame a will. Anselm's God, however, is too imperious and demanding to wait, and so he forces an all-or-nothing decision on his creatures the instant they come into existence.

As in *Why God Became Human,* we are dealing with a God who has become the devil—not in the abstract sense of being somehow evil or unfair but in the very precise sense of conforming to the traditional narrative of the devil's fall that we saw in Gregory of Nyssa. Just as God must redeem us from God in *Why God Became Human,* here God rebels against an aspect of his own plan—in this case the unrestrained freedom of creaturely wills— as a threat to his position in the ontological hierarchy. And just as the devil takes out his anger on humanity in the traditional fall narrative, God's pride drives him to lash out at his subordinates, condemning them to a damaged life. Unlike in the misguided rivalry between the devil and humanity, however, there is no higher court of appeal and therefore no hope of salvation.

THE TRAP OF GRACE

Thomas Aquinas's account of the fall of the devil in the *Summa Theologiae* initially has a much more positive cast,[1] insofar as it begins with the experience of the good angels. In discussing the happiness or beatitude of the angels, for instance, he claims that happiness is twofold:

> The first is one which it can procure of its own natural power; and this is in a measure called beatitude or happiness. . . . Above this happiness there is still another, which we look forward to in the future, whereby "we shall see God as He is." This is beyond the nature of every created intellect. (1a, q. 62, a. 1)

Already the tone seems to have shifted radically in comparison with Anselm, insofar as the accent is on God's generosity and abundance. God initially provides his creatures with a natural happiness and then adds an *even greater* happiness that exceeds nature. With this division in mind, Aquinas claims that the angels are initially created in perfect natural happiness, but because the second level of happiness "is no part of their nature, but its end; . . . consequently they ought not to have it immediately from the beginning" (q. 62, a. 1).

To this division within happiness corresponds a division between two forms of capacity for happiness. The first is nature, which consists of the creatures' own internal resources, and the second is grace, whereby God supernaturally grants them the opportunity to rise to the higher level of happiness attainable only in him (q. 62, a. 2). While Aquinas entertains the possibility that angels were created only in the natural state, he concludes that it "seems more probable, and more in keeping with the sayings of holy men, that they were created in sanctifying grace" (q. 62, a. 3).

Yet this grace does not automatically lead to perfect beatitude. Rather, it puts the angel into a position where it can *merit* beatitude. Here Aquinas seems to distantly echo Anselm's division between the amoral animal will and the will to rectitude, insofar as "free-will is not the sufficient cause of merit; and, consequently, an act cannot be meritorious as coming from free-will, except insofar as it is informed by grace" (q. 62, a. 4). As in Anselm, then, the will requires a divine supplement in order to attain moral rectitude, the angels' morally relevant act occurs instantly (q. 62, a. 5) and with permanent consequences:

> The beatified angels cannot sin. The reason for this is, because their beatitude consists in seeing God through His essence. Now, God's essence is the very essence of goodness. Consequently the angel beholding God is disposed towards God in the same way as anyone else not seeing God is to the common form of goodness. Now it is impossible for any man either to will or to do anything except aiming at what is good; or for him to wish to turn away from good precisely as such. (q. 62, a. 8)

Utterly captivated by God, then, the good angel remains invincibly enraptured in beatitude for all eternity. God's favor is its own reward.

Only after having established the blessed condition of the angels does Aquinas turn to the topic of angelic sin. Here it immediately becomes clear that while a rational creature requires grace to earn *merit* before God, it is perfectly capable of sinning all on its own, because, as in Anselm, "sinning is nothing else than a deviation from that rectitude which an act ought to have; whether we speak of sin in nature, art, or morals" (q. 63, a. 1). If the creature's own nature were the point of reference, then the creature could not possibly fall short of that standard and hence could not sin. However, only God has the privilege of serving as his own standard. In contrast,

> every created will has rectitude of act so far only as it is regulated according to the Divine will, to which the last end is to be referred: as every desire of a subordinate ought to be regulated by the will of his superior; for instance, the soldier's will, according to the will of his commanding officer. Thus only in the Divine will can there be no sin; whereas there can be sin in the will of every creature, considering the condition of its nature. (q. 63, a. 1)

The division between nature and grace, which at first looked like a tribute to God's superabundant generosity, here begins to look like a trap, holding God's creatures to an intrinsically impossible standard.

Although the talk of earning merit may put one in mind of positive and creative acts, it is clear that for Aquinas, as for Anselm, merit consists simply in subordination. Aquinas reinforces this impression by specifying that the first sin logically available to angels is pride, which he defines as "not to be subject to a superior when subjection is due" (q. 63, a. 2). More specifically, he claims that the devil attempted to usurp God's prerogative "by desiring, as his last end of beatitude, something which he could attain by the virtue of his own nature, turning his appetite away from supernatural beatitude, which is attained by God's grace" (q. 63, a. 3)—a view that he explicitly attributes to Anselm, even if he has phrased it according to his own idiosyncratic vocabulary. And indeed, the remainder of Question 63 could be read as a systematization and clarification of Anselm's arguments, focused on establishing a firm division between the first moment in which the angels were all created good and the second moment in which the demons fell at Satan's behest.

What is new in his discussion, other than its greater clarity and argumentative rigor, is Aquinas's subtle attempts to make the devil as individually blameworthy as possible. In his discussion of the sin of pride, Aquinas establishes that if we are speaking in terms of guilt, "all sins are in the demons; since by leading human beings to sin they incur the guilt of all sins" (q. 63, a. 2). He further argues that all the other demons sinned at the devil's behest, and so by extension, the devil is personally responsible for literally every sin ever committed by anyone, angel or human. Yet this notion puts considerable pressure on Aquinas's claim that all the demons fell simultaneously in the second instant of creation, and he makes use of uncharacteristically ad hoc reasoning to save that point:

> Although the demons all sinned in the one instant, yet the sin of one could be the cause of the rest sinning. For the angel needs no delay of time for choice, exhortation, or consent, as man, who requires deliberation in order to choose and consent, and vocal speech in order to exhort; both of which are the work of time. . . . Taking away, then, the time for speech and delib- eration which is required in us; in the same instant in which the highest angel expressed his affection by intelligible speech, it was possible for the others to consent thereto. (q. 63, a. 8)

Just when the tradition had compressed the devil's fall into the narrow- est conceivable space of time, here it suddenly explodes into a narrative on the level of Gregory of Nyssa's account. Furthermore, this narrative is an explicitly political one, as Aquinas goes on to imagine the demons in- stantaneously deliberating as to whether there might be some otherwise unattainable "advantage" in accepting the devil "as their prince and leader" (q. 63, a. 8). But in the following article, he embraces a purely aleatoric model, claiming that only a minority of demons fell, because "that which is against the natural order happens with less frequency" (q. 63, a. 9)—in other words, in God's dice roll of angelic free will, there was a slight statistical bias against sinning.

Once the die has been cast, those excluded from divine beatitude are not simply in a state of natural indifference. Rather, they are already being punished even now, with no hope of escape. In this way, they anticipate the condition of humans in hell, who have lost all hope of redemption: "all the mortal sins of men, grave or less grave, are pardonable before death; whereas after death they are without remission and endure for ever" (q. 64, a. 2).

Yet there is one difference, because the demons continue to add to the tally of their sinfulness, while (as we will see later), the damned have the dubious benefit of no longer accruing sins while they are being punished. Indeed, sin and punishment seem to overlap completely for the demons. Discussing the question of whether sorrow exists for demons, Aquinas concedes that purely spiritual beings cannot feel human emotions, yet

> it must be said that there is sorrow in them; because sorrow, as denoting a simple act of the will, is nothing else than the resistance of the will to what is, or to what is not. Now it is evident that the demons would wish many things not to be, which are, and others to be, which are not: for, out of envy, they would wish others to be damned, who are saved. Consequently, sorrow must be said to exist in them: and especially because it is of the very notion of punishment for it to be repugnant to the will. Moreover, they are deprived of happiness, which they desire naturally; and their wicked will is curbed in many respects. (q. 64, a. 3)

The very site of their sin, the will, is precisely the site of their torment, in the form of frustration, envy, and disappointed spite. One could even see a kind of feedback loop here, insofar as it is the very constraint of their wills, which have been "locked in" after their fall, that produces all their sins. The limits of their will thus represent both their fault and their punishment.

Nonetheless, the demons have a positive contribution to make through their very wickedness. For God has consigned them initially to earth as their place of punishment so that they would tempt human beings and allow them to test their spiritual mettle. In this latter role, they contribute directly to the "procuring of humanity's welfare," an outcome that is appropriate, "lest they should cease to be of service in the natural order" (q. 64, a. 4). In addition to this service, some demons are already hard at work anticipating their ultimate role "in hell, to torment those whom they have led astray," just as some good angels are in heaven ministering to the saints. Yet heaven and hell will not be fully populated until "judgment day: consequently, the ministry of the angels and wrestling with demons endure until then" (q. 64 a. 4). Now and forever, then, the devil and his legions serve God through their very rebellion against him.

FOUNDING THE EARTHLY CITY

Both Anselm and Aquinas's accounts of the devil's fall are extremely abstract. Taking place on a purely spiritual plane within the space of a single instant, both arguments are full of seemingly bloodless metaphysical contortions. Yet profound existential and political questions lurk beneath the surface, questions about the nature and legitimacy of God's governance over his creation and about the meaning and role of creaturely freedom. The evil that Anselm and Aquinas are trying to account for is not simply a mistake or an injury but a specifically *political* evil—the evil of rebellion and disobedience in the face of legitimate authority.

This political thrust is just as much a part of the Augustinian heritage as the complex problem of predestination. Indeed, the two are inseparably intertwined in his greatest work, *City of God*,[2] which can be read as a kind of pendant to Athanasius's two-part treatise made up of *Against the Nations* and *On the Incarnation*. Despite its singular title, Augustine's work is also double, with a polemical first half and a more creative theological second half. Both texts are also addressing the relationship between Christianity and Roman society. But where Athanasius is writing at the dawn of the Constantinian era of alliance between church and empire, Augustine is writing just as that settlement is beginning to unravel. The Roman world had been rocked by the sack of Rome by the Goths in 410, and many observers began to question whether the embrace of Christianity was somehow to blame for that humiliating defeat. In response to these critics, Augustine set out to write a demonstration that the Romans had no one but themselves to blame for their downfall (Books I–X). Only later did he broaden the scope of the work to encompass a systematic account of the Christian alternative to the follies of pagan history (Books XI–XII).

Even apart from its context, the title clearly announces a political theme—the very word "politics" derives, after all, from the Greek *polis*, city. In his preface, he announces that his ultimate intent is to discuss "the glorious city of God," and the way he describes it recalls the prophetic theme of exile and the apocalyptic hope of eschatological fulfillment. The city of

God is "a city surpassingly glorious, whether we view it as it still lives by faith in this fleeting course of time, and sojourns as a stranger in the midst of the ungodly, or as it shall dwell in the fixed stability of its eternal seat, which it now with patience waits for." At the same time, as a kind of negative corollary, this discussion will require that he "speak also of the earthly city, which, though it be mistress of the nations, is itself ruled by its lust of rule" (I, preface). The imagery here recalls the Whore of Babylon, a symbol of Rome from Revelation, and while the earthly city is clearly not *reducible* to Rome, it is clear from the start that Rome is its most important contemporary representative from Augustine's perspective.

In short, the apocalyptic alliance between earthly rulers and the demonic is back in play. And in keeping with the project of rereading the scriptural heritage from an apocalyptic perspective, Augustine traces the rivalry between the two cities all the way back to the very creation of the world. In Augustine's account, the earthly city is founded almost simultaneously with the heavenly, albeit as its shadow and negation. And as we will see, this move severely exacerbates the tensions of the problem of evil, insofar as it continually flirts with the dreaded possibility that God is the direct founder of the earthly city as well as the heavenly.

Augustine acknowledges that in the Genesis account, "it is not plainly said whether or when the angels were created," but he argues that they must have been created on the first day (XI.9), when God created light and then "separated the light from the darkness," calling them Day and Night, respectively (Genesis 1:3–5). For Augustine, these short verses offer a compressed account not only of the creation of all the angels but of the fall of the demons. The fact that God is not said to "create" darkness, but only to separate and designate it, is interpreted as a biblical endorsement of the theory that we have already seen in Gregory, according to which "evil has no positive nature, but the loss of good has received the name 'evil'" (XI.9).

Hence the fall of the demons must have come about before the material world was created. This means that a narrative account like Gregory of Nyssa's, where the fall comes about due to jealousy of humanity, is essentially impossible. Augustine is the first to present himself with this complex theological problem, and as is often the case when great thinkers are mapping uncharted conceptual territory, the argument is convoluted and difficult to follow. Thus, I chose to start anachronistically with Anselm and Aquinas, who present the same basic account much more straight-forwardly. Rather than reconstruct Augustine's argument in detail, then, I propose to show how the more explicitly political context of *City of God* clarifies its stakes.

I have frequently observed that accounts of the devil's fall proceed by way of division. Again and again, Anselm and Aquinas deploy fine con-ceptual distinctions, which just as frequently break down. The same is true of Augustine, who contributes an important distinction that is not equally emphasized by his intellectual descendants. At one point he recognizes that his position, whereby the devil sinned from nearly the very instant of being created, is only a hair's breadth from what he characterizes as the Manichean position that "the devil has derived from some adverse evil principle a nature proper to himself" (XI.13). This view is conceptually in-coherent, however, because "if sin be natural, it is not sin at all," and hence "it is not to be supposed that [the devil] sinned from the beginning of his created existence, but from the beginning of his sin, when by his pride he had once commenced to sin" (XI.15). In other words, the devil's created nature, *as* created, cannot be sinful; what is sinful is his refusal to occupy his appropriate place in the created order, a refusal that is the devil's sole responsibility.

In the first chapter, I connected the problem of evil to Carl Schmitt's very influential account of sovereignty. Here I think it would be helpful to connect Augustine's specific inflection of the problem to Giorgio Agam-ben's critique and reworking of Schmitt's theory.[3] Agamben displaces the central question of sovereignty from the decision on the exception to the application of political power to life. This application is made possible by a division within the concept of life itself, between natural life (*zoè*) and politically qualified life (*bios*)—between the fact of being alive in general and the various rights and privileges that allow us to live our everyday life in society. In the ancient Greek city-state, Agamben argued, *zoè* made its dwelling in the household, which was a necessary precondition for the political realm but did not yet belong to it. *Bios*, in contrast, could be achieved only for one who is recognized as part of the city. To translate Augustine's division into Agamben's terms, we might be initially tempted to say that the devil's *zoè* is necessarily good insofar as it comes from God, but it is the rebellious and derelict form that his *bios* takes that renders him sinful.

Yet things are not quite that simple. In Agamben's theory, when someone is expelled from the city, as the devil has been from the heavenly city, this act of exclusion produces a third form of life, which Agamben calls "bare life." Bare life is the life of someone who was once part of the political realm but has been stripped of that dignity—and is therefore stripped of any political protections against violence. Bare life seems to be nothing more than natural life, but it remains marked by the political in its very exclusion. In bare life, then, the distinction between *zoè* and *bios* breaks down.

A similar confusion of categories appears in Augustine, when he declares that "departure from God would be no vice, unless in a *nature whose property it was* to abide with God" (XI.17, emphasis added). Augustine's entire argument up to this point had depended on a division between the devil's nature as a created being and his abiding permanently with God. Yet just as in Agamben's concept of bare life, the two categories collapse together precisely in the case of the person excluded. That is, after the act of exclusion, the devil's very nature (*zoè*) seems to be marked by his political obligation (*bios*). And just as the act of exclusion founds sovereign power in Agamben, so too in Augustine does God's exclusion of the devil reinforce his reign:

> But God, as he is the supremely good Creator of good natures, so is He of evil wills the most just ruler; so that, while they make an ill use of good natures, he makes a good use even of evil wills. Accordingly he caused the devil (good by God's creation, wicked by his own will) to be cast down from his high position, and to become the mockery of his angels—that is, he caused his temptations to benefit those whom he wishes to injure by them. (XI.17)

Indeed, after having placed this act of exclusion on the very first day of creation, as a necessary concomitant of God's very first act in founding his great city, Augustine veers perilously close to reassigning the blame for evil to God:

> For God would never have created any, I do not say angel, but even human, whose future wickedness he foreknew, unless he had equally known to what uses in behalf of the good he could turn him, thus embellishing the course of the ages, as it were an exquisite poem set off with antitheses. . . . So the beauty of the course of this world is achieved by the opposition of contraries, arranged, as it were, by an eloquence not of words, but of things. (XI.18)

Evil is no longer justified punishment, or beneficial purification, or even a mysteriously necessary part of God's divine plan: "to the eye that has skill to discern it," evil is beautiful (XI.23). The separation between the earthly and heavenly cities seems to be breaking down, as the latter requires the former to fully actualize its glorious beauty.

The cushion of plausible deniability separating God from outright responsibility for evil seems to be wearing very thin. Yet this framing may obscure Augustine's actual purpose. In reality, over the course of his investigation, Augustine's goal gradually shifts away from accounting for how the devil could have sinned and instead becomes a question of *making sure that the devil can be counted as sinful.* Augustine's comments on the contribution evil makes to the beauty of the universe seem to suggest that God somehow *needs* an evil being to define himself against. Thus, free will, which in Gregory of Nyssa was presented as the necessary precondition of our fellowship with God, instead becomes an apparatus for guaranteeing the existence of his permanently excluded foe.

DEMONOLOGY, SLAVERY, AND RACIALIZATION

This strange recruitment of the enemy to enhance God's glory recalls the dynamics not so much of sovereignty as of slavery. In his classic study, *Slavery and Social Death,*[4] Orlando Patterson notes that ownership of slaves was a source of "honor and glory" for members of the master class (p. 99).

Just as the existence of evil highlights God's good creation, so too does the domination over a permanently degraded person who is definitionally incapable of honor emphasize the honor of his master. The connection with slavery is strengthened when we recall that the fall of the devil is envisioned as a war in the Book of Revelation, as it will be in Milton's *Paradise Lost*. As Patterson notes, "Archetypically, slavery was a substitute for death in war" (p. 5), and it results in a strange third space between life and death that he calls "social death." The connection with Agamben's concept of bare life is clear, even if, as Alexander Weheliye points out, Agamben fails to make that connection explicit.[5] Furthermore, the fallen angels are forced to work against their will for the greater glory of God, like a slave—and the humiliation they experience in their involuntary service is, as Athanasius's *Life of Antony* makes abundantly clear, very much the point.

In the course of his critique of Agamben, Weheliye highlights another concomitant of bare life: racialization, which he characterizes as "an assemblage of forces that must continuously articulate nonwhite subjects as non-quite-human" (p. 19). While the reference to whiteness is anachronistic in a medieval context, here too there is a parallel, insofar as the rebellious angels become demons, a new subspecies of not-quite-angels. Like subordinate races under modern white hegemony, the demons are associated—despite the apparent incongruity—with the body or the animal rather than the rational. Given that they are incapable of sexual reproduction, they are "natally isolated" in a particularly radical way (to use Patterson's term for the slave's separation from existing family ties and inability to form socially recognized families)—a point that proved crucial in Anselm's attempt to guarantee that their derelict status was irreversible. Nevertheless, they still constitute something like a distinctive "race" of angels.

The thrust of all three of these contemporary arguments is that the subordinate term is actually foundational rather than a deviation: for Agamben, bare life is the foundation of the political order; for Patterson, the slave is actually the logical presupposition for the "free" individual, insofar as it is only the experience of slavery that would allow "freedom" to appear valuable in itself; and for Weheliye, blackness represents a more authentic humanity (what he calls "the flesh") in contrast to the imposture of Western Man. And the same must be said for the angels in the three medieval accounts: though the demonic state is characterized as a fall or a lack, it actually represents the baseline condition. In that first instant, all the angels are incipiently demons, driven solely by their animal wills and as yet uninitiated into the realm of rectitude or grace. Only by adding something to their original angelic natures does God render them "proper" angels, while leaving the demons in their initial state. God created all the angels in a state of slavery, in other words, and he rewards the good angels with their freedom only when he is sure they will never use it against him.

Insofar as God is rewarding those who obey him and punishing those who rebel, the divine order could initially appear to be a meritocracy. Yet Augustine's argumentation ultimately undercuts this perception. The decisive moment comes when Augustine is trying to establish that in order to create this ostensibly beautiful order of good and evil, of obedient servants and derelict slaves, God must proceed indirectly. Here again, however, Augustine's emphasis falls not on God's desire to insulate himself from responsibility for evil but on conceptual necessity. If God had directly created the devil as evil, he would not have been evil at all: "For no one is punished for natural, but for voluntary vices. For even the vice which by the force of habit and long continuance has become a second nature, had its origin in the will" (XII.3). The only possible source of evil is the will, which as in Anselm is radically self-causing: "If the . . . question be asked, What was the efficient cause of their evil will? there is none. For what is it which makes the will bad, when it is the will itself which makes the action bad? And consequently the bad will is the cause of any bad action, but nothing is the efficient cause of the bad will" (XII.6).

Augustine ties this notion of the self-causing will together with his recurrent theme of remaining in one's appropriate place in the created order: "For when the will abandons what is above itself, and turns to what is lower, it becomes evil—not because that is evil to which it turns, but because the turning itself is wicked" (XII.6). Yet he is careful to specify that the context within which a sinful act of will occurs does not "cause" the will to incline toward evil. To clarify this point, he sets up a thought experiment in which two rational creatures (human or angel) are tempted equally, in precisely identical circumstances. If one gives in while the other persists in righteousness, nothing but their wills can account for the difference: "However minutely we examine the case . . . , we can discern nothing which caused the will of the one to be evil" (XII.6). Hence Augustine claims that if we must speak of causation in connection with evil acts of will, we should think in terms of a new category of causes that are "not efficient, but deficient" (XII.7).

Though Augustine does not say it in so many words, the conclusion is inescapable: If we ask why the devil fell, the only possible answer is *for no reason*. He fell because he fell, in a purely spontaneous and arbitrary act of will. The quest to deprive the devil of any mitigating circumstances for his fall has ended by depriving his fall of any meaning or sense whatsoever. The devil's choice seems less like the authentic expression of freedom and more like a purely random impulse. The rebellion of the demons—or, for that matter, the loyalty of the good angels—becomes less a dramatic political struggle for mastery in the heavenly realm and more a simple roll of the dice. And from this perspective, the order of the universe, which is founded on God's providential response to that dice roll, appears utterly amoral and meaningless.

THE EMPTY SPACE OF FREEDOM

In the two chapters that follow, we will look more closely at the devil's work on earth and in hell, respectively. For the moment, however, I would like to linger in the empty space we have been exploring in this chapter—first of all by gathering together some of the tangled threads of argument. I have pointed out that Augustine, Anselm, and Aquinas all arrive at a broadly similar account of the devil's fall: he fell at the earliest possible moment, due to an act of will that was inexplicably insubordinate to God. Hence, as I noted in the introduction to this chapter, he is as evil as possible (choosing evil with no mitigating circumstances and quite literally for no reason) for as long as possible (from the beginning of time through to eternity, save the one instant necessary to insulate God from direct responsibility for the devil's sin). Further, all three proceed by creating a series of divisions that aim to cordon off the devil's rebellion into a conceptual space excluded from God's realm of direct responsibility.

In all three accounts of the devil's fall, free will proves to be the decisive factor in establishing the devil's responsibility for his own state. Yet without any meaningful context and history, the devil's choice seems to be more an act of sheer arbitrariness and randomness than an authentically free choice in any meaningful sense. Indeed, it can even seem as though God is setting the devil up to fall. After all, for Augustine, evil emerges as a necessary and even beautiful part of the created order.

In any case, we are confronted with a strange and disturbing view of the function of free will. In this theological scheme, freedom does not exist to enhance the devil's dignity or enable his fellowship with God—instead, it provides the pretext for his depravity and exclusion. In light of the randomness of his choice, the devil's freedom has meaning only retrospectively, as a way of justifying his present state of exclusion. In other words, free will is an apparatus for producing blameworthiness.

This theological account may seem to be as far as possible from modern views on freedom. Yet—as we would expect given that God increasingly takes on the role of the devil in the ransom theory—there are uncanny parallels between the fall of the devil and the accounts of the foundation of the modern earthly city in the social contract tradition. Both mobilize the distinction between an original state and a politically qualified state, and both require the surrender of unrestrained freedom in order to enter into the realm of the commonwealth. Both treat contemporary citizens as though they have assented to the laws of the commonwealth, as a way of making them morally accountable for submission. This feature is especially prominent in Hobbes, who goes to great lengths to establish the notion that already in the state of nature, we are fully accountable for fulfilling our promises—even promises made under duress.

The two traditions also share a common trajectory toward greater abstraction. In classical social contract theory, the authors typically provide some kind of narrative account purporting to explain how the transition from the state of nature to the political state might have come about. The overall impression for the reader of Hobbes, Locke, and Rousseau is that we are dealing with *real events*, even if they are necessarily described only approximately. At some point in primeval history, human beings really did come together to form a social contract, in much the same way that modern societies staged the explicit ratification of their written constitutions.

Over time, however, the social contract was more openly put forth as a thought experiment, as when Kant proposes the social contract as a regulative ideal for thinking about our moral obligation to contemporary societies. The tradition arguably culminates with John Rawls, who stages the ratification of the hypothetical social contract as a scene every bit as abstract as the accounts of the devil's fall we have been investigating.[6] All participants are stripped of any historical and contextual specificity and treated as pure reasoning beings. Although the assumption is that they will take on some specific place in human society once it is founded, within the space of Rawls's thought experiment, they are functionally identical to the purely spiritual and intellectual angels of medieval theology. In this abstract space, Rawls's angels are asked to deliberate on the general shape of society, without knowing where they will end up in the heavenly dice roll that will assign them their specific politically qualified form of life (*bios*). If we can imagine these hypothetical angelic humans consenting to enter into a social order with no guarantee of where they will wind up in the social hierarchy, that society is retrospectively viewed as just and legitimate.

Rawls's thought experiment initially seems to cut against the implicit identification of free will and random chance in medieval accounts of the fall of the devil. The two moments are clearly separated—first there is the abstract deliberation, and then everyone is assigned a lot in life. Yet this neat division collapses on further scrutiny, because the condition for judging a society to be just is that a reasonable person would accept any place in society, even the very lowest. That is, each reasoning being has in principle consented to *every* possible social role, meaning that individuals can be treated as consenting to the role in which they in fact wound up. Furthermore, it has seemed clear to most readers of Rawls that he expects that the Western political settlement of his time, in which capitalist inequalities are tempered by a strong interventionist state, will pass the test—which means that, at least for his historical context, all people can be justly treated as if they had consented freely to the political order in some decontextualized and ahistorical realm.

Here there is a slight deviation from the medieval model, in that there is some space for evaluation and judgment of the social order in Rawls's account, whereas the original angels must simply assent to God's chosen order without question. At the same time, the comparison with Rawls helps to highlight the fact that the angels are treated as though they had somehow *already* consented to be under God's rule—as though they are already slaves who are subject to God's will. This is the only way to make sense of the idea that the devil and his comrades are *rebelling* against God rather than simply choosing not to join his side—and more generally, it is the only way to ensure that obedience to God is a morally relevant act rather than an automatic outgrowth of the angelic nature. Like the good angel, the Rawlsian subject is granted freedom only on condition of a prior submission (to the terms of the thought experiment).

It is not surprising that modernity's founding political myth would end up in this empty space discovered by medieval theology when one realizes that its founding philosophical myth had also been staged there. I am speaking, of course, of René Descartes' *Meditations on First Philosophy*.[7] In the first of his famous exercises in methodological doubt, Descartes makes quick work of his long-standing belief in his own perceptions and even his own body, and he assents just as quickly to the truths of mathematics. But he displays much more hesitation in rejecting God. He concedes that the nonexistence of God does make it "more likely ... that I am so imperfect as to be deceived all the time" and hence decides to include God within the field of doubt (p. 78).

At this point Descartes seems to have thoroughly covered the territory of the doubtable, but as a way of making sure he does not grow complacent and too hastily assent to a questionable truth, he decides to "turn [his] will in completely the opposite direction and deceive [himself], by pretending for a time that these former opinions of [his] are utterly false and imaginary" (p. 79). To aid him in this task, he lays down the following assumption:

> I will suppose therefore that not God, who is supremely good and the source of truth, but rather some malicious demon of the utmost power and cunning has implied all his energies in order to deceive me. (p. 79)

Despite these apparently unfavorable circumstances, Descartes is confident that he can overcome this evil demon.

> I shall stubbornly and firmly persist in this meditation; and, even if it is not in my power to know any truth, I shall at least do what is in my power, that is, resolutely guard against assenting to any falsehoods, so that the deceiver, however powerful and cunning he may be, will be unable to impose on me in the slightest degree. (p. 79)

And in the Second Meditation, he hits upon precisely the point at which the demon cannot deceive him:

> I too undoubtedly exist, if he is deceiving me; and let him deceive me as much as he can, he will never bring it about that I am nothing so long as I think I am something. So after considering everything very thoroughly, I must finally conclude that this proposition, *I am, I exist*, is necessarily true whenever it is put forward by me or conceived in my mind. (p. 80)

This realization puts him on the path back to the truth, leading him to grasp the noncorporeal nature of his mind and, in the Third Meditation, the necessity of the existence of a good God. Once the latter is established, he is well on his way to a proper foundation for his everyday knowledge, including an account of why it is possible for him to err in his judgments.

In short, this foundational text of modern philosophy is the story of a disembodied reasoning being who resists the devil and turns instead to God. It is not exactly a retelling of the fall of the devil, but it takes place within the same milieu. And much like Rawls's hypothetical consenting citizens, Descartes is playing the role of a good angel who rejects Satan's wiles and instead chooses the path of reason.

There is considerable evidence that some kind of medieval connection is intentional on Descartes' part. His use of Aristotelian terminology recalls the tradition of medieval Scholasticism initiated by Aquinas, and it is well known that he reworks Anselm's famous proof of the existence of God—the so-called ontological proof, which argues that there is something inherent in the very concept of God that constrains us to affirm his existence—in the Third Meditation. Perhaps less well known is that medieval thinkers in both the Christian and Islamic traditions had arrived at Descartes' principle of "I think, therefore I am." One such instance occurs only pages away from the passages on the fall of the devil in *City of God* discussed previously, where Augustine refutes philosophical skepticism:

> For if I am deceived, I am. For he who is not, cannot be deceived; and if I am deceived, by this same token I am. And since I am if I am deceived, how am I deceived in believing that I am? For it is certain that I am if I am deceived. Since, therefore, I, the person deceived, should be, even if I were deceived, certainly I am not deceived in this knowledge that I am. And, consequently, neither am I deceived in knowing that I know. (XI.26)

This argument then serves as a foundation for Augustine's theory that human beings retain an "image of God" within their soul—a close parallel with Descartes' notion of "the idea of the infinite in me," which serves as the starting point for his demonstration of the existence of God.

The parallels with the fall-of-the-devil scenario go deeper than these tacit references to Augustine, Anselm, and Aquinas, however. Once Descartes establishes that God exists and has created him, he must contend with his own version of the problem of evil. In his case, it is restricted to the sphere of knowledge, and so he asks not why suffering and evil happen but why he is able to make errors in his intellectual judgments. Like his medieval predecessors, he believes that God is not responsible for the existence of error, and to help establish this, he draws on the notion of evil as privation: "I understand, then, that error as such is not something real which depends on God, but merely a defect. Hence my going wrong does not require me to have a faculty specially bestowed on me by God; it simply happens as a result of the fact that the faculty of true judgment which I have from God is in my case not infinite" (p. 100).

This faculty of judgment is a subset of free will, which chooses whether or not to assent to a given intellectual judgment, and as in the medieval concept of free will, it is inherently unlimited and hence potentially in rivalry with God:

> I cannot complain that the will or freedom of choice which I received from God is not sufficiently extensive or perfect, since I know that it is beyond my understanding. . . . It is only the will, or freedom of choice, which I experience within me to be so great that the idea of any greater faculty is beyond my grasp; so much so that it is above all in virtue of the will that I understand myself to bear in some way the image and likeness of God. For although God's will is incomparably greater than mine . . . nevertheless it does not seem any greater than mine when considered as will in the essential and strict sense. (p. 101)

This infinite human will must be disciplined, however, by remaining within the proper limits established by God's "natural light." If it errs, then, it is not due to God's negligence but results from the fact that

> the scope of the will is wider than that of the intellect; but instead of restricting it within the same limits, I extend its use to matters which I do not understand. Since the will is indifferent in such cases, it easily turns aside from what is true and good, and this is the source of my error and sin. (p. 102)

And as the remainder of the text shows, the primary temptations to fall into "error and sin" (a surprising description of the act of making incorrect judgments) come from the promptings of the senses, whose perceptions can never be "clear and distinct" enough to guarantee their truthfulness.

Whatever Descartes' intentions in making use of medieval theological concepts and terminology, his text is profoundly medieval in the sense that I established in the previous chapter. Its focus on knowledge and true belief is in line with the patristic side of the medieval heritage, while its distrust of the body—and its implicit equation of the body with the "evil demon,"

insofar as both are deceivers—places it in the tradition of monastic spirituality. He is seeking natural scientific truth rather than doctrinal truth, but
his approach would be recognizable to Anselm. In short, the content is undoubtedly modern, but the form of this purportedly foundational modern
text is unmistakably medieval.

If Descartes is an angel, though, what of the demons? They are those
who reject reason and give in to madness. As Foucault puts it, with imagery
that is surely meant to recall the "evil demon" who would systematically
deceive Descartes, "the Cartesian formula of doubt is certainly the great
exorcism of madness."[8] Derrida has claimed that Foucault is too hasty in
characterizing Descartes' operation as one of pure expulsion,[9] arguing that
madness is much more integral to Cartesian reason. If I am correct to situ-
ate Descartes' investigation within the milieu of the medieval fall of the
devil, however, the difference between these two views is less important than
the fact that they agree that madness is playing the demonic role—hence we
would expect that it is strangely included through its very exclusion.

And what about the political analogue? If Rawls is the angel, who are
the demons? If the prior social contract theory is any indication, there
are plenty of individuals and populations that cannot or will not accede to
the order of reason, plenty of classes of the not-quite-human. For instance,
there are women, who have enough reason to assent to a marriage contract
but are too mired down in the merely bodily to participate in the political
sphere, as Carole Pateman reminds us in her critique of the social contract.[10]
There are also the enslavable racialized populations whose foundational
role for the Western social contract Charles Mills has highlighted.[11] If modernity has tried to stage the founding of the heavenly city here below, its
earthly shadow has never been far behind. It is therefore to the citizens of
that earthly city—the devil and all his many allies—that we now turn.

CHAPTER 5

THE EARTHLY CITY

As we have seen, Augustine's two cities are each made up of two distinct groups, one angelic and one human. The fall of the devil and his followers divided the angels into two subgroups, both of which are "locked into" their respective moral orientations. The good angels, who constantly enjoy the complete satisfaction that comes from the presence of God, will never turn away from God, never cease to be loyal—and they have been granted their freedom in the assurance that they will never misuse it. The demons, however, are condemned to have their will perpetually frustrated, and they can never rejoin their blessed former comrades. Although their wills can never divert from their course, the actions of both groups remain morally relevant because their will is still *their will*, and the will is the seat of moral accountability. The good angels therefore continue to make use of God's grace in order to build up merits, while the demons are digging themselves ever deeper into the abyss of sinfulness. And even though the demons' actions objectively fulfill God's plan, their deeds are still evil, because they are intended and willed as acts of rebellion.

As medieval theologians often explained, the reason that angels and demons experience their moral lock-in is that they are purely spiritual beings. Once they choose their moral orientation, therefore, there is no room for any countervailing force within their nature to fight against it—they choose all at once, all the way. Our compound nature as a union of body and soul renders our case more complicated, though the end result is much the same: after Adam and Eve's sin, human beings are incapable of willing other than sinfully on their own. But as in the demonic case, because the problem is with our *will*, which is the seat of moral accountability, our inevitable sins still heap condemnation upon us.

To account for this predicament, theologians engaged in ever more elaborate interpretations of the narrative of the fall of humanity in Genesis 3. As Rosemary Radford Ruether has pointed out, it could initially seem strange that the tradition "has taken this rather odd folktale with consummate theological seriousness." She notes that the story

> is never referred to at any other place in Hebrew Scripture as the basis of the etiology of evil. For Judaism, the primary myth of evil lies in the story of God's election of Israel and its subsequent apostasy from God by seeking idols. It is this drama of good and evil, and not the Eve story, that shapes Hebrew thought.[1]

The same could be said of the Qur'an, which includes several versions of the fall of the devil (called Iblis) and his subsequent temptation of the first humans, but does not embrace anything like a doctrine of original sin.[2]

In short, the emphasis on Genesis 3 is a Christian peculiarity. Its biblical roots can be found in the fifth chapter of Paul's Letter to the Romans, which argues that Christ is the "second Adam" whose redemptive work reverses the destructive effects of the first Adam's sin. The appeal of the story of our first parents is perhaps obvious for a religion that is trying to find grounds in the Hebrew Bible for a universal appeal to all nations. Yet in keeping with his purpose of finding common ground between Jews and Christians, Paul himself placed greater emphasis, in both Romans and Galatians, on God's covenant with Abraham, which occurred prior to the promulgation of the Law of Moses. Only once it became clear that a majority of Jews were never going to accept Jesus as the messiah did the focus turn to Adam and Eve.

As we saw in Chapter 3, many early Christian writers, in keeping with the apocalyptic roots of Christianity, understood the fall narrative in political terms. By submitting to the devil rather than God, our first parents were effectively entering into a social contract with the devil, who became their ruler. This condition of subjection was passed down to subsequent generations of humans in much the same way that the status of citizenship or slavery is inherited. By subverting the devil's regime from within, Jesus redeems us—and, at least in Gregory of Nyssa's account, the devil as well.

We also noted how Anselm took up and transformed this basic scheme in *Why God Became Human*, where Christ comes to redeem us, not from the devil but from our inescapable indebtedness to God. Anselm does still conceive the situation as political to some degree, but it is not a question of forming a government under the devil's rule. God's rule is absolute, with no room for even the provisional recognition of an alternative regime. Hence both the devil and his human co-conspirators are rebels and runaway slaves, who are guilty of failing to honor God by obeying him.

Anselm's approach solves the perceived problem of granting too much legitimacy to the devil, but it also raises the question of why subsequent generations should share in Adam and Eve's condition—after all, there is no valid condition of citizenship or slavery to be passed down. And in order to close this conceptual gap, the tradition transformed the political problem of bondage to the devil to the quasi-biological one of the bondage of the will, in which all of humanity paradoxically becomes racialized in Weheliye's sense, consigned to the vagaries of the flesh.

ORIGINAL SIN AND THE RESTRAINER

Augustine's contribution is decisive here. In *City of God*, he hypothesizes that part of humanity's punishment was that their bodies began to rebel against them. Drawing on the biblical claim that Adam and Eve became ashamed of their nakedness, Augustine connects this bodily rebellion to sexuality in specific: "Then began the flesh to lust against the Spirit, in which strife we are born, deriving from the first transgression a seed of death, and bearing in our members, and in our vitiated nature, the contest or even victory of the flesh" (XIII.13). As with the moral lock-in experienced by the demons, this apparent change in human nature is humanity's sole responsibility, not God's, because "God, the author of natures, not of vices, created man upright; but man, being of his own will corrupted, and justly condemned, begot corrupted and condemned children" (XIII.14).

The goal of this argument is to demonstrate that every human being is born in a state of rebellion against God—or, on a more personal note, to account for Augustine's unmistakable experience of being unable to will his conversion without divine intervention. From this perspective, however, Augustine's own solution arguably misses the mark. Drawing on the ancient medical theory where the man provides all the relevant reproductive material while the woman serves as a passive incubator, he claims that when Adam sinned, "already the seminal nature [of all of us] was there from which we were to be propagated" (XIII.14)—that is to say, the seed from which every human individual would grow was present in Adam's body. This questionable biological claim may explain why we are born corrupted but not why we are *morally responsible* for our own corruption, since reproductive material has no moral agency.

Arguably more robust is Anselm's account in *On the Virgin Conception and Original Sin*. In his view, Adam's decision to disobey God introduced a distortion into his will, which he could not restore to its original upright state through his own power. Like Augustine, he draws a distinction between the authentic human nature and humans as we experience them in fact: "If human nature had not sinned, it would have been propagated as God had made it: thus after its sin it is propagated according to what it has made of itself by sinning" (§ 2). In Weheliye's terms, it is paradoxically the case that nearly every human being who has ever existed is "not-quite-human" or racialized. To explain how this occurs, Anselm draws on the same theory of reproduction as Augustine but specifies that the corrupted version of human sexuality leads to an inborn corruption of each individual human *will*, which prevents humans from ever attaining the state of moral rectitude on their own (§ 7). The racialization of humanity is simultaneously a moral degradation.

Now as we know, for Anselm human beings owe it to God to have their wills in a state of submission to him. Failure to fulfill this obligation represents an injustice to God and therefore a sin, and thus "all infants are equally unjust, because they have none of the justice which it is each man's duty to have" (§ 24). Anselm is very clear that the sheer fact of being in a state of original sin, insofar as it involves the will, is a sin in the same sense as any active sin we commit—or at least has the same consequence, damnation (§ 28). Baptism allows infants to be *forgiven* of this sin and grants them access to forgiveness for subsequent sins as well (§ 29), but failing this, even an infant is worthy of damnation. And just as with the demons and their fatally flawed wills, this theory works because the problem is one of a misaligned will, and the will is the source of moral accountability. Yet again, free will proves to be an apparatus for generating blameworthiness.

Thus, instead of the political bond to the devil posited by the ransom theory, we get a kind of de facto kinship of renegade angels and corrupted humans, who all share a distorted will irrevocably oriented away from the good. This displacement from the political to the bodily represents a universalization of the monastic paradigm, in which the body becomes the primary site of struggle with the devil. Unlike in Antony's case, however, this is a struggle that has always already failed—with one notable exception. Christ avoids the corruption of human nature by being born of a virgin (whom God also preserved in a state of original justice for good measure; § 18), which removes the distorting influence of coitus and enables him to be born with an upright will. This means, as we saw in the discussion of *Why God Became Human* in Chapter 3, that Christ, like the good angels, is in a position to accrue merits, which he distributes upon request. Unlike the angelic residents of the heavenly kingdom, however, those who participate in Christ's merits do not gain an irreversibly upright will, at least in this life. Instead, their debt of justice to God is paid vicariously through Christ.

The heavenly city has many human residents, then, but only two—Christ and the Virgin Mary—actually enjoy the full benefits of an upright will. The rest are riding on their coattails, still hobbled by a disordered will, and their ostensible superiority to the sinners around them is thus purely nominal, in a way that anticipates Weheliye's critique of the impostures of Western Man. The human residents of the heavenly city also differ from their angelic counterparts in that they represent a distinct minority of the human population. Aquinas may have reasoned that the majority of angels would choose the good, but the situation with humans is such that *all* of them are affected by Adam's sin. By default, as it were, all of us are heading to hell, and any other outcome requires a special act of grace on God's part.

The idea that the earthly residents of the heavenly city are perpetually a minority is a natural outgrowth of the Hebrew biblical tradition from which Christianity springs. All along, the faithful have been but a small part of the total human population: the nation of Israel, the diasporic Jewish community, the righteous remnant, the messianic community. This sense of being a minority besieged may have momentarily fallen aside in the burst of optimism that followed the recognition of Christianity by the Roman Empire, so that Gregory of Nyssa, for instance, could express confidence that everyone would be saved, even God's demonic foe. In time, however, the inner logic of the apocalyptic framework underlying Christianity asserted itself. In the Middle Ages and well into the early modern period, Christianity largely perceived itself as a religion under siege. Notwithstanding the fact that all European rulers ultimately converted to Christianity, or that ecclesiastical authorities had massive influence and sometimes outright temporal power, or that the monastic ideal represented the moral and intellectual center of medieval society, the earthly representatives of the heavenly city regarded themselves as sojourners in a world that could never be their home.

Christians expected opposition in this world during the apocalyptic interregnum, and in keeping with the medieval synthesis between the patristic and monastic outlooks, they thought primarily in terms of religions opponents (Jews, Muslims, heretics) and bodily temptations (most notably those related to sexuality, particularly that of women). In subsequent sections—in which I discuss texts that show Christianity at its absolute worst—I discuss both of those specific prongs of the devil's offensive against the heavenly city, focusing on Jews and witches, respectively. While the anti-Jewish and misogynistic rhetoric of those texts is extreme and disturbing, I will argue that it grows out of the fundamental presuppositions of the medieval Christian worldview.

From another perspective, however, the opposition the heavenly city experiences is only a symptom, albeit a particularly intense one, of a broader problem: human sinfulness. According to the doctrine of original sin, every human being is born with a predisposition to engage in sinful, destructive acts. We have already noted Gregory of Nyssa's widely shared view that God imposed mortality on humanity as a way of restraining their destructive potential. Over time, a consensus began to emerge that human government plays a similar role. This position draws on Paul's discussion of human authority in Romans:

> Let every person be subject to the governing authorities; for there is no authority except from God, and those authorities that exist have been instituted by God. Therefore whoever resists authority resists what God has appointed, and those who resist will incur judgment. For rulers are not a terror to good conduct, but to bad. Do you wish to have no fear of the authority? Then do what is good, and you will receive its approval; for it is God's servant for your good. But if you do what is wrong, you should be afraid, for the authority does not bear the sword in vain! It is the servant of God to execute wrath on the wrongdoer. (Romans 13:1–4)[3]

In Chapter 2, I noted that from Paul's own perspective, this passage was most likely not meant to indicate that the governing powers had any legitimate authority in the strong sense, only that they played a de facto role in God's plan. And even after patristic and monastic thinkers had disassociated the devil and the earthly rulers—indeed, even after the Roman Empire adopted Christianity—relatively few theologians, at least in the Latin West, were willing to take the next step and identify earthly rulers as God's *direct* instruments in the same sense that the church was. Yet it seemed undeniable that they had some kind of role, not only in the state of emergency that is human existence in a state of original sin but in the apocalyptic sequence as well.

In thinking through the ambiguous place of the de-demonized ruler, theologians turned to an enigmatic passage from the Second Letter to the Thessalonians. This epistle claims to be the work of Paul, but modern scholars believe it to be the product of a later writer posing as the apostle in order to tone down his apocalyptic expectations. The passage reads as follows:

> Let no one deceive you in any way; for that day [of Judgment] will not come unless the rebellion comes first and the lawless one is revealed, the one destined for destruction. He opposes and exalts himself above every so-called god or object of worship, so that he takes his seat in the temple of God, declaring himself to be God. Do you not remember that I told you these things when I was still with you? And you know what is now restraining [*katechon*] him, so that he may be revealed when his time comes. For the mystery of lawlessness is already at work, but only until the one who now restrains [*katechōn*] it is removed. And then the lawless one will be revealed, whom the Lord Jesus will destroy with the breath of his mouth, annihilating him by the manifestation of his coming. (2:3–8)

We will likely never know for sure what the author intended to designate with the words *katechōn* or *katechon* (a personal and impersonal form, respectively, of the same underlying term). According to Augustine, however, "no one doubts that [the term "the lawless one"] means Antichrist" (XX.19)—the devil's final and most powerful representative on earth.

Centuries after the Book of Revelation was written, Augustine is still aware of traditions identifying the Antichrist with "Nero, whose deeds already seemed to be the deeds of the Antichrist" and whom some expected to rise from the dead to serve in that capacity. In this view, Paul would be referring "to the Roman empire" in this passage, though "he was unwilling to use language more explicit" in light of the dangers facing any public critic of the empire. Augustine finds this reading unconvincing and "audacious" but thinks there is a grain of truth to it, insofar as "it is not absurd to believe that these words of the apostle [regarding the restrainer] refer to the Roman empire" (XX.19). Meanwhile, in line with the patristic paradigm, he aligns the Antichrist with religious rather than political opponents to Christianity. Here Augustine is thinking primarily of heretics and other false teachings, while the later medieval tradition will identify the Antichrist as a Jew.

Thus, the apocalyptic role of the earthly ruler is not so much eliminated as displaced. Rome is no longer the Antichrist but the *katechon*, the restrainer. Earthly powers do not merely restrain individuals' evil behavior but somehow serve to restrain or delay the appearance of the ultimate evil in the form of the Antichrist. And by delaying the Antichrist, the ruler is also delaying an event that was to the medieval mind perhaps even more frightening: the Last Judgment itself. What originated as a desperate demand for divine justice was now, in a world where the majority of human beings were destined for eternal damnation, a terrifying prospect. The notion that Christians were perpetual sojourners was much more tolerable, and hence the post-Constantinian political theology centered on the *katechon* could be viewed as an attempt to return to something like the stability of the prophetic paradigm—or at least as close as could be achieved within Christianity's irreducibly apocalyptic framework.

In light of the concept of the *katechon*, as Carl Schmitt notes, "The history of the Middle ages is thus the history of a struggle *for*, not against Rome"[4]—a profound reversal in terms of our previous discussion. Indeed, Schmitt claims that the *katechon* is the only possible basis for a Christian politics:

> I do not believe that any historical concept other than *katechon* would have been possible for the original Christian faith. The belief that a restrainer holds back the end of the world provides the only bridge between the notion of an eschatological paralysis of all human events and a tremendous historical monolith like that of the Christian empire of the Germanic kings. [This grew out of] the conviction that only the Roman Empire and its Christian perpetuation could explain the endurance of the eon and could preserve it against the overwhelming power of evil.[5]

Jacob Taubes once claimed that the *katechon* is not merely of historical interest to Schmitt but serves as a model for his own political outlook:

> Schmitt had one interest: that the Party, that chaos did not win out, that the state stood firm. At whatever cost. . . . That is what he later called the

katechon: the restrainer who holds back the chaos bubbling up from the depths. . . . [Schmitt] sees the apocalypse, in whatever shape or form, as the adversary and does everything to subjugate and suppress it, because, from there, forces may be released that we are incapable of mastering.[6]

The same may be said of Schmitt's great model, Thomas Hobbes, for whom submission to the sovereign serves to stave off interpersonal violence as well as the catastrophe of civil war—which could be viewed as secular equivalents to human sinfulness and the apocalypse, respectively. Like the *katechon*, the Hobbesian sovereign is not positively good but is a necessary evil to head off an even worse fate.

On this basis, one could even say that the *katechon* is the condition of possibility not only for medieval Christian politics but for the secular state, which is meant to persist indefinitely and operates according to its own amoral or extramoral logic. The apocalyptic horizon may be foreclosed in secular modernity, but the *katechon* remains in place—and in an explicit acknowledgment of its apocalyptic roots, the modern state appears in Hobbes precisely as the Leviathan, the beast with whom God wrestles in Job and whom the Christian tradition identified as a symbol of the devil. Yet again, the problem of evil is being tied to the problem of politics, albeit in a strange and ambiguous way.

"THE UNBEARABLE, DEVILISH BURDEN OF THE JEWS"

As we saw in the pervious chapter, the specifically medieval articulation of the problem of evil, centered on the relation between free will and predestination, also carried a political valence. One important political reference goes all the way back to the foundational event of the Hebrew biblical tradition, the Exodus from Egypt. While Moses is attempting to persuade Pharaoh to let the Israelites go, under threat of plagues from God, the biblical author makes frequent mention of the hardness of Pharaoh's heart, which prevents him from acceding to Moses's demand even against his own initial inclination. At times Pharaoh seems to harden his own heart (e.g., Exodus 8:15); at times it is simply stated in the passive voice that his heart "was hardened" (e.g., 8:19); but on a few occasions (e.g., 11:10), the text un-ambiguously states that "the Lord hardened Pharaoh's heart."

Thus, we clearly have a case of divine tampering with an individual's will, which prompts him to commit acts that the biblical author just as clearly expects us to view as morally reprehensible. It is understandable, then, that the hardening of Pharaoh's heart would emerge as an important site—arguably even more important than the fall of the devil—for reflec-tion on the mystery of predestination, from Augustine to John Calvin and beyond. And the most important New Testament passage guiding these re-flections was Romans 9–11, where Paul grappled intensely with the failure of his fellow Jews to embrace Jesus as the messiah. As I discussed in Chapter 2, Paul argues in that passage that the Jews' momentary stubbornness is part of God's plan to include the Gentiles in his promises. Drawing on the history of God's dealings with Israel in the past, he expects that once the Jews see the benefits the Gentiles are enjoying, their jealousy will drive them to turn to Jesus—"and so all Israel will be saved" (11:26). Only then would God's eschatological fulfillment arrive.

Medieval theologians preserved Paul's view that the conversion of at least some critical mass of Jews was necessary to the final apocalyptic se-quence. Yet they were much more focused on Paul's characterization of the situation in the meantime: "they are enemies . . . for your sake" (11:28).[7] This led both theologians and common folklore to incorporate the Jews into the apocalyptic sequence in a very different way, by claiming that the Antichrist—the devil's final and most powerful representative on earth—would be a Jew. And this would be only the crowning achievement in what medieval theology viewed as a comprehensive and unshakable alliance be-tween the devil and the Jews. Thus, in a profound historical irony, a symbol originally developed by Jewish thinkers to characterize their oppressors came to be identified with the Jews themselves—and in keeping with its political roots, comes to perpetuate a view of the Jews *as* oppressors.

The many varied (and sometimes contradictory) forms that supposed oppression took have been documented in Joshua Trachtenberg's classic study *The Devil and the Jews*.[8] Most of the criminal accusations against the

Jews were completely fabricated, as in the "blood libel" myth, according to which Jews kidnapped Christian babies to drink their blood, or the claim that they habitually stole communion wafers in order to desecrate them. Others took an innocent truth—such as the Jewish community's greater access to medical knowledge, due to connections with the more advanced Islamic world—and twisted it so that Jewish court physicians were supposedly aiming to poison their hated Christian employers. The erroneous image of the Jews extended even to claims that the most cursory empirical investigation would show to be utterly ludicrous, such as the idea that Jews have horns or that Jewish men also menstruate.

Trachtenberg's rhetorical strategy centers on portraying medieval ideas about the Jews as completely ridiculous, in order to undermine the modern anti-Semitism that is his ultimate target. As in modern anti-Semitism, he is arguing, medieval anti-Judaism was not "about" real Jews at all. Instead, it reflected the deep tensions and anxieties of medieval Christian society, tensions that became increasingly explosive toward the end of the period.[9] And from our perspective, the centrality of the devil to the medieval conception of the Jew indicates that those anxieties center around fundamental questions of the political theological legitimacy of the medieval Christian order.

That order was ultimately founded on the Hebrew Scriptures, which were the indispensable basis for even making sense of the claim that Jesus was the messiah. By the medieval period, there was a standard repertoire of "prophecies" from those Scriptures, whose reference to Christ was taken to be immediately self-evident by essentially all Christian theologians. Yet the very group who were most devoted to those Scriptures—and to whom it should therefore be inescapably *obvious* that Jesus was their promised redeemer—remained stubbornly opposed to this clear truth. The Jews are therefore paradoxically necessary to Christianity at the same time that they (from the Christian perspective) inexplicably insist on excluding themselves from it. This same insider-outsider dynamic recurs in the contradictory eschatological role of the Jews, whose conversion is necessary to bring on the Last Judgment but who nonetheless also produce God's ultimate human enemy.

Like their "father" the devil, the Jews are necessary in their very exclusion. And like the demons they were supposed to be allied with, the Jews underwent a supplemental racialization over and above the racialization implied by original sin. One scriptural justification for this process is a passage in the Gospel of Matthew, which reports that "the people as a whole" responded to Pilate's incredulity that they wanted to crucify their king by proclaiming: "His blood be on us and on our children!" (27:25). All subsequent Jews were supposed to have inherited this curse for their complicity with Christ's death, just as all human beings inherit the curse God laid upon Adam and Eve. Some theologians took a more radical step, claiming that the very imposition of the divine covenant, far from being a sign of God's favor, was actually a curse meant to entrap the Jews in disobedience. In either case, we are dealing with a redoubling of the inherited moral debility that is at stake in original sin—a double racialization marking Jews as degenerate and accursed, born enemies of Christianity.

Late in the Middle Ages, the entire complex path from Paul's optimistic stance toward his fellow Jews to the paranoid outlook of medieval Christianity was strangely recapitulated and exaggerated in the person of Martin Luther. By most accounts, Luther initially believed that the Jews had failed to accept Christ because of the corruptions and distortions of the gospel introduced by the Catholic Church. Once they learned of his new, purified version of the Christian message, he felt confident that their long-delayed conversion would be at hand. When this failed to occur, Luther rapidly turned on them, ultimately writing one of the most sadly influential anti-Jewish tracts in history: *On the Jews and Their Lies.*[10]

In this lengthy polemic, Luther exerts the full force of his theological creativity to support his vindictive thesis that the Jews must no longer by tolerated and should be driven out of Christian society completely. The result is a text that both compiles and expands upon the core tropes of medieval anti-Judaism. Ultimately addressed to the political authorities of his day, the work's most famous sections include a series of harsh policy recommendations, beginning with an exhortation to "set fire to their synagogues or schools and to bury and cover with dirt whatever will not burn, so that no man will ever again see a stone or cinder of them" (Book 11). Other measures include destruction of their homes and literature, prohibition of rabbinical teaching, denial of safe passage on highways, prohibition of usury, confiscation of wealth (ostensibly for safekeeping, until they convert to Christianity), and forced labor. As in the case of the demons, the Jews in Luther's view are to suffer racialization, exclusion (as in Agamben's figure of the *homo sacer*), and slavery.

All of this is the least they deserve, in Luther's view, for the malicious lies they spread about Christ. He claims that his contemporaries would be the worst traitors to Jesus's cause if they continued to tolerate the Jews: "What a great saint the traitor Judas would be in comparison with us!" And he pauses to implore his royal addressee:

> If my counsel does not please you, find better advice, so that you and we all can be rid of the unbearable, devilish burden of the Jews. Lest we become guilty sharers before God in the lies, the blasphemy, the defamation, and the curses which the mad Jews indulge in so freely and wantonly against the person of our Lord Jesus Christ, his dear mother, all Christians, all authority, and ourselves. (Book 11)

Yet he clearly expects his pleas to fall on deaf ears, due to the perceived influence of Jewish advisers and, more important, Jewish money on political leaders. He even fears that they may be tempted to misapply ostensibly Christian principles of mercy and forgiveness in this case:

> For I observe and have often experienced how indulgent the perverted world is when it should be strict, and, conversely, how harsh it is when it should be merciful. . . . That is the way *the prince of this world* reigns. I suppose that the princes will now wish to show mercy to the Jews, the bloodthirsty foes of our Christian and human name, in order to earn heaven thereby. But that the Jews enmesh us, harass us, torment and distress us poor Christians in every way with the above mentioned devilish and detestable deeds, this they want us to tolerate, and this is a good Christian deed, especially if there is any money involved (which they have filched and stolen from us). (Book 11, emphasis added)

Having clearly identified the devil with the Jews, here Luther seems to fear a possible identification between the Jews and political authorities, and this leads him to edge up to the possibility of completing the circle by identifying earthly princes with "the prince of this world"—the devil.

The foundations for this demonic triad had been laid earlier, when Luther established the Jew-ruler alliance from the Jewish side. The Gospel of John, the most authoritative source for the notion that the Jews are "children of the devil," has the chief priests respond to Pilate's question "Shall I crucify your king?" by claiming, "We have no king but Caesar" (19:15). Gustav Aulén has pointed out that Luther is one of the strongest advocates of the ransom theory of redemption, which he explicitly mentions when he declares Jesus to be the true messiah who is "able to play a trick on the devil and death" (Book 12),[11] and Luther's reading of this verse is deeply consistent with that theory. In essence, he interprets it as a kind of restaging of the social contract in the Garden of Eden, with the Jews (in the person of their legitimate leaders) choosing to submit themselves to the emperor rather than to their covenant with God. As Luther explains, "God had not commanded of them such submission to the emperor; they gave it voluntarily" (Book 11), and when they subsequently rebelled against the emperor, he sent them into diaspora. And in line with the social contract logic, all subsequent Jews of the diaspora are obligated not to the law of Moses—who in Luther's view would "be the first to set fire to the synagogues and houses of the Jews" (Book 11)—but to the law of the emperor.

In this immediate context, Luther again narrowly avoids explicitly identifying the emperor with the devil. Indeed, one of his major complaints about Jewish doctrine is the Jews' supposed embrace of a political messiah, which he deploys in order to associate them with Christianity's great external religious rival, Islam:

> This coincides entirely with the thoughts and teachings of Mohammed. He kills us Christians as the Jews would like to do, occupies the land, and takes over our property, our joys and pleasures. If he were a Jew and not an Ishmaelite [Arabs were supposed to have descended from Isaac's half-

brother Ishmael], the Jews would have accepted him as the Messiah long ago. (Book 12)

In contrast, the completely apolitical message of Jesus won out against even the mightiest of empires:

> The Roman Empire and the whole world abounded with idols to which the Gentiles adhered; the devil was mighty and defended himself vigorously. All swords were against it, and yet the tongue alone purged the entire world of all these idols without a sword. (Book 13)

Here the empire is identified with the devil only insofar as the Romans worshipped idols—in short, Luther is practicing the classic patristic displacement of the political onto the religious. Everywhere, the triad devil-Jews-rulers threatens to form, but only two legs ever come together at once. It is as though Luther is implicitly exhorting the rulers to play their proper role as *katechon* or risk becoming an outright ally to the devil.

In the area of more specifically religious concerns, Luther takes up and intensifies traditional Christian claims to have superseded Judaism. But he takes things a step further by arguing, in a gratuitous gesture of cruelty, that the Jews of his time *do not even practice Judaism* anymore. Already we have seen that toward the end of the text, he argues that they rejected the law of Moses in favor of the law of the empire. That is merely the climax of a much more fine-grained argument, however, which aims to systematically deprive the Jews of any legitimate claim to their own Scriptures or tradition. Most strikingly, the entirety of Book 2 is devoted to demonstrating that, far from being their most distinctive and nonnegotiable religious practice, circumcision is not actually practiced by the Jews *at all*, because at some point they introduced a "devilish supplement" to the circumcision rite that renders it invalid (Book 2). This exaggerates the Christian claim to have superseded the Jewish covenant to the point of making a Christian theologian the judge of proper Jewish religious practice.

More important, for Luther they comprehensively fail to understand the true import of their own Scriptures. The Jews, "a prophet-murdering people" (Book 3), routinely deface the words of the prophets, and even when they leave them in their authentic form, they stubbornly refuse to acknowledge the unmistakable evidence that Jesus is the messiah. For this reason, their possession of the Scriptures only heaps judgment upon their heads:

> If the boast that God spoke with them and that they possess his word or commandment were sufficient so that God would on this basis regard them as his people, then the devils in hell would be much worthier of being God's people than the Jews, yes, than any people. For the devils have God's word and know far better than the Jews that there is a God who created them, whom they are obliged to love with all their heart, to honor, fear, and serve. . . . But what good does it do them to know and to possess God's commandment? (Book 3)

This analogy with the demons is not fortuitous, because the Jews share the demonic condition of being condemned to error and sin. Yet the precise modality of their incapacity to turn toward the good is slightly different from the demons' moral lock-in. Where the demons are forced to serve God's purposes against their will, the Jews delude themselves that they are serving God and so refuse correction:

> God's wrath has consigned them to the presumption that their boasting, their conceit, their slander of God, their cursing of all people are a true and a great service rendered to God—all of which is very fitting and becoming to such noble blood of the fathers and circumcised saints. This they believe despite the fact that they know they are steeped in manifest vices mentally, just as the devils themselves do. (Book 3)

Their very conviction that they are God's chosen people therefore paradoxically renders them the most accursed allies of the devil. Far better, in Luther's view, would have been a more Lutheran response to their calling, emphasizing their unworthiness and reliance on God's grace:

> This boasting must not stem from the idea that Abraham's and his descendants' lineage is worthy of such honor; for that would nullify everything. It

must be based rather on the fact that God chose Abraham's flesh and blood for this purpose out of sheer grace and mercy, although it surely deserved a far different lot. We Gentiles, too, have been honored very highly by being made partakers of the Messiah and the kingdom and by enjoying the blessing promised to Abraham's seed. But if we should boast as though we were deserving of this, and not acknowledge that we owe it to sheer, pure mercy, giving God alone the glory, all would also be spoiled and lost. (Book 13)

Indeed, Luther claims that all the afflictions of the church have stemmed from their inclination to follow the Jewish path of prideful self-righteousness: "Therefore God also delivered us into all sorts of terrible blindness and innumerable false doctrines, and, furthermore, he permitted Muhammad and the pope together with all devils to come upon us" (Book 2). And in this way, the Jews serve as a kind of archetype and rallying point for all God's enemies: external religious foes (Islam), internal heretics (the papacy, in Luther's view), and the demons themselves.

From the other direction, however, heretics sometimes seem to provide the model for the Jews. There is a pervasive notion that, deep down, the Jews really *do* understand that Christianity is true—or even if they don't, that they *should*, that they are obligated to. Even their ignorance, therefore, must be counted as a willful, and therefore culpable, ignorance: "These incorrigible rascals know very well that the New Testament deals with our Lord Jesus Christ, God's Son, while they claim to be unacquainted with its contents. My friend, it is not a question of what you know or what you wish to know, but of what you ought to know, what you are obliged to know." Even if they do not know the details of the New Testament literature, surely they cannot be ignorant of Christianity in general: "The Jews' ignorance is not to be excused, since God has had this proclaimed for almost fifteen hundred years. They are obliged to know it, and God demands this knowledge of them." And just as Luther appears to hold them accountable for his specifically Protestant outlook on unmerited grace, so also does he seem to expect them to be well-acquainted with the finer points of trinitarian doctrine: "Neither Jew nor devil will in any way be able to prove that our belief that the one eternal Godhead is composed of three persons implies that we believe in more than one God" (Book 12).

In short, Jews are to be judged as if they were already Christians, even as they are to be utterly reviled and expelled from the Christian world. Luther says as much in a very strange passage where—in a perhaps unintentional echo of the apocalyptic identification of the devil with the earthly ruler who is the addressee of the rest of the text—he directly addresses Satan himself:

> No, you vile father of such blasphemous Jews, you hellish devil, these are the facts: God has preached long enough to your children, the Jews, publicly and with miraculous signs throughout the world. He has done so for almost fifteen hundred years now, and still preaches. They were and still are obliged to obey him; but they were hardened and ever resisted, blasphemed, and cursed. Therefore we Christians, in turn are obliged not to tolerate their wanton and conscious blasphemy. (Book 12)

Paradoxically, however, the very penalties that Luther recommends to drive the Jews out once and for all can even appear as an effort to convert them:

> I wish and I ask that our rulers who have Jewish subjects exercise a sharp mercy toward these wretched people, as suggested above, to see whether this might not help (though it is doubtful). They must act like a good physician who, when gangrene has set proceeds without mercy to cut, saw, and burn flesh, veins, bone, and marrow. Such a procedure must also be followed in this instance. (Book 12)

In short, the only language they understand is force—and yet there is still a sliver of hope that they might convert. This same sliver of hope comes out in Luther's closing paragraph, which leaps vertiginously from utter demonization to a prayer for the Jews' conversion:

> My essay, I hope, will furnish a Christian (who in any case has no desire to become a Jew) with enough material not only to defend himself against the blind, venomous Jews, but also to become the foe of the Jews' malice, lying, and cursing, and to understand not only that their belief is false but that

they are surely possessed by all devils. May Christ, our dear Lord, convert
them mercifully and preserve us steadfastly and immovably in the knowledge of him, which is eternal life. Amen. (Book 13)

Even the most hateful and perversely inventive of anti-Jewish literature
cannot completely give up on the Jews. Like their father the devil, they
are consummate insider-outsiders of the medieval worldview Luther inherits—a necessary evil at the very foundation of Christianity.

WORSE THAN THE DEVIL

Around the same period that suspicion of the Jews was reaching a fever
pitch—culminating in Ferdinand and Isabella's expulsion of all Jews from
Spain in 1492—many Europeans also believed themselves to be suffering from an unprecedented plague of witchcraft. This perception was
both reflected and bolstered by one of the first great bestsellers in the age
of the printing press: the *Malleus Maleficarum* (Hammer of Witches), a
witch-hunting manual published in 1486 by Heinrich Kramer and James
Sprenger.[12] Kramer, who is widely believed to be the primary if not sole author of the text, was an experienced Inquisitor who had sentenced witches
to torture and death, and even though the official church hierarchy eventually tried to distance itself from the text and the persecutions it inspired,
the *Malleus* initially prompted a letter of commendation from Pope Innocent VIII. Hence the text enjoyed some measure of official legitimacy
in addition to its widespread popularity. But it is clear that Kramer's ambi-
tions extended even further: he wants to make a permanent contribution
to Christian doctrine. This much is at least implied in the bold opening
gambit of the first major division of the *Malleus*, which is to argue force-
fully that "the belief that there are such beings as witches is so essential a
part of the Catholic faith that obstinately to maintain the opposite opinion
manifestly savors of heresy" (p. 1).

These lofty theological pretensions are jarringly incongruous with
much of the rest of the book, which is virulently misogynistic and often
frankly ridiculous. The two qualities are united, for instance, in the lengthy

discussion of precisely how demons are able to impregnate witches. While Kramer concedes that the demons, as angelic beings, do not have bodies or the ability to reproduce, they can nonetheless "assume a body not in order that they may bestow life upon it, but that they may by the means of this body preserve human semen, and pass the semen on to another body" (p. 22). In addition to possessing artificial insemination technology, demons are also expert breeders, able to use their long experience with astrology to single out humans who are "more disposed to work witchcraft than others" and hence to "molest these chiefly for the purposes of such works" (p. 23). Here again, the shadow of racialization appears in the form of a demonic breeding program for their human servants.

In Kramer's view, however, it does not require demonic expertise to discern the group most disposed to witchcraft: women. This is clear from the very grammar of the title. Properly speaking, it should be *Malleus Maleficorum*, insofar as Kramer admits that there are male witches and standard Latin usage dictates that a mixed-gender group should be designated with a masculine noun. The feminine *Maleficarum* unambiguously enshrines women as the normative witches, legitimating a centuries-long campaign of persecution that Andrea Dworkin memorably characterized as "gynecide."[13] This association of witchcraft and women is apparently so taken for granted that the question of "why a greater number of witches is found in the fragile feminine sex than among men" (p. 41) does not arise until nearly halfway through the theological opening third of the *Malleus*. Kramer notes that "it is indeed a fact that it were idle to contradict, since it is accredited by actual experience, apart from the verbal testimony of credible witnesses" (pp. 41–42).

When he does venture an explanation for women's supposed inclination toward witchcraft, he chooses the curious path of explicating a saying of "learned men" to the effect that "there are three things in nature, the Tongue, an Ecclesiastic, and a Woman, which know no moderation in goodness or vice; and when they exceed the bounds of their condition, they reach the greatest heights and the lowers depths of goodness and vice" (p. 42). All three phenomena, in their very different ways, seem to occupy a particularly fraught and sensitive place within the social order, which enable them to have effects disproportionate to their apparent power. Thus, the tongue is a small organ that can cause great edification or great mischief, and church leaders are in a position to do great good but could also easily mislead many people.

The cause of the woman's disproportionate power is less immediately clear, either in Kramer's catalogue of misogynistic sayings from the Bible and classical literature or in his listing of exemplary holy women. The first hint comes in an apparent non sequitur, where he points out women who have converted entire nations to Christianity and then says, "Wherefore in many vituperations that we read against women, the word woman is used to mean the lust of the flesh. As it is said: I have found a woman more bitter than death, and a good woman subject to carnal lust" (p. 43).

The problem, then, stems from the supposed special relationship between women and the body, a conclusion that is borne out by many of the subsequent reasons Kramer provides for their susceptibility to witchcraft. First of all, "they are more credulous, and since the chief aim of the devil is to corrupt faith, therefore he rather attacks them" (p. 43). They are also "more impressionable, and more ready to receive the influence of a disembodied spirit"—a quality that can make them exemplary vehicles of divine power but also ready prey to demons (p. 44). Both of these qualities point to a certain receptivity and passivity, to ideas and to other forms of spiritual influence, respectively. Yet this lack of self-possession can also express itself in aggression, as when Kramer claims that women "have slippery tongues, and are unable to conceal from their fellow-women those things which by evil arts they know." And the reason such arts are tempting is that women "are weak" and "find an easy and secret manner of vindicating themselves by witchcraft" (p. 44).

After exhorting preachers not to discourage women, particularly in light of the sterling example of the Virgin Mary, Kramer proceeds to reiterate similar accusations, this time emphasizing that the weaknesses of women are a direct product of their nature. First, he notes that "as regards intellect, or the understanding of spiritual things, they seem to be of a different nature from men," because "she is more carnal than a man, as is clear from her many carnal abominations." Kramer is even so bold as to critique

God's handiwork in the case of women: "it should be noted that there was a defect in the formation of the first woman, since she was formed from a bent rib, that is, a rib of the breast, which is bent as it were in a contrary direction to a man." Furthermore, her very name, according to a deeply questionable etymology of the Latin *femina*, testifies to her faithlessness, "for *Femina* comes from *Fe* and *Minus*, since she is ever weaker to hold and preserve the faith" (p. 44).

So far, it might seem difficult to hold women responsible for these defects of their nature. Indeed, based on the consensus of Augustine, Anselm, and Aquinas that we saw in the previous chapter, the very idea of a morally flawed nature is incoherent—a creature cannot be morally responsible for being the way God created her. So it is perhaps not accidental that at this point Kramer introduces "her other mental quality, that is, her natural will" (p. 44). As with everything feminine, her will is exceptionally changeable, prone to wild shifts: "when she hates someone whom she formerly loved, then she seethes with anger and impatience in her whole soul" (p. 44). Yet it is still the site of her moral accountability, and so the discussion shifts from natural weakness to morally charged categories like lust, hatred, envy, and betrayal. And although Kramer claims, somewhat puzzlingly, that "nearly all the kingdoms of the world have been overthrown by women" (p. 46), the majority of women's depredations center on sexuality and reproduction. Indeed, he concludes one major section of the discussion by claiming that "all witchcraft comes from carnal lust, which is in women insatiable"—just before thanking God that he has "so far preserved the male sex from so great a crime" (p. 47).

Women's sexual craving is in fact so exaggerated that "for the sake of fulfilling their lusts they consort even with the devils" (p. 47). Kramer concedes that it is difficult to understand exactly how such a thing occurs (p. 41), but as the discussion of demonic artificial insemination makes clear, this is intended literally. Earlier he had enumerated the process by which one became a witch:

> First, most profanely to renounce the Catholic Faith, or at any rate to deny
> certain dogmas of the faith; secondly, to devote themselves body and soul

to all evil; thirdly, to offer up unbaptized children to Satan; fourthly, to indulge in every kind of carnal lust with Incubi and Succubi [certain types of demons] and all manner of filthy delights. (pp. 20–21)

Of all these outrages—one of which, in a striking example of how the characteristics of Satan's allies seem to migrate from one group to another, resembles the Jewish blood libel accusation—the sexual element seems to be most central. Sexuality comes in for the most detailed discussion and routinely plays a strategic role in the argument, as when it concludes the examination of women's weakness that we have been following. The crimes of witches also tend to center on sexual and reproductive matters, as in this list of "seven methods by which they infect with witchcraft the venereal act and the conception of the womb":

first, by inclining the minds of men to inordinate passion; second, by obstructing their generative force; third, by removing the members accommodated to that act; fourth, by changing men into beasts by their magic art; fifth, by destroying the generative force in women; sixth, by procuring abortion; seventh, by offering children to devils. (p. 47)

From this perspective, it seems that the real problem with offering up infants to Satan is not the act of murder but the betrayal of the motherly role. Even when they commit the ultimate sin of murder, then, it is somehow linked with sex and reproduction.

This list appears in the midst of a discussion centered on the three vices characteristic of women: "infidelity, ambition, and lust" (p. 47). What implicitly unites them all is that women refuse to stay in their appropriate place. They defy the marriage contract tying them to a particular man, they aspire to roles above their subordinate station, and they actively seek out sexual fulfillment rather than accept their naturally passive role in the sexual act. In this way, their sin is formally similar to that of the fallen angels, who refused to be subdued and assume their assigned place in the ontological hierarchy. In the divine order, it is not enough simply to *be* in the place God has set out for you—you must *will* it. Thus free will becomes an apparatus not only for generating blameworthiness but for moralizing hierarchy and subordination.

At the same time, this parallel between the devil and witches is to a certain extent misleading, because in one of the most surprising arguments in the history of Christian theology, Kramer claims that the sins of witches are actually *worse* than the devil's. His first argument in favor this bold claim is that "the sins of those who fall from a state of grace, as do the witches by denying the faith which they received in baptism, exceed the sins of the Angels" (p. 82). Kramer even expresses some sympathy with what we have characterized as the devil's moral lock-in: "since Satan is incapable of repentance, therefore he is incapable of pardon; and this is due to his very nature, which, being spiritual, could only be changed once, when he changed it forever; but this is not so with men, in whom the flesh is always warring against the spirit" (pp. 82–83). There are also further mitigating circumstances. He cites Anselm to establish that the devil fell before he could have known about the punishment for sin, in stark contrast to witches who "make light of" God's well-known punishments "and hasten to commit, not the least deadly of sins, as do other sinners who sin through infirmity or wickedness yet not from habitual malice, but rather the most horrible crimes from the deep malice of their hearts" (p. 83). Whereas the devil could fall only once, the witches are willfully falling a second time after receiving the grace of baptism. And while the devil had no access to the compassion and forgiveness of God so that "he keeps his heart hardened against a punisher," "we sin against a merciful persuader" (p. 83).

Compared to the sins of the witches, then, the devil's offense seems almost understandable. The same goes for Adam's sin, for which even more mitigating circumstances are adduced (pp. 83–84). Thus, on top of the inexplicable fall of the devil, which introduced evil into the world, and the fall of Adam, which condemned every subsequent human being to be born in sin, there has arisen a new and more severe form of rebellion against God. Even worse, this evil has steadily grown throughout human history so that "the evils which are perpetrated by modern witches exceed all other sin which God has ever permitted to be done" (p. 74). Alarmingly enough, the witches' wicked deeds have in Kramer's view reached such a pitch that "they seem now to be depopulating the whole of Christianity" (p. 68).

In accounting for these disturbing "facts," the theological treatise that makes up the first major division of the *Malleus Maleficarum* inevitably becomes a meditation on the problem of evil—as is already implied in the title of the section: "The first part treating of the three necessary concomitants of witchcraft, which are the devil, a witch, and the permission of almighty God" (p. 1). The question is unavoidable: Why would God permit such extravagant and obscene evils to be perpetrated in his good creation? When Kramer finally confronts this question directly, his answer is essentially that of Augustine: "God permits evil to be done, though he does not wish it; and this is for the perfecting of the universe" (p. 67). This observation opens out into a general discussion of divine providence:

> Just as all things come from God, so also are all things ordained by him, and are consequently subject to his providence. For the providence of God is to be understood as nothing else than the reason, that is, the cause of the ordering of things to a purpose. Therefore, insofar as all things are part of one purpose, so also are they subject to the providence of God. (p. 69)

God's providence operates at two levels, that of the particular and that of the universal. If he were limited to only the particular level, he

> must of necessity keep away all the harm he can, since he is not able to extract good out of evil. But God is the universal controller of the whole world, and can extract much good from particular evils; as through the persecution of the tyrants came the patience of the martyrs, and through the works of witches comes the purgation or proving of the faith of the just.... Therefore it is not God's purpose to prevent all evil, lest the universe should lack the cause of much good. (p. 69)

As in Luther's discussion of the Jews, the special apocalyptic role of earthly rulers still exercises its influence, but the clear implication is that the "tyrants" whom Christians face today are the witches. In both cases, the outcome of an ostensibly depoliticized apocalyptic is a reactionary and

paranoid politics that views marginal populations as oppressors, legitimating and even necessitating campaigns of persecution *by* Christians—all to
combat their victims' supposed persecution *of* Christians.

THE NECESSARY EVIL

As I have pointed out, one of the most striking features the *Malleus Maleficarum* is its obvious bid for theological respectability. This is clear from the
very first page, where Kramer begins his argument in the style of a traditional
scholastic *disputatio*, which during the medieval period gradually emerged
as a systematic method for weighing arguments and counterarguments and
for resolving apparent conflicts between perceived authorities. The format is
an awkward fit for the material at hand, however, and it is clear that Kramer
is unable to sustain it much beyond the first "question" (on whether it is
heretical to deny the existence of witches).

Yet when it comes to the key concepts of scholastic theology, his presentation is mostly sound. This holds even for an area that is particularly
fraught with complex nuances and fine distinctions: the doctrine of providence. That doctrine is the subject of one of Giorgio Agamben's most
ambitious works, *The Kingdom and the Glory*. It centers on the fate of the
Greek word *oikonomia* (economy), which originally referred to the management of the household and subsequently came to be associated with
the management of a culturally diverse empire and (primarily by means of
its Latin translation *dispositio*) with God's providential management of his
creation. It is the latter that proves most crucial for Agamben's argument, as
he claims that theological reflection on divine providence served as a kind
of laboratory for developing concepts that would later be deployed within
the field of modern economics. Like the present study, then, *The Kingdom
and the Glory* is a genealogical investigation that aims to expose the unexpected theological roots of modern political concepts.

Returning to Kramer, readers of Agamben would anticipate something like the complex providential interplay between the universal and
particular that we briefly discussed in the previous section. They may be sur-
prised, however, to learn of the central role of the problem of evil in those

dynamics—and in this case, the *Malleus Maleficarum* is a better guide to the doctrine of providence than *The Kingdom and the Glory*, because Agamben systematically ignores or downplays questions related to the morality or legitimacy of God's providential acts. This is strange, since only because certain particular providential outcomes appear to be evil or unjustified does a contradiction between the particular and the universal, for instance, arise in the first place. If the "collateral effects" of God's actions were all beneficial, there would be no need to justify them by positing a transcendent and inscrutable divine plan in which everything works together for our good—it would be *immediately obvious* that everything was working together for our good.

What is missing in Agamben's account is the awareness that the experience of evil and suffering is the ultimate root of the doctrine of providence, and it is what gives this baroque theological apparatus its existential pull. More than that, however, evil and suffering are increasingly the motor of the providential apparatus itself. In the *Malleus Maleficarum*, it can seem that, beyond merely being *able* to create good out of evil, God actively *prefers* to do his good by way of evil. And while the *Malleus* is admittedly an extreme case in some ways, in other ways it is a natural outgrowth of the medieval emphasis on the redemptive value of suffering, to the near exclusion of any other form of meritorious action. We can see this in Kramer's example of the persecution of tyrants leading to the faithfulness of martyrs—in other words, the suffering inflicted by unjust rulers was beneficial because it led people to heroically submit to suffering. Suffering provides the opportunity for more suffering.

The apparatus of free will of course has a key role here. By permitting rather than actively willing evil acts, God avoids responsibility for them, and by wisely integrating them into his providential plan, he enhances his glory. Agamben notes the crucial role of freedom in the providential model, which he characterizes as a democratic, nondespotic mode of governance.[14] This reinforces the connection he seeks to make between theological providence and modern theories of government. This connection is actually further reinforced if we give due attention to the moral element that Agamben neglects, because in both the economic realm proper and the realm of democratic governance, it is above all our *evil* choices that work together for the greater good. The invisible hand does not simply coordinate whatever choices we happen to make. Rather, it depends primarily on qualities that are morally questionable at best, above all greed. Similarly, in democratic republics built on the principle of the division of powers, the assumption is that everyone involved will be power hungry and self-seeking, and the governmental structure is designed to harness those vices toward the public good.

Any reader of the *Federalist Papers* will be familiar with such arguments. One of the most frequently quoted adages from that text is found in *Federalist No. 51*, which briefly elaborates the angelology of the American Founders: "If men were angels, no government would be necessary. If angels were to govern men, neither external nor internal controls on government would be necessary."[15] This quotation does not seem to account for the role of fallen angels, but it is clear enough that we are dealing with the same kind of corrupted human beings that we have encountered in the medieval earthly city. The medieval theological framework lives on, with one significant change: the reference to the heavenly city, which throughout the medieval period grew ever more vestigial in any case, has now been dispensed with completely. We are henceforth in the land of the necessary evil, with no further reference to the good.

The indirect logic of divine providence is not the only link between the *Malleus Maleficarum* and the "necessary evils" at the foundation of the modern world. As Silvia Federici argues in *Caliban and the Witch*,[16] the witch trials—far from being an unfortunate medieval holdover in early modernity—were a systematic campaign of terror aimed at reducing the European population into docile workers and harnessing their sexual energies solely toward reproductive ends. This mass demonization provided the template for subduing native populations in the New World and Africa. This unexpected connection between witch hunts and colonization is reinforced by Eduardo Viveiros de Castro's study of Jesuit missionaries' perception of Brazilian natives.[17] Echoing Kramer's description of women, they describe the natives as inconstant and impulsive—a constitutional moral failing that legitimizes violent repression of the native way of life.

Modernity also takes up Luther's anti-Judaism, which mutates into an explicitly racialized anti-Semitism. This of course culminates in the horrors of the Shoah, where Jews were reduced to bare life in a way that Agamben singles out as exemplary—and are simultaneously, as Weheliye points out, enslaved and racialized.[18] This extreme threefold degradation is shared by the African populations kidnapped and enslaved in the New World, leading Weheliye to suggest that racial slavery would serve as a better starting point than the Shoah for understanding "the manifold modes in which extreme brutality and directed killing frequently and peacefully coexist with other forms of coercion and noncoercion within the scope of the normal juridio-political order" in modernity.[19] And just as the plantation and concentration camp are closely related, so too have many black scholars—among them Willie Jennings, J. Kameron Carter, and Vincent Lloyd—pointed out the ways in which secular modernity has implicated blacks in a racializing logic that echoes the dynamics of medieval Christianity's twisted view of Judaism.[20] Just as the Jews serve as the excluded foundation for the medieval Christian order, so too do blacks serve as the excluded foundation of the order of whiteness—a role that, as in the case of the Jews, has been legitimated by a supposed biblical curse against all those of African descent.[21] Here, too, racialization implies an inherited moral failing on the model of original sin.

Secular modernity thus still has its own demons, and for those demonized populations, the modern earthly city is surely a living hell. In this diagnosis, Agamben agrees—though for characteristically abstract and disembodied reasons. In a chapter of *The Kingdom and the Glory* entitled "Angelology and Bureaucracy," Agamben describes the angelic hosts as a kind of divine middle management, performing essential administrative functions in the providential apparatus. Unlike modern forms of management and administration, however, the providential machine is oriented toward a goal, the Last Judgment. After that point, governance by means of necessary evil will be obsolete—with one important exception: hell. There, the demons will continue to execute God's providential plan by punishing the damned for all eternity.

Agamben takes advantage of this observation to make a rare joke: "from the perspective of Christian theology, the idea of eternal government (which is the paradigm of modern politics) is truly infernal."[22] In other words, the modern secular world, governed indefinitely by the providential apparatuses of economy and democracy, is a living hell. From the perspective of the unspeakable crimes of modernity, this quip may seem inappropriately glib— yet insofar as it posits that the "normal" run of things is *also* fundamentally hellish, it suggests that hell could be the staging ground for a radical critique of secular modernity as a whole. In order to assess this claim, however, we will need to spend much more time in hell than Agamben does.

CHAPTER 6

LIFE IN HELL

The devil's fall, as we have seen, took but an instant. And while his career on earth is to last millennia, that time is vanishingly brief compared to the eternity he will spend as chief guard and chief inmate in hell. At the same time, the biblical documentation on his career in hell—though not non-existent, as in the case of his fall—is scant, because, as with the devil himself, the notion of eternal damnation arose only with the emergence of the apocalyptic paradigm. Only when this world seems unredeemable does the afterlife become a site of systematic theological reflection, and only when God's chosen people face an implacably evil foe does the notion of infinite punishment begin to sound plausible.

The majority of the materials in the Hebrew Bible are compiled from sources that originated prior to the apocalyptic breakthrough. What speculations they contain about the afterlife center on a vague and shadowy realm known as "Sheol," which houses the good and the evil alike. Perhaps surprisingly from a contemporary Christian perspective, many references to the realm of Sheol center precisely on its theological *irrelevance*. For instance, in a passage from the Book of Isaiah in which King Hezekiah of Judah is begging God to spare him and his kingdom, he reminds God that "Sheol cannot thank you, death cannot praise you; those who go down to the Pit cannot hope for your faithfulness" (38:18). If God wants to derive glory from his servants, he must do so while they are alive—after death, it seems, they are beyond his grasp.

In contrast, the bulk of the New Testament literature clearly presupposes some notion of eternal damnation. This is clearest in the Book of Revelation, where we learn that the devil and his minions are to be "thrown alive into the lake of fire that burns with sculpture" (19:20) and where the joy of the blessed is counterposed with the sufferings of the damned: "But as for the cowardly, the faithless, the polluted, the murderers, the fornicators, the sorcerers, the idolaters, and all liars, their place will be in the lake that burns with fire and sulfur, which is the second death" (21:8). Several other passages speak of the existence of fire in hell, often connected with Jesus's characteristic description of the abode of the damned as a place "where there will be weeping and gnashing of teeth" (e.g., Matthew 13:42; Luke 13:28).

In short, the devil will be there, fire will be involved, and there will be suffering. More detailed information is difficult to come by. The majority of New Testament authors are more focused on the fate of the blessed than the damned, and much of that discussion takes the form of enigmatic allegories. This is above all the case for the parables of Jesus, which generally use metaphor and other forms of indirect communication to highlight the ways in which the Kingdom of Heaven subverts the customary expectations of this world.

There is, however, one apparent exception: Jesus's parable of the Rich Man and Lazarus. While its overall message—centered on the reversal of worldly status hierarchies and the continuity of Jesus's message with the Hebrew biblical tradition—could be found in any number of parables, its topographical description of heaven and hell is unique:

> There was a rich man who was dressed in purple and fine linen and who feasted sumptuously every day. And at his gate lay a poor man named Lazarus, covered with sores, who longed to satisfy his hunger with what fell from the rich man's table; even the dogs would come and lick his sores. The poor man died and was carried away by the angels to be with Abraham.

The rich man also died and was buried. In Hades, where he was in tor-ment,[1] he looked up and saw Abraham far away with Lazarus by his side. He called out, "Father Abraham, have mercy on me, and send Lazarus to dip the tip of his finger in water and cool my tongue; for I am in agony in these flames." But Abraham said, "Child, remember that during your lifetime you received your good things, and Lazarus in like manner evil things; but now he is comforted here, and you are in agony. Besides all this, between you and us a great chasm has been fixed, so that those who might want to pass from here to you cannot do so, and no one can cross from there to us." He said, "Then, father, I beg you to send him to my father's house—for I have five brothers—that he may warn them, so that they will not also come into this place of torment." Abraham replied, "They have Moses and the prophets; they should listen to them." He said, "No, father Abraham; but if someone goes to them from the dead, they will repent." He said to him, "If they do not listen to Moses and the prophets, neither will they be convinced even if someone rises from the dead." (Luke 16:19–31)

Whether originally intended to be taken literally or not, this vision of heaven and hell served as a central point of reference for theological speculation about our ultimate destiny. And the key point that it seems to establish is that the residents of heaven and hell can see each other and communicate in some way, even if they cannot affect each other otherwise.

Hence this passage serves as the biblical basis for Tertullian's claim that the blessed in heaven get to enjoy the spectacle of the torments of the damned. As disturbing as this vindictive attitude seems from a modern standpoint—and as unsupported as it is in the text, where Abraham and Lazarus take no pleasure in the rich man's suffering—it actually represented the hegemonic view in the Latin West. It is in fact so pervasive that it shows up quite unexpectedly even where it seems to be blissfully absent.

Such is the case in Augustine's *City of God*. Though he notes in the final book of his great work that the residents of the heavenly city will be intellectually aware of "the eternal sufferings of the lost" (XXII.30), there is no direct indication that they will enjoy the vision of their torments. Yet there is something curious about the penultimate book, devoted exclusively to the topic of hell, where Augustine focuses on establishing and justifying the eternal nature of hell's torments. Since the resurrection of the dead is to occur before the Last Judgment, it implies that the punishments in hell will be bodily. Noting that "it seems to be more incredible that bodies endure in everlasting torments than that they continue to exist without any pain in everlasting felicity"—which he also cites as his primary reason for discussing hell before heaven (XXI.1)—Augustine first turns to the problem of the sheer physical possibility of eternal suffering. This discussion quite unexpectedly opens out into a general consideration of the many marvels of God's creation. Though many of them have to do with fire or unexpected longevity, he also discusses less immediately relevant wonders such as magnets (XXI.4). Toward the middle of this section, he challenges his skeptical interlocutors:

> Why, then, cannot God effect both that the bodies of the dead shall rise, and that the bodies of the damned shall be tormented in everlasting fire— God, who made the world full of countless miracles in sky, earth, air, and waters, which itself is a miracle unquestionably greater and more admirable than all the marvels it is filled with? (XXI.7)

The argumentative point is clear enough, and difficult to dispute: if God can do anything, he can also create an eternally tormentable body. The affect and tone, however, are unmistakably enthusiastic—clearly for Augustine the body of the damned belongs to the series of God's most impressive and awe-inspiring miracles. Thus, when he declares that the blessed in heaven will view the world "in such a way that we shall most distinctly recognize God everywhere present and governing all things, material as well as spiritual" (XXII.29), it seems like a fair extrapolation to assume that this vision will include the damned as well. The theme of the infernal spectacle is not truly absent but hovering just beneath the surface.

Even if the New Testament provides the grounds for the notion of hell as a spectacle, however, there is one key feature of the medieval vision of hell that is completely missing from the biblical evidence: the notion that the devil is not merely an inmate in hell but a guard and torturer. But even if explicit evidence is lacking, the idea of God using his enemy to carry out punishments has deep biblical roots. Above all, it serves as one of the core claims of the prophetic paradigm, which I argued could be seen as a model for the post-Constantinian political theology centered around the concept of the *katechon*. And indeed, the idea of the devil as guard as well as inmate seems to have developed only after the Constantinian settlement.[2] By that point, the political "devil" had already been pressed into God's service here below, so why not extend the same logic to the earthly ruler's theological doublet? After all, we know from Revelation that "the kings of the earth will bring their glory into" the New Jerusalem for all eternity (21:24)—and it seems only fair that the Prince of this World should also be expected to make a contribution of his own to God's glory.

THE SOCIOPATHY OF THE REDEEMED

Aquinas is clear that what is at stake in the sufferings of the damned is indeed the glory of God. In his discussion of the question "whether the blessed in heaven will see the sufferings of the damned," the textual support for his positive response is unambiguous and brutal: "It is written (Isaiah 66:24): 'They shall go out and see the carcasses of the men that have transgressed against Me'; and a gloss says: 'The elect will go out by understanding or seeing manifestly, so that they may be urged the more to praise God'" (IIIa supp., q. 94, a. 1). The biblical citation figures God as a military conqueror, and the medieval commentary clarifies that the appropriate response to the divine carnage is to glorify God.

Aquinas clarifies the exact reason for this praise in his "answer" (the section of the *disputatio* that synthesizes his initial response with the elements of truth in the view the author is rejecting):

Nothing should be denied the blessed that belongs to the perfection of their beatitude. Now everything is known the more for being compared with its contrary, because when contraries are placed beside one another they become more conspicuous. Wherefore in order that the happiness of

the saints may be more delightful to them and that they may render more
copious thanks to God for it, they are allowed to see perfectly the sufferings
of the damned. (q. 94, a. 1)

The situation is not exactly like that envisioned in Tertullian, where the
blessed are deriving direct enjoyment from the entertaining spectacle of
their enemies' torment. Just as God does not will the evil that happens in
the world but indirectly uses it to enhance the world's beauty, so too do the
saints in heaven make indirect use of the contrast between their state and
that of the damned to enhance the enjoyment of their own blessings. Aquinas reinforces this parallel with God's stance toward evil in the third article
of this question, which asks "whether the blessed rejoice in the punishment
of the wicked." As in the discussion of the fall of the devil, he proceeds by
establishing a duality or division that serves to shield the blessed from the
ugliest implications of rejoicing in the suffering of the damned:

> A thing may be a matter of rejoicing in two ways. First directly, when one
> rejoices in a thing as such: and thus the saints will not rejoice in the punish-
> ment of the wicked. Secondly, indirectly, by reason namely of something
> annexed to it: and in this way the saints will rejoice in the punishment of
> the wicked, by considering therein the order of Divine justice and their own
> deliverance, which will fill them with joy. And thus the Divine justice and
> their own deliverance will be the direct cause of the joy of the blessed: while
> the punishment of the damned will cause it indirectly. (q. 94, a. 3)

Far from reveling in the spectacle of hell, as the initial biblical citation
seemed to indicate, the saints' attitude toward the damned could appear to
be a very literal "there but by the grace of God go I."

The immediately preceding article complicates this picture, however,
because it unambiguously excludes the empathy that is implied in that
common saying. To the question of "whether the blessed pity the unhappiness of the damned," Aquinas affirms, "Whoever pities another shares
somewhat in his unhappiness. But the blessed cannot share in any unhappiness. Therefore they do not pity the afflictions of the damned." In his

"response" he establishes another duality, that between "mercy or compassion . . . by way of passion" and "by way of choice." Here, however, the purpose is to exclude both sides of the duality. It is clear enough the blessed will be free of all passions, including spontaneous compassion, because undergoing passion is considered to be a form of suffering. Choosing to take pity is excluded as well, however, because Aquinas views it as logically inconsistent. On the one hand, "mercy or compassion comes of the reason's choice when a person wishes another's evil to be dispelled." Hence it is possible to wish for the salvation of the damned while they are sojourning on earth, because we can imagine the evil of their sinful state being removed. On the other hand, "in those things which, in accordance with reason, we do not wish to be dispelled, we have no such compassion." The sufferings of the damned belong in this category, because relief of their sufferings "would be contrary to divine justice" (q. 94, a. 2).

Like their heavenly fellow citizens the good angels, redeemed human beings come to enjoy a state of moral lock-in, a total and irrevocable submission to divine justice. Understandably enough, their counterparts in hell react in exactly the opposite way, forever rebelling against the divine justice to which they are unwillingly subjected. Aquinas draws a direct parallel to the moral lock-in of the demons, citing the authority of John of Damascus: "As Damascene says, 'death is to men what their fall was to the angels.' Now after their fall the angels could not be restored. Therefore neither can man after death: and thus the punishment of the damned will have no end." Further down, he expands on the implications of this quotation: "For just as the demons are obstinate in wickedness and therefore have to be punished forever, so too are the souls of men who die without charity" (q. 99, a. 3).

This obstinacy of the damned is both cause and effect of their condition. On the one hand, it is the obstinacy of their evil will that brought them to hell in the first place, but on the other hand, the experience of hell guarantees that their will remains forever opposed to the God who put them there. Therefore, while their will remains formally good insofar as it is the creation of God, every concrete act of their will "is in them always evil: and this because they are completely turned away from the last end of a right will, nor can a will be good except it be directed to that same end" (q. 98, a. 1). And—in yet another duality that spares God the appearance of outright injustice—though they "repent indirectly, inasmuch as they will suffer from the punishment inflicted on them for sin," they "will not repent of their sins directly, because consent in the malice of sin will remain in them" (q. 98, a.2). A similar division pertains to their hatred of God, whom it is impossible to hate "in himself" (since the vision of God is immediately enrapturing) but who can be hated "by reason of his effects" (q. 98, a. 5). Presumably if the damned could ever see God for what he truly is, they would immediately embrace him—but deprivation of the vision of God is a central part of their punishment. It is perhaps in this sense that Aquinas understands his claim that "the perverse will of the damned proceeds from their obstinacy which is their punishment" (q. 98, a. 6).

The latter point comes up in the context of a discussion of "whether the damned demerit." Aquinas answers that "all are agreed that after the judgment day there will be neither merit nor demerit"—in other words, all moral striving and moral evaluation come radically to an end with the Last Judgment. "Consequently," he concludes, "good will in the blessed will not be a merit but a reward, and evil will in the damned will be not a demerit but a punishment only" (q. 98, a. 6). In this way, the human residents of the two cities are assimilated to their angelic counterparts, who reached the uttermost limits of merit and demerit with their first acts (submission and rebellion, respectively) and were subsequently confirmed in their respective moral orientations for all eternity.

In both cases, this disconnection from the realm of moral striving threatens to render the two groups' moral evaluations meaningless or arbitrary. How does it make sense to regard someone as good or evil in an ongoing way when they are unable to will anything else? As we noted in our discussion of the *Malleus Maleficarum*, even Kramer could find it in his heart to sympathize with the devil's plight of being unable to repent. The moral distinction becomes even more difficult to support when we observe that the damned seem to be in a much more sympathetic situation, insofar as God is actively depriving them of any grounds for repentance, while the blessed display a sociopathic lack of compassion toward precisely those who are suffering the worst conceivable pain. It is not simply that the grounds for moral evaluation are lacking—on an intuitive level, one is tempted to say that the moral evaluations should, if anything, be reversed.

Even if we stop short of that reversal, it is difficult not to conclude that the only salient difference between the blessed and the damned is God's inscrutable decision to favor the members of one group and reject the others. And when we recall that Aquinas, like essentially all mainstream medieval theologians, fully embraced the doctrine of predestination, that conclusion becomes absolutely inescapable. From the perspective of eternity, the distinction between the first instant in which God creates and the second instant in which the devil and his comrades inexplicably rebel collapses into a single instant, and the conflict between the divine and demonic wills collapses into the single act of will by which God at once created and predestined his creation.

Even if God's decree of election remains inscrutable, however, the situation in hell was well known to theologians by the late medieval period. Indeed, Aquinas has a great deal to say about the torments to be found there: dividing them between the punishments of the soul (in many respects shared with the demons) and of the body (including fire and darkness), speculating on hell's physical location (an inescapable corollary of the resurrection of the dead; q. 97, a. 7), and pondering the implications of the damned's vision of the blessed (q. 98, a. 9). Except as a point of comparison with the human damned, however, the demons are strangely absent from his account. In his discussion of the fall of the devil, he had made reference to the fact that some demons "are even now in hell, to torment those whom they have led astray" (Ia, q. 64, a. 4). Yet when it comes time to describe the torments of the damned, he never explicitly mentions the role of the demons as their fellow prisoners and torturers.

Now admittedly Aquinas's *Summa Theologiae* is an incomplete work, and so he may have intended to add a further series of questions about the demons' role as torturers. At the same time, there is something appropriate about the absence of the demons in his discussion of hell, because by this time the demons have already done their job. They have insulated God—if only by the breadth of a single instant—from active responsibility for the evil that pervades creation. For Aquinas as for medieval Christianity as a whole, in contrast, there is ultimately no need to provide God with that kind of plausible deniability for the punishments he doles out to sinners. Offenses against an infinite God demand infinite punishment (IIIa, supp., q. 99, a. 1), and those God has redeemed and rewarded will rejoice in the execution of his terrible will, eternally undistracted by pity or compassion.

"THE GREAT FUNDAMENT OF THE WORLD"

The demonic torturers may play a subdued role in Aquinas's discussion of hell, but they feature prominently in a literary masterpiece inspired by his theology: Dante's *Inferno*.[3] In this great poetic vision of hell, which perhaps more than any other text has shaped Christian views of the fate of the damned, the demons are eager participants in the ingenious punishments devised for their fellow rebels against God. In one curious incident, they even set their sights on Dante and his guide, Virgil, as a group attempts to capture them and tear them to pieces (see cantos 22 and 23). Divided against themselves by their pride and petty rivalries, however, they allow the poets to escape their grasp.[4] The damned may be utterly at their mercy, but demons are powerless against those God has favored.

Though we could view this discord among themselves as part of their punishment, it seems fair to say that the demons are more tormenting than tormented in hell—with one exception: Satan himself. Everything about his situation is calculated to render him miserable, as well as to upend the reader's expectations about the nature of hell. Some of these overturned assumptions could have been drawn from Dante's own account, most notably the gleeful mobility of the demons. In contrast, Satan is utterly trapped and stationary, weighed down by a body of unimaginably gargantuan proportions, the culmination of the paradoxical embodiment of this originally purely spiritual being. On entering the lowest level of hell, Dante had seen four towering giants keeping watch over the nether realms (34.31–32), and when he sees the devil, he declares that "to his arm alone the giants were /

less comparable than to a giant I" (34.30–31). Even worse, the body in which "that creature fairest once of the sons of light" (34.18) is entombed is hideously ugly. His head has three faces of various hues (34.37–45), under each of which are "two great wings that well / befitted such a monstrous bird as that" (34.46–47). The wings are "plumeless and like the pinions of a bat" (34.49), but the rest of his body is covered in shaggy hair (34.73–74).

This vast, malformed body is encased in ice up to its chest (34.29), a punishment that is self-inflicted, because as his wings "flapped and whipped / three winds went rushing over the icy flat / and froze up all Cocytus" (34.50–52). This deepest region of hell is not hot but unbearably cold, and the many traitors he meets there all share the devil's icy entombment to a degree proportionate to their crime. Yet the three greatest traitors in Dante's accounting—Judas Iscariot, who betrayed Christ, along with Brutus and Cassius, who both betrayed Julius Caesar—are not embedded in the ice so much as embedded in Satan himself, who perpetually chews on all three in his three great mouths, supplementing Judas's punishment with his scraping claws (34.55–60). As he carries out his grim duties, the devil "wept / from his six eyes, and down his triple chin / Runnels of tears and bloody slaver dripped" (34.52–54)—a graphic and repulsive mixture of the fruits of the torments he both suffers and carries out.

In her creative rereading of the *Inferno*, Laurel Schneider has pointed out how foundational the devil is to the world Dante has constructed, on a very literal level. First, the ice in the deepest level of hell, which Dante describes as "the great / fundament of the world" (32.6–7), "is not in fact integral to the place, but it is the product of continuous effort on the part of the so-called Prince of the prisoners."[5] Were he to cease in his labors, then presumably the whole vast edifice of creation would come crashing down as the ice melted. More than that, the center of gravity of the entire universe is found at the pelvic region of the devil's body—and as Schneider argues, Dante's language seems to imply that the weight of the world converges on either the devil's anus or even his vagina (an organ that would be no less incongruous for a spiritual being than the penis his male figuration would imply; p. 98). In Schneider's words, "Satan is the foundation of the universe. His position is pivotal not only as an axis in the world, but the hairy place where hip meets thigh is apparently the point upon which the edifices of Purgatory and Heaven—the whole realm and creation of God— are built" (p. 99).

For Schneider, this cosmological structure represents an implicit critique of the metaphysical assumptions of medieval Christianity. Above all, she highlights the uncanny overlap between the absolute stasis at the heart of hell and the ideal of changeless heavenly eternity, which indicates that "eternity is the essence of damnation" (p. 97). Drawing on Catherine Keller's *Face of the Deep*, she argues that the fact that the core of the universe is made precisely of *ice* demonstrates the artificiality of the cosmic order, which must still the roiling motions of the waters that in the biblical tradition represent the forces of primordial chaos (p. 91). She even playfully suggests that Dante and Virgil's climb down the body of Satan to the center of gravity and thence up the inverted legs of Satan could instead be read as a journey into the devil's anal or vaginal cavity, so that "heaven lies in the body of Satan" (p. 98). In short, she claims, "at the center of Hell Dante inadvertently (it is inadvertent?) exposes the lie of traditional Christian metaphysics" (p. 103).

The same symbolism could of course be read very differently. Instead of being the foundation of the world, it could be that the center of hell is so desolate because, in a spherical world, the center is the point furthest from God. And if we accept Schneider's contention that Dante is placing the center of gravity precisely at the devil's anus or vagina, the symbolism has a similar effect. If we conceive of it simply as a hole, then it is a lack of being, which is the furthest possible thing from the divine superabundance. If we view the orifice as vaginal, then it emphasizes the devil's sterility in a world order where only God is capable of authentically creative acts. And if we conceive of it a conduit for waste, then it is one that goes unused, because the devil's relentless consumption of his victims does not result in digestion. The implication would then be that nothing finally goes to waste in God's creation.

In short, everything, no matter how repulsive and evil it may seem, is articulated into God's overarching plan for the universe. In the declaration posted at its entryway, a strangely personified hell proclaims that this rule holds above all for its ghastly realms:

> Through me the road to the City of Desolation,
> Through me the road to sorrows diuturnal,
> Through me the road among the lost creation.
>
> Justice moved my great Maker; God eternal
> Wrought me: the power, and the unsearchably
> High wisdom, and the primal love supernal.
>
> Nothing ere I was made was made to be
> Save things eterne, and I eterne abide;
> Lay down all hope, you that go in by me. (3.1–9)

In keeping with her critique of the concept of eternity, Schneider focuses on the final stanza: "This is a remarkable theological claim: *nothing* but eternity itself (God, presumably) existed before Hell and its gates. Eternity created Hell first, out of itself, perhaps because Hell is all that Eternity *can* create" (p. 95). Yet the second stanza is if anything even more damning, attributing the creation of hell to God's justice, power, wisdom, and—worst of all—love. If we are to read Dante as a critic of Christianity, then it is a harsh critique indeed, one that seems, at least from a modern perspective, to reveal God's love for his creation to be a cruel lie.

Now the question of authorial intent is never the last word on a great work of literature. Whether or not Dante intended them, the implicit critiques that Schneider points out are there to be seen. At the same time, I believe it is worth attending to Dante's likely intention as a way of building on the potentially "inadvertent" critique of Christianity Schneider sees in the *Inferno*. The key question in determining whether Dante actually intended his text to be read as a critique of Christianity is what he thinks of the institution of hell. Clearly he is frightened and repulsed by what he sees there, but is he outraged? He has a certain degree of sympathy and respect for many of his damned interlocutors, but do we have any indication that he believes their treatment is unjust?

The answer to both questions, I believe, is no. Even if he sometimes expresses surprise or disbelief at someone's placement in hell, Dante never overtly questions the wisdom of the sentence. This is doubtless in part because hell proves to match up so remarkably well with Dante's own political opinions. The uncanny correspondence is perhaps most striking in the mouth of the devil, where Dante sees *two* traitors to the Roman Empire but only one traitor against Christ—an arrangement that reflects Dante's own somewhat idiosyncratic desire, expressed most clearly in *De Monarchia*, to vindicate the role of the Roman Empire as God's ordained worldly ruler.

More than simply submitting to God's wisdom in dealing out punishments, however, Dante sometimes joins in on the cruelty in hell. In one case, having been taunted by a particularly unpleasant member of a rival faction, Dante expresses his desire to see him completely submerged in the mud in which he is wallowing (8.52–54). Virgil approves of the idea (8.55–57), and Dante's wish is fulfilled, prompting him to "praise and thank my God" (8.60). Later, in the face of much more severe penalties, Dante begins to weep with pity, and Virgil rebukes him:

> Why!
> And art thou too like all the other fools?
>
> Here pity, or here piety, must die
> If the other lives; who's wickeder than one
> That's agonized by God's high equity? (8.26–30)

By the time they reach the lowest level of hell, Dante has clearly learned his lesson, as he threatens to tear off the scalp of one of the traitors trapped in the ice unless he tells his story (32.97–102)—and he proves his willingness to carry out his threat by "wrench[ing] away a tuft or two" before the sinner finally gives in to his demands (32.104).

Even if Dante does not always attain it, then, the ideal is to contemplate the sufferings of the damned with the same dispassionate gratification as the blessed in heaven enjoy. The sympathy and respect that so attracts modern readers to Dante is ultimately a temptation that must be overcome, lest we be counted among "all the other fools." Already in Aquinas's account, the sociopathic detachment of the blessed could appear disturbing, but insofar as Dante is joining in with the devil's henchmen in tormenting the damned, here the ideal is quite literally demonic. A God who has become the devil turns his followers into demons.

CARCERAL CHRISTIANITY

It is nonetheless difficult to give up the possibility that Dante could see beyond the medieval worldview his *Divine Comedy* so brilliantly encapsulates because Dante seems to be proto-modern in so many ways. His decision to write his great epic in the vernacular Italian rather than Latin, for instance, looks ahead to the modern era, with its various national literatures. His politics, too, can appear proto-modern. Admittedly, his emphasis on the independent dignity and legitimacy of imperial power is from one perspective the most extreme illustration of Carl Schmitt's previously quoted dictum that "the history of the Middle ages is thus the history of a struggle *for*, not against Rome."[6] Yet with the benefit of hindsight, Dante's plea for a secular power to counterbalance the excesses of the church seems to anticipate the rise of the autonomous modern state and the subordination of ecclesiastical power that is characteristic of secular modernity.

What strikes many readers as most modern in Dante, however, is his careful attention to individuality. The characters he meets in hell are not broad moral archetypes but very specific historical individuals, whom Dante allows to speak about their experiences in their own voice. And his interlocutors are eager to tell their stories because Dante is offering them the unique opportunity to influence their reputations from beyond the grave, granting them access to something like a secular public sphere whose values do not always match up with those expressed in hell.

Accordingly, the most unforgettable among them tell stories that are at best only indirectly related to the sin that has eternally marked them. This is above all the case for the tragic story of Count Ugolino (33.4–75). Though he occupies one of the very lowest rungs of hell, his harrowing account of being locked in a tower with his sons and left to starve to death threatens to render his sufferings in hell exorbitant or even redundant. The operative ideal may be to extinguish compassion, but even the lowest of the low in hell can reawaken that response—in the reader as in Dante, who pauses to castigate Ugolino's native city of Pisa for allowing such outrages (33.79–84). The damned can also evoke feelings of genuine admiration, as in Ulysses' account of his final hopeless voyage (26.90–142), where his defining character trait is not the fraud for which he has been sentenced but his insatiable appetite for adventure.

Thus, we have trouble believing that Dante cannot see beyond the horizon of hell because he so often allows his characters to present themselves in terms that are not reducible to the logic of their damnation. Whatever evil deeds Ugolino has committed, surely he has suffered enough, and whatever Ulysses' character flaws, his remarkable heroism seems incompatible with being just another face in the crowd of the damned. In these and many other examples, vividly human individuals manage to exceed the divine verdict on their lives. If attention to richly imagined individuality is a distinctive trait of modernity, there can be little doubt that Dante is protomodern in this sense. But what does it mean that something like modern individualism emerges precisely in the depths of hell?

In Chapter 4, we saw how the emergence of the modern subject could be read as a repetition of the angels' choice between good and evil. The legitimacy of modern knowledge and modern political institutions alike shares in the logic of the fall of the devil, with its complex dynamics of retroactive responsibility. In both cases, the idealized modern subject chooses the side of the angels, and though I suggested that the process implied the production of the correlative demons (madness and those excluded from the social contract, respectively), that element was not explicitly thematized in the texts of Descartes and Rawls. What is striking from the perspective of our current question is how deindividualized the angelic modern subject is in both traditions. For Descartes as for Rawls, the ideal subject is one who has been stripped of all idiosyncrasies and attachments, allowing it to issue perfectly neutral and generic judgments that would be accepted by any other purely rational subject. If recognizable individuality is to emerge anywhere, then, it seems it must be among the demons.

A similar dynamic can be seen in Dante, where the rich individuality of the *Inferno* gives way to a much more generic uniformity in the *Paradiso*. This difference no doubt accounts for the greater popularity of the *Inferno* (and to a much lesser extent, the *Purgatorio*) compared to the *Paradiso*. As Schneider puts it, "*Paradiso* is as frozen in its bright circles of light as Satan is in ice" (p. 101). For Schneider, what is missing in heaven above all, what deprives heaven of the strangely joyful dynamism of hell, is the messiness of embodiment: "Without excrement, effort, blood, noise, upside-down church officials, the challenge of escape, or the pull of desire there can also be no life, and certainly no humor" (p. 102). It seems reasonable to assume, then, that there is some necessary connection between the concreteness of the body and the idiosyncratic depth of the modern individual. Once again, however, these are not just any bodies but precisely bodies that have been subjected to punishment.

The connection between individuality, punishment, and embodiment would come as no surprise to Nietzsche. In the second essay of *Genealogy of Morals*, he attempts to defamiliarize modern values by tracing their roots to the complex dynamics of cruelty. It is in the confrontation between the masters, who revel in violence and cruelty, and the slaves, whose suffering produces a durable *ressentiment*, that something like modern subjectivity emerges. For Nietzsche the decisive trait of modern subjectivity is the "bad conscience," which he describes as "the serious illness that man was bound to contract under the stress of the most fundamental change he ever experienced—that change which occurred when he found himself finally enclosed within the walls of society and peace."[7] In this situation, "suddenly all their instincts were disvalued and 'suspended,'" and "as a rule they had to seek new and, as it were, subterranean gratifications" (p. 520). As in Hobbes's theory of the state, the peace of the state that has enclosed them is founded on violence, and like the medieval God, this state demands unconditional obedience: "the oldest 'state' thus appeared as a fearful tyranny, as an oppressive and remorseless machine, and went on working until this raw material of people and semi-animals was at last not only thoroughly kneaded and pliant but also *formed*" (p. 522). Only when the "instinct for freedom" has been thoroughly subdued, to the point where it is "pushed back and repressed, incarcerated within and finally able to discharge and vent itself only on itself" can a genuine internal life be said to exist. It is not the body as such that gives rise to an internal life, then, but the enslaved, punished body (p. 522).

In Nietzsche's admittedly speculative analysis, the connection with the modern subject is mainly implicit. Though he clearly believes that the slave morality centered on *ressentiment* still dominates modernity, the second essay gets only as far as the advent of Christianity (see pp. 527–28). The basic logic of Nietzsche's account is extended into modernity, with much greater attention to concrete historical practices, in Michel Foucault's *Discipline and Punish*. Foucault presents his study as "a correlative history of the modern soul and of a new power to judge."[8] As Foucault claims—by means of a contrast with Christianity that seems questionable in light of our investigation—the modern soul,

> unlike the soul represented by Christian theology, is not born in sin and subject to punishment, but is born rather out of methods of punishment, supervision, and constraint. This real, noncorporal soul is not a substance; it is the element in which are articulated the effects of a certain type of power and the reference of a certain type of knowledge, the machinery by which the power relations give rise to a possible corpus of knowledge, and knowledge extends and reinforces the effects of this power. (p. 29)

As in Nietzsche's account, punishment is central to the emergence of something like modern subjectivity, but for Foucault that cruelty is necessarily tied to a certain observability and knowability. All of these elements come together in the famous illustration of the Panopticon. In this perfect prison imagined by Bentham, all the cells would be completely visible from a central guard tower, but the prisoners would be unable to see the guard. Without the ability to know whether they are being observed at any particular moment, they would be forced to assume that they are always being watched—and hence to internalize the perspective of the guards, continually judging their own behavior by the guards' standards. Here again, it is only in the milieu of punishment that self-reflexive individuality emerges.

This self-disciplining individual has an objective correlate in the increasingly fine-grained knowledge that disciplinary power is able to extract from him. As Foucault says,

> For a long time ordinary individuality—the everyday individuality of everybody—remained below the threshold of description. To be looked at, observed, described in detail, followed from day to day by an uninterrupted writing, was a privilege. . . . The disciplinary methods reversed this relation, lowered the threshold of describable individuality, and made of this description a means of control and a method of domination. It is no longer a monument for future memory, but a document for future use. (p. 191)

Dante's hell exhibits a similar attention to detail, as the "terrible art which justice here conceives" (14.6) is deployed in the service of rigorously individualized punishments. Even though every sinner belongs to a broad category—something that also holds for the prison, where delinquents are relentlessly classified (p. 253)—the precise degree and nature of their punishment are always carefully calibrated to match their crime. Seen from this angle, Dante's demand for information from the damned could appear less as a departure from the logic of hell than as form of participation in it, perhaps no less cruel than his overt acts of violence. In any case, the experience of the damned parallels that of the modern delinquent, who

> is to be distinguished from the offender by the fact that it is not so much his act as his life that is relevant in characterizing him. The penitentiary operation, if it is to be a genuine reeducation, must become the sum total existence of the delinquent, making of the prison a sort of artificial and coercive theater in which his life will be examined from top to bottom. (pp. 252–53)

What is being punished in hell as in prison is not so much what the person has done but what the person *is*. And both achieve this by continually transforming the prisoners into what they ostensibly are. Just as the very experience of hell ensures that the damned will remain unrepentant for all eternity, so too does the prison produce the delinquents on whom it exercises its disciplinary techniques.

I have frequently suggested that the medieval Christian God needs
evil, needs rebellion, needs the devil, and so contrives to make sure that
they are all produced. Foucault's disturbing investigation suggests that
much the same must be true of modern society—it must *need* delinquents
in some way:

> The prison, apparently "failing," does not miss its target; on the contrary, it
> reaches it, insofar as it gives rise to one particular form of illegality in the
> midst of others, which it is able to isolate, to place in full light, and to or-
> ganize as a relatively enclosed, but penetrable, milieu. It helps to establish
> an open illegality, irreducible at a certain level and secretly useful, at once
> refractory and docile; it isolates, outlines, brings out a form of illegality
> that seems to sum up symbolically all the others, but which makes it pos-
> sible to leave in the shade those that one wishes to—or must—tolerate.
> (pp. 276–77)

Like hell, the entire vast apparatus of disciplinary punishment serves as a
spectacle. This is not to discount the lives that it destroys, the resources it
wastes, the racist structures of oppression it reproduces and reinforces. The
spectacle is integral to all those destructive effects, distracting us from the
plain fact that prison produces rather than simply punishes criminals—and
in Foucault's view, the even more disturbing fact that the logic of the prison
forms *all* modern subjects, not just those in hell. In a strange way, then, the
spectacle of prison serves as a distraction from the fact that modern society
as a whole can be conceived of as a prison, or in other words, it serves as a
distraction *from itself*.

THE GLORY OF THE LORD

In *The Kingdom and the Glory*, Agamben's brief discussion of hell is followed
immediately by an investigation of the role of spectacle in political life. He
addresses the oppressively baroque public ceremonials of the late Byzan-
tine emperors, the revival of public acclamations by early twentieth-century
fascism, and the realm of public opinion, which he reveals to be a kind of
liturgy for the modern world. But never once in these later chapters does he

address the spectacle of hell itself. After studiously ignoring the moral valuations that pervade the doctrine of providence, at the crucial turning point in his argument he chooses good over evil, heaven over hell.

This is not to say that Agamben is taking God's side, however. His goal is not to praise God but to pull back the curtain and uncover what the glory of God is concealing. This hidden element, which the spectacle of glory serves both to conceal and reveal, is what Agamben calls "inoperativity." Though he never directly defines this key term, he describes its function:

> Human life is inoperative and without purpose, but precisely this *argia* [lack of work] and this absence of aim make the incomparable operativity of the human species possible. Man has dedicated himself to production and labor, because in his essence he is completely devoid of work, because he is the Sabbatical animal par excellence.[9]

Humanity's very lack of a pregiven purpose thus leads it to submit to the forces that would govern it: "The governmental apparatus functions because it has captured in its empty center the inoperativity of the human essence. This inoperativity is the political substance of the Occident, the glorious nutrient of all power" (p. 246).

This reference to a "nutrient" is puzzling, because a void or lack in human nature would not seem to be very nutritious. Within the terms of the theological system Agamben is analyzing, however, a lack is never simply a lack. Every lack carries with it a moral valence: it is evil, the deprivation of good. As we have seen repeatedly in recent chapters, evil represents above all a lack of divine agency, the outside of his active will that God is nonetheless able to recover for the inside. And using Agamben's own concepts, I have claimed that the dynamics of the production of this strange inside-outside are homologous to the production of bare life by sovereign power.

Agamben never mentions bare life in this discussion, but he makes much of the notion of eternal life, the Greek term for which, *zōē aiōnios*, uses the word for prepolitical, natural life (p. 247). Yet who in the eternal realm is truly alive? Schneider suggests that the residents of hell are more alive than their heavenly counterparts, and coming at the problem from a

different angle, Augustine also insists in *City of God* that hell is a place for
the living:

> For though it be a question whether that which suffers can continue to live
> forever, yet it is certain that everything which suffers pain does live, and
> that pain can exist only in a living subject. It is necessary, therefore, that he
> who is pained be living, not necessary that pain kill him; for every pain does
> not kill even those mortal bodies of ours which are destined to die. (21.2)

The life of the damned, like that of their more blessed peers, is far from a
merely natural and prepolitical life—both live, after all, precisely in a *city*,
complete with a hierarchical organization and a governmental structure.
And after the entry into the political space has occurred, there are only two
modes of life available: the "normal" politically qualified life, which Agamben designates with the Greek term *bios*, and the life that is included in its
very exclusion from the political sphere, which he calls bare life.

In the Christian vision of the afterlife, heaven is clearly the realm of
"normal" political life and hell the realm of bare life. In turning away from
the spectacle of the damned, Agamben is turning away from the spectacle
of bare life. And if the heavenly realm enjoys an eternal Sabbath rest, then
that means that the sole and exclusive work of God for all of eternity is
the continual production and reproduction of bare life *as the spectacle of hell*.
This activity does perhaps reveal a certain "inoperativity," insofar as it seems
to be completely pointless—after all, the damned will never repent and
will never be destroyed, so their endless punishment aims at no rational
end. Yet it also suggests another candidate for "the glorious nutrient of all
power": suffering.

At every step in our investigation, suffering has been the motive force
behind the development of the theological apparatus: the suffering of the
Jews in exile, the suffering of the victims of Antiochus and Nero, the sufferings of Christ. The theological apparatus cannot truly prevent or extinguish
suffering, but it can transform it by giving it meaning: as punishment, as
purification, as the darkness before the dawn. Within the indefinitely extended apocalyptic horizon of Christianity, however, something strange

happened: suffering was not given meaning but was put forward *as* meaning. The God who was called upon to transform his followers' suffering into meaning then mutated into a God who demanded suffering as an end in itself and created an endless spectacle of suffering. God had once promised to defeat an implacable adversary who viciously persecuted and murdered his people out of sheer love of cruelty, but he eventually recruited that adversary as an ally and became indistinguishable from him. And the monument to this God who has become the devil, the concrete and eternal instantiation of the glory of the Lord, is hell.

Earlier I claimed that the spectacle of hell, like that of prison in Foucault's account, is a distraction. But what is hell a distraction *from*? Just as in the case of the prison, it is ultimately a distraction *from itself*. First of all, as in the case of a specific institution known as a prison, the specific institution known as hell distracts from the fact that, in Schneider's words, "Hell is all that Eternity *can* create" (p. 95). In Foucault's terms, this would be equivalent to noting that the particular articulation of power that created the prison can create only prisons, that all of modern society is in some way modeled on the prison. The heavenly prison system can mobilize suffering and discipline to rehabilitate the sinner, as in purgatory, but the only alternative to suffering that it can offer is the absolute stasis of heaven, which is indistinguishable from death. The only place with room for life is the site of absolute suffering.

Is suffering really all that is going on here, though? Is this all, without exception, "part of the plan"? There is reason to be suspicious. Think of our discussion of Schmitt in the first chapter—the sovereign legitimates himself by claiming control over the state of emergency, but an authentic emergency is by definition beyond anyone's control. In this way, the sovereign converts his own impotence into the basis for his power. Only from a perspective (like Schmitt's) fully identified with that of the sovereign could the unruly reality of an emergency appear as a mere "exception" over which the sovereign maintains unalloyed agency. Weheliye levels a similar critique of Agamben's reflections on the most degraded victims of the concentration camps, known as "Muselmänner" to their fellow inmates (a racial slur against Muslims that may have suggested itself here due to the traditional Christian misconception that Islam was a religion of total fatalism). Where Agamben portrays them as utterly and irrevocably defeated, Weheliye points out the abundant evidence that they actively rebelled against their state. Agamben ignores these facts, Weheliye claims, because he "cannot conceive of the Muselmänner as actual, complicated, breathing, living, ravenous, and desiring beings," because he too readily buys into the Western politico-juridical order's claims to wield "genocidal violence" as "an absolute force of law from above that negates all other dimensions of the existence and subjectivity of the oppressed."[10]

Even in the living hell of the concentration camp, just as in the living hell of the plantation and in all the other sites where the modern order deploys its most extreme forms of coercion, there is a resistance that can be broken only by death—an option that does not exist in hell. In Weheliye's terms, this means that the production of bare life as pure victimization is never the last word, because underlying it is the unruliness that he calls the "flesh" but that medieval theologians would have called the rebellious will. Far from being the monument to God's absolute control, then, hell becomes the spectacle of all that he can never finally control. We can see this in the eternal tormenting activities of the demons, which are directed at no rational end and can serve no possible redemptive purpose. We can see this in the defiance of the human inmates, who consistently refuse to identify with the verdict of God. Power can shape unruly bodies into rational subjects and delinquent individuals, and as the spectacle of hell shows us, that work of shaping can have very durable effects. But as Foucault expresses more clearly in *The History of Sexuality* than in *Discipline and Punish*, the subjectivities and identities that power has produced will always continue to produce their own creative and unpredictable new modes of resistance.

We could continue to call this unruliness that forever eludes the divine control "inoperativity,"[11] but as we have seen, only from a God's-eye view could this unworking of the divine works appear merely as absence and lack, as an inert substance or nutrient. For those who can embrace their demons, inoperativity is the ungovernable power of life itself. And if we dwell on the spectacle of hell, we will find that this truth has been hiding in plain sight. All along, the Christian God has legitimated himself more and more by converting what he does not will or control—the evil that issues from unruly wills—into the foundation of his glorious rule. The presentation of this infernal spectacle as the definitive proof of his almighty power is the ultimate bluff. For all its regimented hierarchical structure, hell is finally the location of all that God *cannot* control. And even when that unruliness can express itself only as defiant suffering, it is preferable to the eternal stasis of death—a truth to which God and his angels and saints implicitly testify as they remain forever entranced by the spectacle of hell.

THE LEGACY OF THE DEVIL

Secular modernity has remained fascinated by the devil. Even as his theological role grew more and more marginal in mainstream churches, encounters with the devil proved formative for the modern world. This holds above all for the Romantics' embrace of Milton's Satan as the true hero of *Paradise Lost* and for the decisive influence that Goethe's *Faust* would have on the milieu that produced German idealism. The devil has had a prolific career in literature, opera, and film, in addition to enjoying a theological resurgence among more marginal and populist religious groups in the late twentieth century.

Tracing the secular afterlife of the figure of the devil is beyond the scope of the present study. My goal here is to point to a less literal, more subterranean legacy of the devil—a deeper legacy that can help to account for the ongoing interest in the figure of the devil but cannot be reduced to it. Throughout my investigation, I have highlighted connections between the theological concepts that came to surround the devil and the central concepts of modernity, particularly modern political thought. If we accept Schmitt's dictum that "all significant concepts of the modern theory of the state are secularized theological concepts,"[1] then it appears that the devil has served as a privileged conduit for that conceptual transfer.

While it would be a mistake to exaggerate its role in this process, Milton's *Paradise Lost* provides tools for thinking it through. This is in part due to the perceived ambiguity of the text. Milton's stated purpose is to "assert Eternal Providence / and justify the ways of God to men,"[2] but it is by now a commonplace that his portrayal of the devil is so rich and seductive that Milton must be, in William Blake's words, "of the Devil's party without knowing it."[3] This ambivalence at the literary level finds biographical support in Milton's involvement in Cromwell's revolutionary government as a propagandist. Written after the Restoration of the monarchy, *Paradise Lost* would in this reading represent the reflections of a failed revolutionary trying to come to grips with his movement's defeat. This political connection is only reinforced by Milton's departure from the medieval tradition of extreme abstraction in depicting the fall of the devil. Instead, he presents the devil as a charismatic political leader who rallies his troops to fight a quite literal war—and still inspires loyalty even after a crushing defeat.

I cannot pretend to make an original contribution to this long-standing debate. I would like to focus instead on another, subtler ambivalence in the final lines of the poem. Before being expelled from the Garden of Eden, Adam is granted an overview of all of human history, up to the Last Judgment, which will "dissolve / Satan with his perverted world" and usher in a new heaven and a new earth (12.546–547). Adam learns the intended lesson that "to obey is best" (12.561), and his angelic guide encourages him to keep the faith so that he will "not be loath / to leave this Paradise," since he will "possess / a paradise within [him], happier far" (12.585–87). After waking Eve (12.594), Adam summarizes the message of his vision for her, and Eve proclaims that Adam's companionship is paradise enough before citing the "further consolation" that "though all by me is lost, / such favor I unworthy am vouchsafed, / by me the promised Seed shall all restore" (12.620–23).

In this light, their departure from paradise takes on a perhaps unexpectedly optimistic aspect, as expressed in the poem's concluding lines:

> The world was all before them, where to choose
> Their place of rest, and Providence their guide.

They hand in hand with wand'ring steps and slow
Through Eden took their solitary way. (12.646–49)

In the most natural reading of these lines, they know God is in control, they have each other, and so everything will ultimately turn out for the best. At the same time, these lines could be read as containing a strange contradiction: In what sense are they "solitary" if they have providence as a guide? Further, given that "Satan with his perverted world" will be dissolved only at the end of time, it seems relevant to recall that the Prince of this World had promised that he would offer them a particularly intimate companionship:

League with you I seek
And mutual amity so strait, so close,
That I with you must dwell or you with me
Henceforth. (4.375–79)

From a theological perspective, of course, we know that the devil plays a privileged role in divine providence—hence, having providence as guide necessarily entails having the devil as a traveling companion. Yet if it makes sense theologically, humanity's "mutual amity" with the devil only compounds the question of what is meant by their "solitary way."

I would like to suggest that focusing on this ambivalence allows us to read Milton's text less as an implicit critique or attempted vindication of Christianity than as a kind of fable of the transition from Christianity to secular modernity. Modern Western humanity ultimately believed itself to be embarking on its "solitary way" beyond the borders of the dubious paradise of Christian faith. Like Adam and Eve, it carried with it the memory of the entire Christian narrative—from creation and fall to the Last Judgment—but sought its own path. Instead of living in the tension between the earthly and heavenly city, it sought to found a new secular city. The foundation of that city was neither obedience to God nor rebellion against him but a new form of social bond forged in indifference to the claims of any historical revelation (at least in principle). And the basis of that social bond was ultimately *freedom*—the free consent of the community to join together and choose their own form of government.

Yet the "solitary way" of the modern West was not so solitary after all. Like Adam and Eve, we still have providence as guide, and that necessarily entails the continued companionship of the devil. This situation is not a matter of sheer contingent happenstance. It is not a question of the personal bias of important modern thinkers inadvertently setting us on an imperfectly secular course. We are not dealing here with mere cultural baggage that can be discarded at will. We cannot simply shed the Christian shell in order to get at the kernel, because it is precisely the core value of Western modernity that has bequeathed to us the entire grim apparatus of providence with its devilish supplement.

THE TRAP OF FREEDOM

That value is freedom. It legitimates our governments and our economic structures alike. It shapes how we think of our deepest spiritual convictions and our most intimate relationships. It absolutely saturates everything we do and say.

As we have seen, freedom plays an equally important role in the medieval theological paradigm. Freedom is crucial to medieval strategies for coping with the problem of evil, meaning that freedom is also a principle of legitimation for medieval Christianity. It serves as the ground for every moral judgment, and those moral judgments ultimately determine one's eternal fate. In the meantime, free will is crucial for the constitution of social identity, which in theological terms is determined by the choice either to embrace Christianity and the role it allots you or else to rebel against it and assume a marginalized identity.

Clearly not every free choice is equal in Christian terms. As shown most vividly in Aquinas's account of the fall of the devil, there is a fundamental asymmetry in the Christian view of free choice: we can choose rightly only with the aid of the grace of God. Any choice we make independently is always by definition wrong, because only God enjoys the privilege of making choices that are unconstrained by any higher authority. This means that

God effectively gets all the credit for our good choices, while we take the blame for our bad choices—which remain blameworthy despite the fact that God enhances his glory by bringing good out of the evil we do. This logic comes out clearly in the term "heretic," which derives from a Greek word meaning simply "choice": to choose is always to choose wrongly.

In short, within the medieval theological paradigm, freedom is a trap. It functions as an apparatus for generating blameworthiness. It achieves this through a logic of retroactive responsibility, most dramatically when the angels' first act of will is treated as if they had somehow *already* consented to God's will. And because the right choice is always the choice to submit to another's will (God's, in the last analysis), freedom serves to moralize social hierarchy. The demon, the witch, the Jew, the heretic—none of them know their place.

At first glance, the medieval conception of freedom may appear worlds apart from our most cherished modern value, just as much as the medieval obsession with doctrinal truth appears to be opposed to the modern valorization of scientific knowledge. Yet in the latter case, Nietzsche has famously argued that modernity is less a repudiation of Christianity than a further deployment of Christianity's own "will to truth." Hence, atheism is "only one of the latest phases of its evolution, one of its terminal forms and inner consequences—it is the awe-inspiring *catastrophe* of two thousand years of training in truthfulness that finally forbids itself the *lie involved in belief in God*."[4] As one might expect given the deep connection between the two themes in Descartes' foundational *Meditations on First Philosophy*, the situation is the same with freedom: modernity may have declared its freedom from Christianity, but it did so using *Christianity's freedom*.

Modern freedom is Christian freedom with the opposite moral valuations. The free expression of an unrestrained will is no longer a sign of moral degradation but the essence of human dignity. By the same token, unquestioning conformity to a higher power is viewed not as the pinnacle of ethical perfection but as inauthentic at best and highly dangerous at worst. This reversal comes out in the fetishization of the rebel, of the subversive and irreverent—or more literally, of the devil and of heresy.

Yet modern freedom is not simply negative, not solely freedom from restraint. Like Christian freedom, it is a *governed* freedom. Ideally, our lives are governed by two powers: the state, which translates our will into law, and the invisible hand of the market, which transmutes our self-interested choices into the social good. As in the medieval paradigm, the legitimation behind these restraints on our will is itself a will—but in the modern version of providence, God's will is replaced by our own collective will.

This shift from God to humanity is certainly a radical secularization of the medieval paradigm, but it results in a claustrophobia that is if anything even more extreme than that of the medieval paradigm. What initially appears as an opening to the infinite horizon of creative self-determination collapses into an endlessly tautologous justification of the way things are. And this is because freedom remains the modern answer to the problem of evil.

Why is our society so disordered and violent? It is what we have chosen, what we have voted for—or from another angle, we have not mustered up the will necessary to change it. Why are we given unhealthy food to eat, produced using revolting and inhumane methods? It is what we have chosen to purchase, what the market demands, and so what we must want. Why is capitalist production destroying the material conditions for human survival? It is what we have all collectively chosen through the globalized market.

Over and over, we have no one but ourselves to blame. Modern freedom remains an apparatus for generating blameworthiness. Like the medieval freedom it secularizes, modern freedom still operates through a logic of retroactive responsibility—whatever is, *must* be what we have collectively willed (or at least not willed to change). And if we shift to the level of the individual, we can see that it still serves to moralize social hierarchy. For instance, why do a few people enjoy unprecedented superabundance, while others face increasing deprivation? Some people have made good choices and the market has rewarded them, while others have made bad choices and must face the consequences. Why are some racial groups subordinate while others enjoy comfort and privilege? They have chosen to participate in a faulty culture, chosen to commit crimes or turn a blind eye to those who commit crimes.

In light of these parallels, it should be no surprise that the modern paradigm includes its own mechanisms of demonization. And by this I do not *simply* mean scapegoating and exclusion. Our investigation allows us to be more precise about the mechanism of demonization: eliciting and even *forcing* the very choices for which an individual or group is to be judged morally inferior and worthy of punishment.

The model here is the moral lock-in of the rebellious angels, which finds its echo in the structure of hell, where the inmates are continually deprived of any means for willing anything but the rejection of God. We saw a similar logic in Foucault's account of the production of delinquents in the prison system, an account that we can extend on the basis of American experience where racialized populations—black Americans above all—are collectively criminalized.[5] This is why Michael Brown could "look like a demon" to the police officer who murdered him: the mechanism by which blacks are included in American society through their very exclusion is a secularized version of the mechanism that produced demons and their allies in the medieval paradigm. We can hear the echo in the seemingly instinctive response to the ever-growing list of similar cases of racist police violence: in the mainstream media debate I analyzed previously, victims are *always* presumptively to blame for their own death. They could have appeared less frightening or aggressive; they could have been more obedient and submissive—in short, they had a *choice*.

We could extend the same analysis to the international level, where the War on Terror seems calculated to produce despair and resentment in the very populations it is supposedly pacifying. And a similar dynamic is at work on the economic level, where debt—a contract freely entered into!—becomes a lever for extracting ever more resources from debtors (whether individuals or nations), setting up a vicious cycle where creditors demand measures that will ensure that the debt can never be repaid.

In the medieval paradigm, the dynamics of demonization found their ultimate expression in the spectacle of hell, which I characterized as the spectacle of the production of bare life. In *The Kingdom and the Glory*, Agamben argues that the sphere of public opinion is the secularized version of the sphere of divine glory. From the perspective of this investigation, it is therefore not surprising how much of what we see in that public sphere is a spectacle of suffering and death—and how often war is presented as a kind of spectacle, as a way of "sending a message" to the enemy, of showing our strength. For people actually living in a war zone, however, there is no spectacle because there is no room for calm contemplation. They may be the targets of the "shock and awe" campaign, but they are not its intended audience. The whole thing is staged for the viewer back home, just as hell is staged for the righteous and redeemed.

The modern world could therefore be viewed as a secularized version of the medieval world structure. At the foundation is hell, where bare life is produced and reproduced, while the pinnacle is the global elect, that small minority on whose behalf all the glory is extracted from the damned. In between, there is the aspirational zone of purgatory, where by dint of hard work and sacrifice, we can all make it to heaven—assuming we have all of eternity to work off their debt. In this secularized version, heaven, hell, and purgatory are not separate regions belonging to a transcendent realm beyond this world but are distributed throughout our world itself at all levels. As the dominant world power, the United States as a whole obviously belongs in the category of heaven, for instance, but it also includes its own burgeoning hell in the form of an ever-expanding archipelago of prisons.

NOTES TOWARD A NEW PARADIGM

In the medieval apparatus, the spectacle of hell served as a distraction from two unpalatable truths. The first is that the apparatus of freedom can *only* punish and control—that hell is the truth of heaven. The second and more radical is that in the last analysis, there is something that this apparatus *cannot* control, something that eternally resists and frustrates it. We can say the same of the modern apparatus of freedom, whose promise of human flourishing has run aground in a global order that can do nothing but discipline, extract, and destroy. Yet for all its power, this apparatus of freedom has proven unable to exercise the control necessary to prevent unprecedented and potentially catastrophic changes to the material forces that condition its survival—much less to master the forces of protest and resistance that continue to dog it at every step despite seemingly endless displays of force.

In both cases, the apparatus that can do nothing but control finally *cannot* control everything. The two situations are not identical, however. Within the medieval version of this paradigm, the displacement of the apparatus into the transcendent, otherworldly realm opened up the possibility of imagining some other space, if only a provisional one. We know from medieval sources that many and perhaps most people were able to live their day-to-day lives in relative indifference to the doctrinal claims of the church. Even the residents of Dante's hell, whose fates are absolutely and irrevocably sealed in the terms of the theological apparatus, are able to imagine an alternative fate for themselves—an alternative afterlife—in the sphere of reputation.

That possibility is foreclosed in the secularized version, wherein the apparatus of freedom comes to permeate the very fabric of our everyday lives. This renders it much more powerful and destructive than its medieval counterpart, because it is seemingly inescapable. As Agamben warns in *The Use of Bodies*, "The shift in level worked out by secularization often coincides not with a weakening, but with an absolutization of the secularized paradigm."[6] At the same time that it becomes stronger, however, it becomes infinitely more fragile, because it does not have the luxury of eternity. It is making an open-ended demand to extract and destroy in a finite world, to discipline and reshape human beings who are not infinitely plastic.

For some, my analysis may point toward a "return" to Christianity, as a preferable alternative to modernity. The only concrete model for what this would mean in practice, however, is the political project of fundamentalist Christianity, which demands that laws be changed to conform to purportedly "biblical" mandates, that the privilege of Christianity be more openly recognized, and so forth. If secular modernity brings the *form* of the theological apparatus down to earth, these Christian extremists desire to refit it with what they consider more overtly Christian *content*. Clearly such a program is no alternative to modernity. It would succeed only in making the world more of a living hell, by exposing more populations to criminalization.

It would be just as much of a mistake to claim that the answer is to completely purge the Christian elements of our heritage and thereby finally achieve a *true* secularism. As I have argued, however, the modern world order does not contain Christian "elements" but is "Christianity-shaped" through and through. A campaign to finally expel the religious other—who willfully persists in irrational beliefs despite the manifest benefits of secular modernity—would represent yet another demonization campaign within Western countries, alongside the ongoing demonization of Muslims at the geopolitical level. Such campaigns are necessarily endless, as the demonizer always needs the demon as a means of self-definition and self-legitimation.

The choice between religious extremism and Enlightenment values is a false one, but at the same time, we must not imagine that we can start from scratch. Both the medieval and the modern paradigms have long since occupied the empty space of sheer freedom, deploying it as part of their apparatus for producing angels and demons. The fantasy of starting from absolute zero, of *creatio ex nihilo*, is the fantasy of a pure freedom that is at the same time a pure order. I have noted that the truth of hell is that an order that can do nothing but control ultimately cannot control everything. It also shows an obverse truth: there is no pure spontaneity that finally escapes all control. That is what the modern rebels who identified with the devil missed—even the devil is shaped by the divine order he rejects. If we are to build an alternative order, we must recognize that we are shaped by that order and that we can only use materials that have been shaped by that order.

I do not have the final answer to what should be done, but I do have an idea of where to look for *the kind of thing* that should be done. I have traced a path from ancient Israel through Christianity to modernity, but that is only one trajectory within the broader tradition of monotheism. Even within the Christian mainstream, we have seen one attractive attempt to break the cycle of demonization in Gregory of Nyssa's bold suggestion that even the devil could be redeemed—precisely by being deprived of his despotic power. This idea was ultimately not taken up, but it could serve as a resource for current efforts to rethink the Christian tradition and its secular aftermath. There are many other "roads not taken" within the Christian tradition itself, including those represented by heretical and other marginal movements. Contemporary liberation theologies, grounded in the experience of the oppressed, should be central to this investigation, because far from representing a nihilistic "return" to Christianity, they are an attempt to create a new and unprecedented Christianity in the wreckage of Christianity's modern afterlife.

One could also read Judaism and Islam as something like an "alternative history" of what monotheism could be become. What I have in mind here is not primarily to mine those traditions for specific ideas and practices that could be adopted, though that may prove beneficial. More important is to attend to the *form* of what they are doing to the monotheistic heritage, in the hopes of achieving a similar gesture in our own context.

Particularly promising from this perspective is the gesture of classical rabbinic Judaism. After the catastrophe of the Roman destruction of Jerusalem and its Temple in 70 CE, both the apocalyptic paradigm and the various militant attempts to restore the Deuteronomistic situation had been utterly discredited. I have noted before that the prophetic paradigm continues to define the political strategy of the mainstream Jewish community in the wake of that disaster, but there was one crucial, if tacit, shift: it was a prophetic paradigm with no immediate expectation of restoration. For the indefinite future, there would be no Jewish self-rule on a large scale, no rebuilding of the Temple—in short, no possibility of returning to the way things were.

Rather than discard their heritage, however, the intellectual elites of the Jewish community found a new use for it. They converted their laws into an object of study and creative commentary. While it served as the basis for discussions of community norms, the final word was the consensus among the interpretive community itself. The ostensible content of their religion—the Torah and other Scriptures—remained unchanged, but the form had radically changed.

Beyond any of the concrete ideas and practices found in rabbinic Judaism, the appeal of this model is that it shows that there is an alternative to the gesture of doubling down. Furthermore, though it suggests that the space for such an alternative may open up only when the path of doubling down has ended in disaster, it gives us an alternative that is viable and sustainable, as Jewish communities, against great odds, have survived and often flourished under the rabbinic paradigm for centuries.

The conditions of the Jewish tradition in first-century Rome and the modern Western tradition under present-day democratic capitalism are of course radically different. One is a tradition of the oppressed, while the other is the heritage of the oppressor. That makes it admittedly difficult to imagine what kind of crisis could open up the space for such a reconceptualization within the modern West. Even in the wake of the greatest economic disaster in generations and amid unmistakable evidence of the effects of climate change, our world order remains addicted to doubling down—using capitalism to save us from the environmental damage caused by capitalism, going to war to solve the problems caused by our last war, solving debt crises with yet another consolidation loan.

At the risk of adopting an apocalyptic tone, this order is surely demonic, endlessly flapping its wings to keep itself irrevocably stuck in the same place, interminably consuming its victims without ever being satisfied. We all know how to wish that this devil could be defeated, punished, and held up to ridicule. That wish is a deeply human one, but the story of the devil shows that indulging it can only lead to the installation of a new and more powerful devil. If our heritage is demonic, then finding a new use for it may mean thinking in a different and far riskier direction. It may mean asking what it would look like to free the devil of the burden of being the devil—in other words, what it would mean for the devil to be saved.

NOTES

INTRODUCTION

1. Quoted in Emily Wax-Thibodeaux, "Wilson Said the Unarmed Teen Looked like a 'Demon.' Experts Say His testimony Was Dehumanizing and 'Super-humanizing,'" *Washington Post*, November 25, 2014, http://www.washingtonpost .com/news/post-nation/wp/2014/11/25/wilson-said-the-unarmed-teen-looked-like-a -demon-experts-say-his-testimony-was-dehumanizing-and-super -humanizing/.

2. See, for instance, James Cone, *God of the Oppressed*, rev. ed. (Maryknoll, NY: Orbis, 1997), particularly chap. 10. As I suggest in later chapters, this parallel is far from fortuitous.

3. While I favor the use of gender-inclusive language for contemporary constructive theological projects, I maintain masculine pronouns in reference to God when discussing the traditional view, to reflect the historical reality that the traditional God has been figured as male.

4. The figure of *ha-satan* does put in an appearance at certain key moments in the Hebrew Scriptures—a fact that is somewhat obscured by many conventional biblical translations—though it is unclear how these other references relate to the more fully fleshed-out character in the Book of Job. See Elaine Pagels, *The Origin of Satan: How Christians Demonized Jews, Pagans, and Heretics* (New York: Vintage, 1995), pp. 39–44, for an overview of the passages in which *ha-satan* appears.

5. For an example of this approach to the devil in specific, see Philip C. Almond, *The Devil: A New Biography* (New York: I. B. Tauris, 2014), particularly chap. 1.

6. Friedrich Nietzsche, *Genealogy of Morals*, in *Basic Writings of Nietzsche*, ed. Walter Kaufmann (New York: Modern Library, 1992), p. 513 (emphasis in original).

7. Michel Foucault, *Discipline and Punish: The Birth of the Prison*, trans. Alan Sheridan (New York: Vintage, 1995).

8. Giorgio Agamben, *The Kingdom and the Glory: For a Theological Genealogy of Economy and Government*, trans. Lorenzo Chiesa and Matteo Mandarini (Stanford, CA: Stanford University Press, 2011), p. 36.

9. Carl Schmitt, *Political Theology: Four Chapters on the Concept of Sovereignty*, trans. George Schwab (Chicago: University of Chicago Press, 2005), p. 36.

10. Ibid., p. 44.

11. Ibid., p. 45.

12. Michel Foucault, *The Order of Things: An Archeology of the Human Sciences* (New York: Vintage, 1995), p. 158.

13. Catherine Keller, *Face of the Deep: A Theology of Becoming* (New York: Routledge, 2003).

14. Laurel C. Schneider, *Beyond Monotheism: A Theology of Multiplicity* (New York: Routledge, 2008).

15. See Adam Kotsko, *Politics of Redemption: The Social Logic of Salvation* (New York: T&T Clark, 2010), particularly the concluding chapter.

16. One unfortunate side effect of this approach is a neglect of historical sources by women, which I attempt to compensate for by embracing a "preferential option" for contemporary works by women as dialogue partners.

17. Nietzsche, *Genealogy*, p. 531 (emphasis in original).

CHAPTER 1

1. Pagels, *Origin of Satan*, pp. 45–46.

2. Ibid., chap. 5.

3. Schmitt, *Political Theology*, p. 5.

CHAPTER 2

1. See Daniel Boyarin, *The Jewish Gospels: The Story of the Jewish Christ* (New York: New Press, 2012).

2. My understanding of Paul—and the political-theological context of the first century more broadly—has been deeply shaped by Theodore W. Jennings Jr., *Outlaw Justice: The Messianic Politics of Paul* (Stanford, CA: Stanford University Press, 2013); Brigitte Kahl, *Galatians Re-imagined: Reading with the Eyes of the Vanquished* (Minneapolis: Fortress, 2010); and Neil Elliott, *Liberating Paul: The Justice of God and the Politics of the Apostle* (Minneapolis: Fortress, 1994).

3. Alain Badiou exaggerates this fact to claim that for Paul, the cross is a matter of almost total indifference. See Alain Badiou, *Saint Paul: The Foundation of*

Universalism, trans. Ray Brassier (Stanford, CA: Stanford University Press, 2003), chap. 6.

4. For a thorough discussion of the Pauline notion of the "as if not" or *hōs mē*, tying it to modern political debates, see Giorgio Agamben, *The Time That Remains: A Commentary on the Letter to the Romans*, trans. Patricia Dailey (Stanford, CA: Stanford University Press, 2005), pp. 19–43.

5. Nietzsche, *Genealogy*, pp. 488–89.

6. Friedrich Engels, "On the History of Early Christianity," trans. Institute of Marxism-Leninism, in *Marx-Engels Archive*, accessed May 6, 2015, https://www .marxists.org/archive/marx/works/1894/early-christianity/.

7. Elizabeth Schüssler Fiorenza, *Revelation: Vision of a Just World* (Minneapolis: Fortress, 1991), pp. 7–12.

8. Tradition identifies this John with Jesus's beloved disciple, as well as with the author of the Gospel of John and the New Testament Epistles of John, but virtually all scholars believe that this attribution is both false and unintended by the author of Revelation.

9. Schüssler Fiorenza, *Revelation*, p. 83.

10. Ibid.

11. Ibid., p. 89.

12. For a study of this strain of biblical imagery and its legacy in Christianity and modernity, see Keller, *Face of the Deep*.

13. My reading of Mark relies heavily on Theodore Jennings, *Insurrection of the Crucified: The Gospel of Mark as Theological Manifesto* (Chicago: Exploration Press, 2003).

14. See, for example, Amy-Jill Levine, *The Misunderstood Jew: The Scandal of the Jewish Jesus* (New York: Harper, 2007); and John P. Meier, *A Marginal Jew: Rethinking the Historical Jesus*, 4 vols. (New Haven, CT: Yale University Press, 1991–2009), in addition to Boyarin's *The Jewish Gospels*.

15. In reality, the history is much more complex, and communities of Jewish followers of Jesus continued to exist centuries into the Christian era.

16. See Giorgio Agamben, *Pilate and Jesus*, trans. Adam Kotsko (Stanford, CA: Stanford University Press, 2015).

17. Karl Barth, *The Epistle to the Romans*, 6th ed., trans. Edwyn C. Hoskyns (New York: Oxford University Press, 1968), pp. 475–85.

18. Jacob Taubes, *The Political Theology of Paul*, trans. Dana Hollander (Stanford, CA: Stanford University Press, 2004), p. 16 (emphasis in original).

19. Irenaeus, *Against Heresies*, trans. Alexander Roberts and James Donaldson, in *The Ante-Nicene Fathers*, vol. 1, ed. Alexander Roberts, James Donaldson, and

Cleveland Coxe (Grand Rapids, MI: Eerdmans, 1885), pp. 841–1391. All subsequent references to *Against Heresies* and other premodern Christian texts will be in text, following the standard divisions.

20. See in particular Elaine Pagels, *The Gnostic Gospels* (New York: Vintage, 1979); and Karen King, *What Is Gnosticism?* (Cambridge, MA: Harvard University Press, 2003).

21. Tertullian, *De Spectaculis* [On the shows], trans. S. Thelwall, in *Ante-Nicene Fathers*, vol. 3, ed. Alexander Roberts, James Donaldson, and A. Cleveland Coxe (Buffalo, NY: Christian Literature Publishing, 1885), pp. 157–91.

22. For a different genealogy of the Christian invention of "religion" as a distinctive sphere of human activity, see Daniel Colucciello Barber, *On Diaspora: Christianity, Religion, and Secularity* (Eugene, OR: Cascade, 2011).

23. Athanasius, *On the Incarnation of the Word*, trans. Archibald Robertson, in *Christology of the Later Fathers*, ed. Edward R. Hardy (Philadelphia: Westminster, 1954), pp. 55–110.

24. Jacques Derrida, *The Gift of Death*, trans. David Wills (Chicago: University of Chicago Press, 1995), pp. 97–102.

CHAPTER 3

1. Gregory of Nyssa, "An Address on Religious Instruction," ed. and trans. Cyril C. Richardson, in *Christology of the Later Fathers*, ed. Edward R. Hardy (Philadelphia: Westminster, 1954), pp. 268–325.

2. For the classic statement, see Gustav Aulén, *Christus Victor: An Historical Study of the Three Main Types of the Idea of the Atonement*, trans. A. G. Herbert (London: Society for Promoting Christian Knowledge, 1931). I critique Aulén's account at length in chapter 3 of *Politics of Redemption*. For a reading of the ransom theory from a feminist/liberationist standpoint, see Darby Ray, *Deceiving the Devil: Atonement, Abuse, and Ransom* (Cleveland: Pilgrim, 1998).

3. Athanasius, *The Life of Antony and the Letter to Marcellinus*, trans. Robert C. Gregg (Mahwah, NJ: Paulist, 1980).

4. See Giorgio Agamben, *The Highest Poverty: Monastic Rules and Form-of-Life*, trans. Adam Kotsko (Stanford, CA: Stanford University Press, 2013), pp. 9–11.

5. Ibid., p. 53.

6. Ibid., pp. 37–45.

7. Carole Pateman, *The Sexual Contract* (Stanford, CA: Stanford University Press, 1988).

8. John of Damascus, *The Orthodox Faith*, in *Writings*, trans. Frederic H. Chase Jr. (New York: Fathers of the Church, 1958), III.27.

9. Anselm of Canterbury, *Why God Became Man*, in *Major Works*, ed. Brian Davies and Gillian Evans (New York: Oxford University Press, 1998). All subsequent citations from Anselm's works derive from this translation, which has sometimes been altered for inclusive language.

10. Peter of Poitiers, *Sententiae* 1.16, qtd. in Giorgio Agamben, *Opus Dei: An Archeology of Duty*, trans. Adam Kotsko (Stanford, CA: Stanford University Press, 2013), p. 23.

11. Peter Abelard, *Commentary on the Epistle to the Romans*, trans. Steven R. Cartwright (Washington, DC: Catholic University of America Press, 2011), p. 165.

CHAPTER 4

1. Thomas Aquinas, *The Summa Theologica of St. Thomas Aquinas*, 2nd rev. ed., trans. Fathers of the English Dominican Province (1920), New Advent, 2008, http://www.newadvent.org/summa.

2. Augustine, *The City of God*, trans. Marcus Dods (New York: Modern Library, 1993).

3. See Giorgio Agamben, *Homo Sacer: Sovereign Power and Bare Life*, trans. David Heller-Roazen (Stanford, CA: Stanford University Press, 1998).

4. Orlando Patterson, *Slavery and Social Death: A Comparative Study* (Cambridge, MA: Harvard University Press, 1982). Subsequent page citations are in the text.

5. See Alexander G. Weheliye, *Habeas Viscus: Racializing Assemblages, Biopolitics, and Black Feminist Theories of the Human* (Durham, NC: Duke University Press, 2014). Subsequent page citations are in the text.

6. See John Rawls, *Theory of Justice* (Cambridge, MA: Belknap Press, 1971).

7. René Descartes, *Meditations on First Philosophy*, in *Selected Philosophical Writings*, trans. John Cottingham and Robert Stoothoff (New York: Cambridge University Press, 1998). In-text citations refer to the page numbers in this edition.

8. Michel Foucault, *Madness and Civilization: A History of Insanity in the Age of Reason*, trans. Richard Howard (New York: Vintage, 1965), p. 108.

9. See Jacques Derrida, "Cogito and the History of Madness," in *Writing and Difference*, trans. Alan Bass (Chicago: University of Chicago Press, 1978), pp. 31–63.

10. See Pateman, *The Sexual Contract*.

11. See Charles W. Mills, *The Racial Contract* (Ithaca, NY: Cornell University Press, 1999).

CHAPTER 5

1. Rosemary Radford Ruether, *Sexism and God-Talk: Toward a Feminist Theology* (Boston: Beacon, 1983), p. 166.

2. See, for example, Asma Barlas, *"Believing Women" in Islam: Unreading Patriarchal Interpretations of the Qur'an* (Austin: University of Texas Press, 2009), pp. 138–39.

3. Here I maintain the New Revised Standard Version (NRSV) translation, which reflects the medieval interpretation of Paul's views.

4. Carl Schmitt, *The Nomos of the Earth in the International Law of the Jus Publicum Europaeum*, ed. and trans. G. L. Ulmen (New York: Telos, 2003), p. 59.

5. Ibid., p. 60.

6. Jacob Taubes, *To Carl Schmitt: Letters and Reflections*, trans. Keith Tribe (New York: Columbia University Press, 2013), p. 54.

7. The NRSV translation supplies "enemies *of God*," despite conceding in the footnotes that this phrase has no explicit basis in the Greek text.

8. Joshua Trachtenberg, *The Devil and the Jews: The Medieval Conception of the Jew and Its Relation to Modern Anti-Semitism* (Philadelphia: Jewish Publication Society, 1983).

9. Ibid., p. 159.

10. Martin Luther, "On the Jews and Their Lies," trans. Martin H. Bertram, in *Luther's Works*, vol. 47 (Philadelphia: Fortress Press, 1971), accessed June 26, 2015, http://jdstone.org/cr/pages/sss_mluther.html. Subsequent citations are given in the text.

11. See Aulén, *Christus Victor*.

12. Heinrich Kramer and James Sprenger, *Malleus Maleficarum*, trans. Montague Summers (New York: Dover, 1971). In-text references are to the page numbers of this edition. I also treat Kramer as the sole author, though this is solely for convenience and should not be misconstrued as any kind of strong claim about the actual composition process of the text.

13. See Andrea Dworkin, *Women Hating* (New York: Plume, 1974), chap. 7.

14. Agamben, *Kingdom and the Glory*, p. 141.

15. *Federalist No. 51*, Constitution Society, accessed July 7, 2015, http://www.constitution.org/fed/federa51.htm.

16. Silvia Federici, *Caliban and the Witch: Women, the Body, and Primitive Accumulation*, 2nd ed. (New York: Autonomedia, 2014).

17. Eduardo Viveiros de Castro, *The Inconstancy of the Indian Soul: The Encounter of Catholics and Cannibals in 16th-Century Brazil*, trans. Gregory Duff Morton (Chicago: Prickly Paradigm, 2011).

18. See Weheliye, *Habeas Viscus*, particularly chap. 2.

19. Ibid., p. 37.

20. See Willie James Jennings, *The Christian Imagination: Theology and the Origins of Race* (New Haven, CT: Yale University Press, 2010); J. Kameron Carter, *Race: A Theological Account* (New York: Oxford, 2008); and Vincent W. Lloyd, *The*

Problem with Grace: Reconfiguring Political Theology (Stanford, CA: Stanford University Press, 2011).

21. See Genesis 9:20–27, where Noah actually curses his grandson Canaan for an ill-defined disrespectful action taken by Ham (Noah's son, Canaan's father), who is supposed to be the primeval ancestor of all those of African descent. Extracting the supposed "Curse of Ham" completely misrepresents the text, which obviously intends to legitimate the Israelite conquest of Canaan and never mentions skin color or Africa.

22. Agamben, *Kingdom and the Glory*, p. 164.

CHAPTER 6

1. The NRSV has "where he was being tormented," but neither the original Greek text nor the Latin Vulgate translation actually includes a passive-voice construction implying any particular agent executing his torments. Both simply indicate that he existed in the midst of torments (Greek: *huparkōn en basanois*; Latin: *esset in tormentis*).

2. See the discussion of this theme's textual origins in *The Gospel of Nicodemus* (ca. 555 CE), in Almond, *The Devil*, pp. 57–59.

3. I will be using the Sayers translation: Dante, *The Divine Comedy I: Hell*, trans. Dorothy Sayers (New York: Penguin, 1949). In-text references refer to the canto, followed by the verse number in this translation (which closely follows the original).

4. See Sayers' commentary on p. 211.

5. Schneider, *Beyond Monotheism*, p. 97. Subsequent page citations are in the text.

6. Schmitt, *Nomos of the Earth*, p. 59.

7. Nietzsche, *Genealogy*, p. 520. Subsequent page citations are in the text.

8. Foucault, *Discipline and Punish*, p. 23. Subsequent page citations are in the text.

9. Agamben, *Kingdom and the Glory*, pp. 245–46. Subsequent page citations are in the text.

10. Weheliye, *Habeas Viscus*, p. 122.

11. I have argued that another potential designation is the Freudian category of drive in my essay "Perhaps Psychoanalysis?," in *Agamben's Coming Philosophy: Finding a New Use for Theology*, by Colby Dickinson and Adam Kotsko (New York: Rowman & Littlefield, 2015), pp. 137–54.

CONCLUSION

1. Schmitt, *Political Theology*, p. 36.

2. John Milton, *Paradise Lost: A Norton Critical Edition*, ed. Gordon Teskey (New York: Norton, 2005), 1.25–26. Subsequent citations are in the text.

3. Quoted in ibid., p. 389.

4. Nietzsche, *Genealogy*, p. 596.

5. The standard reference here is Michelle Alexander, *The New Jim Crow: Mass Incarceration in an Age of Colorblindness* (New York: New Press, 2012).

6. Giorgio Agamben, *The Use of Bodies*, trans. Adam Kotsko (Stanford, CA: Stanford University Press, 2016), p. 45.

BIBLIOGRAPHY

Abelard, Peter, *Commentary on the Epistle to the Romans*, trans. Steven R. Cartwright (Washington, DC: Catholic University of America Press, 2011).

Agamben, Giorgio, *The Highest Poverty: Monastic Rules and Form-of-Life*, trans. Adam Kotsko (Stanford, CA: Stanford University Press, 2013).

————, *Homo Sacer: Sovereign Power and Bare Life*, trans. David Heller-Roazen (Stanford, CA: Stanford University Press, 1998).

————, *The Kingdom and the Glory: For a Theological Genealogy of Economy and Government*, trans. Lorenzo Chiesa and Matteo Mandarini (Stanford, CA: Stanford University Press, 2011).

————, *Opus Dei: An Archeology of Duty*, trans. Adam Kotsko (Stanford, CA: Stanford University Press, 2013).

————, *Pilate and Jesus*, trans. Adam Kotsko (Stanford, CA: Stanford University Press, 2015).

————, *The Time That Remains: A Commentary on the Letter to the Romans*, trans. Patricia Dailey (Stanford, CA: Stanford University Press, 2005).

————, *The Use of Bodies*, trans. Adam Kotsko (Stanford, CA: Stanford University Press, 2016).

Alexander, Michelle, *The New Jim Crow: Mass Incarceration in an Age of Colorblindness* (New York: New Press, 2012).

Almond, Philip C., *The Devil: A New Biography* (New York: I. B. Tauris, 2014).

Anselm of Canterbury, *The Major Works*, ed. Brian Davies and Gillian Evans (New York: Oxford University Press, 1998).

Athanasius, *The Life of Antony and the Letter to Marcellinus*, trans. Robert C. Gregg (Mahwah, NJ: Paulist, 1980).

————, *On the Incarnation of the Word*, trans. Archibald Robertson, in *Christology of the Later Fathers*, ed. Edward R. Hardy (Philadelphia: Westminster, 1954), pp. 55–110.

Augustine, *The City of God*, trans. Marcus Dods (New York: Modern Library, 1993).

Aulén, Gustav, *Christus Victor: An Historical Study of the Three Main Types of the Idea of the Atonement*, trans. A. G. Herbert (London: Society for Promoting Christian Knowledge, 1931).

Badiou, Alain, *Saint Paul: The Foundation of Universalism*, trans. Ray Brassier (Stanford, CA: Stanford University Press, 2003).

Barber, Daniel Colucciello, *On Diaspora: Christianity, Religion, and Secularity* (Eugene, OR: Cascade, 2011).

Barlas, Asma, *"Believing Women" in Islam: Unreading Patriarchal Interpretations of the Qur'an* (Austin: University of Texas Press, 2009).

Barth, Karl, *The Epistle to the Romans*, 6th ed., trans. Edwyn C. Hoskyns (New York: Oxford University Press, 1968).

Boyarin, Daniel, *The Jewish Gospels: The Story of the Jewish Christ* (New York: New Press, 2012).

Carter, J. Kameron, *Race: A Theological Account* (New York: Oxford, 2008)

Cone, James, *God of the Oppressed*, rev. ed. (Maryknoll, NY: Orbis, 1997).

Dante, *The Divine Comedy I: Hell*, trans. Dorothy Sayers (New York: Penguin, 1949).

Derrida, Jacques, *The Gift of Death*, trans. David Wills (Chicago: University of Chicago Press, 1995).

————, *Writing and Difference*, trans. Alan Bass (Chicago: University of Chicago Press, 1978).

Descartes, René, *Meditations on First Philosophy*, in *Selected Philosophical Writings*, trans. John Cottingham and Robert Stoothoff (New York: Cambridge University Press, 1998), pp. 73–122.

Dworkin, Andrea, *Women Hating* (New York: Plume, 1974).

Elliott, Neil, *Liberating Paul: The Justice of God and the Politics of the Apostle* (Minneapolis: Fortress, 1994).

Engels, Friedrich, "On the History of Early Christianity," trans. Institute of Marxism-Leninism, in *Marx-Engels Archive*, accessed May 6, 2015, https://www.marxists.org/archive/marx/works/1894/early-christianity/.

Federalist No. 51, Constitution Society, accessed July 7, 2015, http://www.constitution.org/fed/federa51.htm.

Federici, Silvia, *Caliban and the Witch: Women, the Body, and Primitive Accumulation*, 2nd ed. (New York: Autonomedia, 2014).

Foucault, Michel, *Discipline and Punish: The Birth of the Prison*, trans. Alan Sheridan (New York: Vintage, 1995).

———, *Madness and Civilization: A History of Insanity in the Age of Reason*, trans. Richard Howard (New York: Vintage, 1965).

———, *The Order of Things: An Archeology of the Human Sciences* (New York: Vintage, 1995).

Gregory of Nyssa, "An Address on Religious Instruction," ed. and trans. Cyril C. Richardson, in *Christology of the Later Fathers*, ed. Edward R. Hardy (Philadelphia: Westminster, 1954), pp 268–325.

Irenaeus, *Against Heresies*, trans. Alexander Roberts and James Donaldson, in *The Ante-Nicene Fathers*, vol. 1, ed. Alexander Roberts, James Donaldson, and Cleveland Coxe (Grand Rapids, MI: Eerdmans, 1885), pp. 841–1391.

Jennings, Theodore W., Jr., *Insurrection of the Crucified: The Gospel of Mark as Theological Manifesto* (Chicago: Exploration Press, 2003).

———, *Outlaw Justice: The Messianic Politics of Paul* (Stanford, CA: Stanford University Press, 2013).

Jennings, Willie James, *The Christian Imagination: Theology and the Origins of Race* (New Haven, CT: Yale University Press, 2010).

John of Damascus, *The Orthodox Faith*, in *Writings*, trans. Frederic H. Chase Jr. (New York: Fathers of the Church, 1958), pp. 165–406.

Kahl, Brigitte, *Galatians Re-imagined: Reading with the Eyes of the Vanquished* (Minneapolis: Fortress, 2010).

Keller, Catherine, *Face of the Deep: A Theology of Becoming* (New York: Routledge, 2003).

King, Karen, *What Is Gnosticism?* (Cambridge, MA: Harvard University Press, 2003).

Kotsko, Adam, "Perhaps Psychoanalysis?," in *Agamben's Coming Philosophy: Finding a New Use for Theology*, by Colby Dickinson and Adam Kotsko (New York: Rowman & Littlefield, 2015), pp. 137–54.

———, *Politics of Redemption: The Social Logic of Salvation* (New York: T&T Clark, 2010).

Kramer, Heinrich, and James Sprenger, *Malleus Maleficarum*, trans. Montague Summers (New York: Dover, 1971).

Levine, Amy-Jill, *The Misunderstood Jew: The Scandal of the Jewish Jesus* (New York: Harper, 2007).

Lloyd, Vincent W., *The Problem with Grace: Reconfiguring Political Theology* (Stanford, CA: Stanford University Press, 2011).

Luther, Martin, "On the Jews and Their Lies," trans. Martin H. Bertram, in *Luther's Works*, vol. 47 (Philadelphia: Fortress Press, 1971), http://jdstone.org/cr/pages/sss_mluther.html.

Meier, John P., *A Marginal Jew: Rethinking the Historical Jesus*, 4 vols. (New Haven, CT: Yale University Press, 1991–2009).

Mills, Charles W., *The Racial Contract* (Ithaca, NY: Cornell University Press, 1999).

Milton, John, *Paradise Lost: A Norton Critical Edition*, ed. Gordon Teskey (New York: Norton, 2005).

Nietzsche, Friedrich, *Genealogy of Morals*, in *Basic Writings of Nietzsche*, ed. Walter Kaufmann (New York: Modern Library, 1992).

Pagels, Elaine, *The Gnostic Gospels* (New York: Vintage, 1979).

———, *The Origin of Satan: How Christians Demonized Jews, Pagans, and Heretics* (New York: Vintage, 1995).

Pateman, Carole, *The Sexual Contract* (Stanford, CA: Stanford University Press, 1988).

Patterson, Orlando, *Slavery and Social Death: A Comparative Study* (Cambridge, MA: Harvard University Press, 1982).

Rawls, John, *Theory of Justice* (Cambridge, MA: Belknap Press, 1971).

Ray, Darby, *Deceiving the Devil: Atonement, Abuse, and Ransom* (Cleveland: Pilgrim, 1998).

Ruether, Rosemary Radford, *Sexism and God-Talk: Toward a Feminist Theology* (Boston: Beacon, 1983).

Schmitt, Carl, *The Nomos of the Earth in the International Law of the Jus Publicum Europaeum*, ed. and trans. G. L. Ulmen (New York: Telos, 2003).

———, *Political Theology: Four Chapters on the Concept of Sovereignty*, trans. George Schwab (Chicago: University of Chicago Press, 2005).

Schneider, Laurel C., *Beyond Monotheism: A Theology of Multiplicity* (New York: Routledge, 2008).

Schüssler Fiorenza, Elizabeth, *Revelation: Vision of a Just World* (Minneapolis: Fortress, 1991).

Taubes, Jacob, *The Political Theology of Paul*, trans. Dana Hollander (Stanford, CA: Stanford University Press, 2004).

———, *To Carl Schmitt: Letters and Reflections*, trans. Keith Tribe (New York: Columbia University Press, 2013).

Tertullian, *De Spectaculis* [On the shows], trans. S. Thelwall, in *Ante-Nicene Fathers*, vol. 3, ed. Alexander Roberts, James Donaldson, and A. Cleveland Coxe (Buffalo, NY: Christian Literature Publishing, 1885), pp. 157–91.

Thomas Aquinas, *The Summa Theologica of St. Thomas Aquinas*, 2nd rev. ed., trans. Fathers of the English Dominican Province (1920), New Advent, 2008, http://www.newadvent.org/summa.

Trachtenberg, Joshua, *The Devil and the Jews: The Medieval Conception of the Jew and Its Relation to Modern Anti-Semitism* (Philadelphia: Jewish Publication Society, 1983).

Viveiros de Castro, Eduardo, *The Inconstancy of the Indian Soul: The Encounter of Catholics and Cannibals in 16th-Century Brazil*, trans. Gregory Duff Morton (Chicago: Prickly Paradigm, 2011).

Wax-Thibodeaux, Emily, "Wilson Said the Unarmed Teen Looked like a 'Demon.' Experts Say His Testimony Was Dehumanizing and 'Super-humanizing,'" *Washington Post*, November 25, 2014, http://www.washingtonpost.com/news/post-nation/wp/2014/11/25/wilson-said-the-unarmed-teen-looked-like-a-demon-experts-say-his-testimony-was-dehumanizing-and-super-humanizing/.

Weheliye, Alexander G., *Habeas Viscus: Racializing Assemblages, Biopolitics, and Black Feminist Theories of the Human* (Durham, NC: Duke University Press, 2014).

INDEX

CPSIA information can be obtained
at www.ICGtesting.com
Printed in the USA
LVHW021712200121
676999LV00010B/1731

9 781503 600201